## DATE DUE

| | | | |
|---|---|---|---|
| | | | |
| | | | |
| | | | |
| | | | |
| | | | |
| | | | |
| | | | |
| | | | |
| | | | |
| | | | |
| | | | |
| | | | |
| | | | |
| | | | |
| | | | |
| | | | |
| | | | |
| | | | |

DEMCO 38-297

# OLD MEN OF THE BOWERY

# OLD MEN OF THE BOWERY
## Strategies for Survival
## Among the Homeless

Carl I. Cohen
SUNY Health Science Center at Brooklyn

Jay Sokolovsky
University of Maryland, Baltimore County

*With the assistance of*
Eric Roth, Jeanne Teresi, and Douglas Holmes

THE GUILFORD PRESS
*New York   London*

*For Uncle Ed, the Fry Cook, and Super-Runner*

© 1989 The Guilford Press
A Division of Guilford Publications, Inc.
72 Spring Street, New York, NY 10012

Printed in the United States of America

Last digit is print number: 9 8 7 6 5 4 3 2 1

Library of Congress Cataloging-in-Publication Data

Cohen, Carl I.
  Old men of the Bowery.

  Bibliography: p.
  Includes index.
  1. Homeless persons—New York (N.Y.) 2. Aged men—
New York (N.Y.) I. Sokolovsky, Jay. II. Title.
HV4506.N6C65 1989      362.5'097471      88-24356
ISBN 0-89862-718-4
ISBN 0-89862-509-2 (pbk.)

Portions of Chapters 5, 6, and 7 appeared in "Survival Strategies of Older Homeless Men" by C. I. Cohen, J. Teresi, D. Holmes, and E. Roth, *The Gerontologist, 28* (1988), pp. 58–65; "The Mental Health of Old Homeless Men" by C. I. Cohen, J. Teresi, and D. Holmes, *Journal of the American Geriatrics Society, 36* (1988), pp. 492–501; and "The Physical Well-Being of Old Homeless Men" by C. I. Cohen, J. Teresi, and D. Holmes, *Journal of Gerontology: Social Sciences, 43* (1988), pp. S121–S128.

All the names mentioned in this book, with the exception of researchers and staff members, have been changed to protect the privacy of the individuals.

# *Preface*

When we began this project in 1982, we weren't sure whether the dramatic rise in homelessness might be a transient phenomena, a glitch in the system. Perhaps with a little recalibration, the problem would disappear. Six years later, shelters are firmly embedded in the urban landscape where they already have been professionalized, bureaucratized, and computerized. Homelessness continues to worsen. A report released in December 1987 by the United States Conference of Mayors found that the demand for emergency food and shelter increased by approximately 20% nationwide over the previous year. In some cities the demand increased by more than twice this national average. Moreover, the percentage of homeless families grew by greater than one-third.

The litany of statistics and outrage, however, has been undermined by a generalized psychic numbing. Along with cold steel fireplugs and ruptured garbage bags, the homeless person has become just one more object on the sidewalk. Newspapers and T.V. now spew forth a daily dose of homeless stories along with the murders, fires, weather, and sports. And subtly, there has been a shift in parlance from "Homelessness"—suggesting a social origin—to "The Homeless Problem," which implies that the cause may be within the homeless person. Experts have contributed to this by labeling the homeless as "loners" or "chronic mentally ill," thereby side-stepping the reality of insufficient housing and impoverishment.

In this work our aim is to refocus the debate. Previous studies of the homeless have tended to be either too system-oriented or too individual-oriented. We have addressed both levels—the personal casualties as well as the systemic causalities. We have combined anthropological, psychological, and sociological methods and have drawn upon the lives of older homeless men not to consign individual blame, but to illuminate the interplay of biography and society. Their life pathways point to where today's young homeless will head if meaningful interventions are not introduced. We have described our experience with a model service program for older homeless men. Although this program can help treat the wounded, our historical reading of the ebb and flow of homelessness leads us to conclude that the problem resides ultimately in broader social forces, in understanding the political economy of our system.

Homelessness evokes many responses—anger, compassion, revulsion. But its most profound response is fear. The homeless expose the flaws in our society. They stand counterpoised to Roosevelt's exhortation for a "freedom from want." That decent housing, a secure job, or adequate income are no longer guaranteed. Recently, when the stock market tumbled, we all shuddered and wondered anxiously what the future held.

Most of us struggle to deny and repress. We may try to view homelessness as individual breakdown and deviancy; often we succumb to psychic numbing. Yet, at times, when our security is threatened and the armor cracks a bit, one eventually must ask: "What if I lost my job or personal tragedy befell me or my family and I couldn't pay my mortgage or the rent, who would help? Would anyone really care?" Above all, for this reason, our fate is integrally linked with the plight of the homeless.

A very special trinity made this study possible. Carole Lefkowitz transcribed tapes, typed and retyped manuscripts, and never (hardly ever) complained. The National Institute of Mental Health, Center for the Mental Disorders of Aging Branch and the Community Support Program provided support for this research project and funding for Project Rescue (Grants RO1 MH37562, H84 MH42443). Within NIMH, Barry Lebowitz and Enid Light offered not only material support (which they never reduced) but enthusiastic encouragement. Finally, the Bowery Residents' Committee provided a base of operation, access to its clients, and various support services.

We also thank Kim Hopper for his helpful comments, especially regarding the historical roots of homelessness, and Eugene Feigelson for giving departmental support. Lastly, for persevering through our many years on the streets, in the flophouses, in SRO hotels, and other skid row haunts—we express our deepest love and gratitude to our families—Katie, Joan, Sara, Zachary, Rebecca, Louise, Shirley, Lou, and Harry.

# Contents

CHAPTER ONE

# Introduction: Three Bowery Men

*The Bow'ry, the Bow'ry*
*They say such things*
*And they do strange things*
*On the Bow'ry, the Bow'ry!*
*I'll never go there any more!*

These popular song lyrics from the 1891 hit show *A Trip to Chinatown* (cited in Bediner, 1961, p. 73) helped introduce New York's Bowery to the American public. They also epitomize the contemporary situation of this urban zone which remains our nation's most infamous skid row. A trip into the world of older men who make this area their home illuminates one of the emerging human tragedies of this decade: there is continuing dramatic growth in poverty and homelessness even as certain sectors of society consolidate their power and grow richer. President Reagan exemplified the attitude of these latter sectors when, in his 1984 State of the Union Address, he proclaimed, "America is back—standing tall, looking to the 80s with courage, confidence, and hope."

As we introduce Uncle Ed, Miles (the Fry Cook), and Roland (the Super-Runner), it will become apparent to the reader that for men who are old and poor, and who rely on the scant resources of the Bowery for survival, each day is likely to inflict a major crisis. These three men do not encompass the total variety of social types on the Bowery. However, the dilemmas they face daily, the paths that led them to the Bowery, and their future prospects constitute key patterns that are repeated in the lives of several hundred men we interviewed while researching this book.

## UNCLE ED, THE CLASSIC BOWERY MAN

It was one of those rare times that Ed showed real anger when he was not drunk. In a rage he shouted, "How could such a freakin' stupid thing happen to someone who is so needy. I need my food stamps back, you stupid bitch!" He lunged awkwardly across the table at the thin, frightened black woman working the computer in Room 301 of the Human Resources Administration, but stumbled, and fell suddenly back in his chair. Feeling the wall of bureaucracy pressing on his head, Ed was embarrassed at the loss of his usually pleasant demeanor. After all, it was his congenial countenance that had earned him his moniker, "Uncle Ed." Without a word he left the office and headed back to the Bowery. Although only 56, Ed has worked to fight off dependent needs and the idleness of old age. The frustration and rage evoked by the bureaucratic wall roused under-lying cravings for a bottle.

Before returning to his tiny cubicle he rested on a park bench and contemplated the oppressive reality of his life. From a monthly check of $277.85, Ed pays $132.18 for a 4 by 7 foot space with thin wooden walls and a chicken wire ceiling. Despite free mission cloth-ing, 25-cent breakfasts and lunches from the Bowery Residents' Committee (BRC), and occasional free cheese distributions, Ed must shell out between five and and six dollars for his daily coffee, cig-arettes, dinner, and incidentals. It is a rare month when he does not need to borrow money at the typical usurious rates: "Get ten dollars and pay back fourteen," as the street proverb states.

Uncle Ed is a jovial caricature of the classic skid row alcoholic. Nick-named by a nurse because of his helpful and affable attitude toward others while he was a patient at a "sobering up station," he tries to show a nonoffensive helpful face to all he meets. A comely clean-shaven person when sober, he is usually dressed in second-hand mission clothes that tend to be misfitted to his bulky frame and pot belly. As he walks the streets of the Bowery hardly five minutes will go by without someone shouting, "Hiya, Uncle Ed." Every other block will find Ed passing some deli or second-hand clothes shop where he has often found casual work running errands. He is a walking encyclopedia of Bowery trivia, color, and history. On his own since the age of 16, he has spent the last 40 years working menial jobs in restaurants, hotels, and construction sites.

Seldom without a cigarette, he chain smokes Camels, lighting up for a few minutes, putting it out delicately with his fingers, clamping the butt securely behind his ear, only to resume smoking a short time later. To emphasize a point, he will crinkle his pug nose, roll his eyes up into the side of his head and discuss in raspy, measured words his life on the streets: "I was one time four months sober and then at another time six months sober, but then I went off the deep end. But this time I'm sober five months."

At the time of writing this book, his last major drunken spree had begun about eight months earlier, following a bitter argument with a woman with whom he had been living for a short time in Philadelphia. As he put it:

During the night, I guess John Barleycorn [alcohol] talked to me. Well fuck it! I'm going back to the bottle. I've already got it in my mind that the only place I can go is back to the bottle. So I drank a bottle. Three-quarters of a fifth of gin. Then I went out to the bus stop and I got on a bus to Penn Station, bought some more gin and came back to the Bowery and this is where I am now. I come right to the Pacific Hotel around three in the morning. I saw the clerk which I know personally. Steve's his name. He said, "What do you want Uncle Ed?" I said I want a room. I gotta sleep this shit off.

As Ed could pay the $3.50 for the night, he was given a cubicle, and he began one of his cyclical trips to oblivion:

I'd wake up in the morning and I'd be so discouraged, depressed, knowing that I just had another goddamned day with a bottle, I never made no plans, everything just came as they came, you know. I'm an early riser, up by six, even when I'm drinking. I'd sleep two hours an' I think I got a good night's sleep. I'd usually see if I've got the dollar and a quarter for the first pint of T-Bird [Thunderbird wine], and if I didn't, I'd go bum a card [panhandle] at Lafayette and Houston Streets. I'd usually walk down Grand Street going up to drivers, and they'd give me a quarter, or wipe his windshield and hope he gives me a quarter.

By eight o'clock [AM] I've made a bottle. I'd take a couple of good shots to kind of settle my nerves, put it in my back pocket and go out and make another one. Usually I make my second before I finish the first. This way I have reinforcements for the next day. I usually like to drink by myself, but sometimes I get despondent and I want someone to talk to. So I go to this park on Spring Street. If I've got a bottle or if I haven't, I go there to see who's got a bottle. Without a doubt I would find myself an associate or two.

Usually, one would say, "Well we need a bottle, Uncle Ed" and I'll say, "Let's go make it."

Ed left Philadelphia with $300, but inside of a week it was gone. He was back on the streets. He spent nights in parks, or darkened doorways. For four nights he slept in Penn Station, crawling behind a partition or sitting in a phone booth until the police finally kicked him out. "I was relatively holding the banner [living on the streets] with money in my pocket because I was drinking around the clock until I went broke and my legs went bad."

For two months he slept at night on the subway and sometimes went to the Holy Name Mission to clean himself up. Finally, in a state of exhaustion and with his feet so swollen that he could not put on his shoes, he was coaxed into a detoxification unit near the Bowery.

While in the detoxification unit a case worker recertified Ed for Supplemental Security Income (SSI) and when he was released nine days later, the Pacific Hotel once again became his home. At an Alcoholics Anonymous (AA) meeting in early August 1985, he celebrated his last five months of sobriety. Each day he wages war against drinking. His daily circuit takes him from his hotel to a local center for older men, for long walks to Greenwich Village where he stops to have coffee and read the newspaper in a quiet park, and finally a visit to one of the several AA groups to which he belongs. He carefully sidesteps the Spring Street Park where his old "bottle gang" usually gathers. Ed talks proudly of the young alcoholic in his hotel whom he recently "twelve stepped," that is, convinced through personal testimony and persuasion to join his AA group.

Constantly poised between hope and despair, Ed occasionally looks for a quiet job. "A night watchman or doorman position would be ideal," he wistfully says, but he has given up looking for the time being. On occasion, to get some money he will "make a run" for the older men in his flophouse who are too frail or too drunk to leave their shabby quarters. After a series of mild heart attacks over the last few years, Ed can no longer play the quick errand boy for local merchants. Ed realizes old age is upon him and each day ends with him wondering if the next morning will find him splayed in the gutter on Spring Street reeking of cheap wine.

## MILES, THE FRY COOK

"It's my own damn fault," Miles says repeatedly to himself as he searches in vain for a comfortable sleeping position on the hard wooden bench. As if it had happened minutes ago, he can still feel the ragged edge of a broken mirror held tautly to his throat as a man he knew only as Paco dashed away with all of his savings. While spending the prior month upstate at Camp LaGuardia, he met Paco amongst a thousand other homeless men. Paco was a friendly type with an easy way about him, and the two quickly become "associates." He had confided to Miles that he could help him get a cheap apartment in the Bronx. He claimed to know the super in the building and Miles would have to put down a deposit immediately. At the beginning of July, Miles returned to the city, cashed his social security check, paid off some loans, and went to meet Paco. He remembers a sudden blow to the head, tumbling to the ground, and then looking up to find Paco holding the glass shard to his neck. Next, he was relieved of the $380 he had brought along—all the money that he had in the world.

It is now a summer day. Miles rises before daybreak from his park bench at East 23rd Street. Despite his tall lean frame and healthy looks, old age hangs on this black man's shoulders like a leaden cloak. At first light he begins what for him is a humiliating task, collecting returnable soda and beer cans. He slept even less than usual during the previous night. At 12:30 AM an old acquaintance, Jack McDonald, wandered into the small park. Jack spotted Miles and offered to share his pint of Wild Irish Rose. Miles politely turned this down, as the cheap wine sometimes made him sick.

When Jack learns of Miles's plan for the coming day, he is indignant, "What are you doing picking up cans for a livin'?" Trying to hide his growing depression, Miles replies, "Tomorrow's my birthday, I'll be 63 and I want to buy myself somethin' real good to drink, get some cigarettes, and maybe go take in a movie uptown." Jack finally dozes off on a nearby bench, but Miles just sits and blankly stares at the other homeless men and women whose darkened outlines stud the park. By 4:00 AM the prostitutes and the cadres of gay men looking for a quick tryst leave the park to the 90 people who make this urban glade their home on this particular warm summer night. Most sleep on the benches, but a few are in small tents on the grass.

Over the next two hours Miles smokes a handful of the tobacco stubs garnered earlier during his daily trek across Manhattan. Every once in a while he mutters to himself, "I can take this carryin' a stick [living on the streets] every once in a while, but I can't take much more pickin' shit wit' these pigeons [scavenging the street for cigarette butts]."

Miles's life had not always been this way. After World War II he began working as a cook's helper at a seafood restaurant that attracted hundreds of patrons daily. Miles became quite adept at cooking fish and within five years he became one of the chief fry cooks. By the late 1940s he had a good apartment in the Bronx and was living with a woman who worked for the electric company.

It was two decades later that his life began to come apart. In 1972, at the age of 50, he had the first of several heart attacks, and shortly after he was released from the hospital, the restaurant closed. Without his old job, and in poor health, he began a pattern of periodic drinking that eventually led to his relinquishing his apartment. Miles then shifted from one run-down single-room-occupancy (SRO) hotel to another on the Upper West Side and in midtown Manhattan. Every few years he was compelled to search for a new place to live as gentrification began to decimate the available low-cost housing stock.

Although this proud man has only twice slept on the Bowery (for very short periods), by the early 1980s he had begun an economic and residential lifestyle common to many of the older skid row men. For most of the spring and summer he would live in cheap hotel rooms and take short-term manual labor jobs around the city or in one of the many hotel resorts in the Catskill Mountains. If his money ran low or when he was forcibly evicted from hotels as they underwent cooperative conversions, he would spend a week or two "carrying the stick" until he could afford another "livable" room. During the winter when jobs were scarcer and he tended to drink more, he would live for several months in upstate New York, staying at various retreats for homeless men. Miles would remain at one such city-run facility, Camp LaGuardia, for up to three months.

When speaking about the Bowery, Miles literally spits out angry words to express his feeling of humiliation:

I told this social worker, I'm not trying to be funny or smart. I refuse to sleep on the Bowery. I don't consider myself Bowery material 'cause I can remember years ago when I used to come down to the Bowery just to have a ball. That's when they had nice bars and shows down here.

He is also quite aware of the continuing *de facto* segregation which offers blacks rooms in only the very worst flophouses. This is an area where even the best accommodations are barely fit for human habitation.

More than anything, Miles is a victim of one of the worst housing crises New York City has ever faced. His last residence for any length of time (26 months) was a run-down SRO hotel with a room rent ($260) that consumed nearly two-thirds of his monthly Social Security check. When he complained about the horrendous conditions in the hotel, he was harassed by the management. He hastily left the hotel after being robbed by thugs hired by the management. Fearing for his life, Miles departed for the "Holy Mountains," a retreat for homeless men in Upstate New York.

Now, three years later, he was currently in the "carrying the stick" segment of his annual cycle. With almost no money in his pockets, he was spending July sleeping in the park in good weather or on the subways when it rained.

Following the incident with Paco, he was able to obtain only $21.50 from the Welfare Department. Miles then went to Tony the "buy and sell" man where he pawned his watch and ring for another $15. Although Miles had not had any contact with his relatives in Alabama since 1960, he still maintained a couple of close friends whom he had known for 40 years. Both these black men were in their late 60s and maintained tiny apartments. One of them kept Miles' suitcase in his apartment. The other man, who worked as a cook's helper at the BRC, talked Miles into going there for the 25-cent lunches. From these friends he was able to borrow about $30 following his robbery.

Miles could have obtained a ticket for a free room through the Muni (the Municipal Shelter for Men) or even paid for a couple of weeks at one of the lesser flophouses. The first option was ruled out because on his last visit to the Muni he had been violently attacked by a young man strung out on drugs. Miles did not even consider paying for a flop since he refused to panhandle, and he wanted to husband his resources in hopes of securing a better place to live in the future.

For now he would sleep in the small park that stretched two square blocks in a neighborhood that was safer for old men than the Bowery. To homeless men who lived in this area, skid row had come to be called "Little Vietnam." In fact, Miles was perpetually scared living anywhere on the streets. He attributed his consumption of a pint of wine a day to this situation. Besides witnessing various brutal attacks on older men by young thugs, twice in the last year he had been robbed and beaten.

The other times Miles had been homeless he had stayed by himself, but this time it was different. After having watched attacks on other older men and having himself been robbed, he slept with a group of three other black men who he had come to know in the last month. Two of them, Walt and John, were his age, while the other, James, was in his mid-30s. He had met John while waiting on a line for sandwiches at the St. Francis of Assisi Church. Miles had offered John a cigarette and, as they struck up a conversation, they not only came to like each other but discovered that they had been sleeping at opposite ends of the same park. Back at the park Miles was introduced to the two other men who had been staying together for about a month, and it was decided they would all sleep together, two men to each long bench.

Miles usually rises earliest in the morning and gently shakes his benchmates to inform them that he will be leaving soon. The four men spend most of their waking hours apart. When they congregate in the early evening they swap the day's news and information about the menus at various soup kitchens, trade surplus food, and usually split a pint of wine. Walt and John have steady jobs while James does household repairs and redeems old soda cans. James had introduced Miles to the latter trade.

The day prior to his birthday had begun badly. Although Miles had enlisted Jack to help with the collection of cans, they had made only about five dollars. Some merchants simply refused to take dirty cans even though the Mayor had declared this unnecessary due to the severe water shortage. As his frustrations mounted, the depressive feelings and suicidal thoughts that had plagued him for the past two decades began to recur. Over the course of the day, however, he encountered three of his oldest friends who each remembered his birthday, and gave him gifts of money totalling $14. Better still, one of these buddies related a rumor that the restaurant might be opening again.

That night in the park, Miles celebrated by sharing several bottles of vodka with Jack and his three benchmates. Perhaps the liquor and the thought of his Social Security check coming next week made him ebullient as he discussed his plans for the coming week. First he would buy a copy of the Amsterdam News and begin scouting for a cheap apartment. Next, he would take the D train to Brooklyn and see if anyone could use a real fine fry cook.

## ROLAND, THE SUPER-RUNNER

"Not even the cops will bother me here," Roland said confidently as he closed the top of his room for the night—a cardboard carton which last housed a new refrigerator. As a final ritual to evoke momentary security he pulled his woolen cap over his gaunt, well-scrubbed cheeks and curled up into a ball.

Satisfied for the moment with his comfort, he was less certain of how he would fare the icy rain predicted for the night. His flimsy shelter had big rips which were difficult to repair with the newspaper he had collected during the day. For the past week he had been scouting out this secret "flop" in a tiny alley off Bleecker Street where a short landing of steps led down to a basement door which was nailed shut. By 1:00 AM, having prepared the steps with cans to warn of intruders, Roland drifted off into a light sleep. His last words that night were, "Just six more months until my 65th birthday, then I dig up my money, start collecting my Social Security checks, and get away from here."

It was the week before Thanksgiving, a time of year which forced the street-dwelling homeless of New York to make life and death decisions. Roland had recently taken to wearing several layers of clothing and using extra caution in choosing his flop for the night. Not only was he now leery of marauding young black skid row men, but the Mayor had declared that all homeless persons would be removed from the streets when the temperature dipped below 32°. Just last month he had been sleeping in a cardboard box set behind a big shrub on a tiny street at the edge of Greenwich Village. The police had stumbled upon his warren and asked him to come along with them. But Roland told himself, "They're not taking me to the hospital and givin' me no electric shock treatment." Despite a strange new pain in his left leg he ran like a frightened rabbit. The two patrolmen just stood there and laughed, glad to have chased another bum out of their patch.

Yet Roland is no ordinary bum. He has the money, and more importantly the connections, to get a room in a flophouse. Many years ago, when he was still drinking, he slept with 400 other men in a dormitory-style flophouse, resting on cloth-covered planks of wood. Periodically he would lose most of his accumulated money either by going on month-long drinking binges or by being robbed in his hotel. Now a decade later he will relate with a slight shudder how he left the flop, began living in an abandoned building uptown, and simply decided that life on the street as a drunk was too dangerous. He ceremoniously broke his remaining bottles of wine and just sat in his room for a week of hell until the tremors from withdrawal had gone away. Since that time the streets have been his home.

Although for the last ten years he has slept somewhere on the streets of New York, he remains meticulously clean. He has, through his own will power, completely stopped drinking and works a steady 40-hour week at various jobs on the Bowery. He is in fact a "super-runner." A runner does errands for cash. Roland is a super-runner in that he has graduated from the "get the bottle and keep the change from the ten" level to only working for social workers, priests, and nuns. He is now an amazingly fit and energetic 64-year-old.

Roland is a "do-gooder" who labors for the charity establishment rather than the tavern owners or hotel managers because he has acquired the social work ethic. Each weekday at noon he becomes the delivery unit of the Bowery's main "meals on wheels" program. Up and down the steps of flophouses he can be seen effortlessly hefting a cart laden with prepared lunches from a local soup kitchen. Moving in a fluid half-run through each building, he deposits a meal, shouts "how ya doin," and accepts the quarter tip he receives in each of the 40 odd rooms he will visit. He is constantly ferreting out hotel-bound and homeless old men who need food and clothing, and he helps bring them together with the Bowery's social service resources. He will not buy a bottle for you but he will get your prescription filled.

Although Roland rapidly moves through the streets with a gait seemingly born from confidence, his active participation in life dangles on a thin thread. In the course of being a super-runner he is asked to operate a machine or deal with a key, often with disastrous results. Not because he is careless. He attacks any job with metronomic precision, but he will always try to avoid work that involves any technology whatsoever. Nevertheless, new employers (the local mission's pastor or a new social worker in an agency he patronizes) will take advantage of his great energy and willingness to help and will press him into locking up or running a dryer or dishwasher. Roland is no worse at these tasks than anyone else, yet when the inevitable happens, when a fan belt breaks or a key is lost, or a fuse goes, Roland becomes frantic. He knows he has broken whatever he was working on. He feels it must be his fault. Invariably he flees and avoids the embarrassment of dealing with his screw-up. His life is cast in cycles of such stories which are used to explain how he came to the Bowery and why he has not had any contact in years with his sister or other relatives in nearby Connecticut.

Roland's affect, motor, and speech patterns are quite unusual. Constantly in motion or asleep, his appetite is prodigious. Not more than 140 pounds, with a wiry body that looks no more than 40 years old, he eats perhaps five times what other older men do. Many of his jobs involve food as well as cash payments. He talks in bursts, as if to verbally mimic his mode of motion and work. A voracious newspaper reader, he readily offers opinions on both front page and obscure items. Obsessed with stories of gore and violence, especially those perpetrated on Bowery men, he is a walking local history of murders and bizarre accidental deaths. If you walk the street with him, every few minutes another sordid story will unfold. For instance, passing a boarded-up paper processing factory, he tells of a drunk old bum who slipped in late one winter night to sleep warmly between layers of cardboard. Unfortunately the man slept too long and was tragically crushed to death when the bailing machines were started up in the morning.

Despite his varied jobs in Bowery institutions he always sleeps alone in one of several places off the Bowery. One is under the Manhattan Bridge, and several others are dispersed on the edges of the Greenwich Village area. Where he flops on a given night depends on the weather and his judgment of its safety, based on a scouting of the area. After spending his day on the Bowery he will walk a winding two-mile route to the West Village where he meets a close associate who attends an AA meeting there. On route he constantly scans the streets for two things, money and muggers. As he passes a garbage can he will quickly examine the top layer of refuse hoping to repeat a recent windfall when he found five $20 bills neatly folded in an empty pack of cigarettes. After a meal at McDonalds with his associate, and an hour or so of casual conversation, the two men will separate, and Roland makes his way to one of his "homes," always arriving around midnight.

Roland had not slept indoors more than a handful of times over the last ten years, giving in only when the winter weather reached arctic dimensions. Now on this late November night, while Roland dozed in his leaking cardboard shelter, the temperature hovered just over freezing, and a mixture of rain, sleet, and hail pelted the city. Virtually paranoid over the possibility that the police would again try to drag him off the street, he would use his secret sleeping place. The bottom of the landing where he lay in dreamless slumber was impossible to see even from a few feet away.

Roland was startled awake at 5:00 AM by stinging pain that ran up and down his left leg and almost made him cry out. Most of his body was soaked and he felt colder than he had been all the previous winter. What frightened him most was that his lithe frame could not be supported by his usually dependable legs. Yet, now it was a great effort to move, let alone walk. A terrifying thought ran through his mind, "My God, have I got AIDS or somethin'?"

Fueled by his mounting fear, Roland willed himself to half crawl, half hop to the Holy Name Mission, one of the several places he worked on the Bowery. After several agonizing hours he managed to negotiate the mile to this sanctuary only to find himself on his hands and knees, totally immobile, directly across the street from the mission doors. He could not move another inch. Fortunately, he did not have to wait long before he could hail a young homeless man seeking an early morning shower. Roland gave him a dollar and asked him to call Father Ahern at the Holy Name. The priest came out with another man and carried Roland into the mission and laid him down on a warm bed.

Later that day a doctor examined Roland and concluded that he was suffering from a possible sciatic nerve inflammation; he prescribed some medicine and several weeks of rest. For the next month, he slept at the Holy Name, and then to the shock of everyone who knew him, Roland checked into the best flophouse on the Bowery. Notwithstanding the bold statements Roland often made about his ability to survive street life, after a decade of "holding the banner," he seemed ready to accept for the time being in an abode more sturdy than tattered cardboard.

## THREE LIVES IN PERSPECTIVE

These three profiles illustrate the world of recurrent crises which confront older Bowery men. These men face acute crises, including falling through holes in the welfare "saftey net," rapid deterioration in health, physical assault, alcohol craving, and loss of shelter. These short-term episodes are embedded within the patterns of chronic crises of impoverishment, alcohol abuse, physical and psychological disability, sporadic work opportunities, a public policy of reduced entitlement programs and destruction of low-income housing stock, and the stigma attached to life on the skids.

It is easy to react to the plight of such individuals through popular stereotypes of the poor skid row derelict who is homeless by choice, unwilling to work, constantly inebriated, possibly psychotic, reluctant to conform to norms of personal hygiene and dress, and beyond redemption. In order to address the problem of homelessness, it is necessary to avoid such popular characterizations and to examine the interweaving of the numerous elements that generate and sustain these individuals.

To many, Uncle Ed must seem like the archetype of a Bowery "bum." In his worst moments, he can be viewed as a hopeless drunk, living for days in the same wine-soaked garments and panhandling quarters for his next bottle. Yet like so many of the older Bowery men in a quest for dignity and enhanced economic stability, he desperately seeks employment beyond the occasional "go for" job. Ed is convivial, articulate, of great support to others, and he maintains a wide range of social relationships including women friends and kin. Despite frequent bouts of severe depression he still nourishes the hope of maintaining sobriety long enough to escape the vicious consequences of his addiction and poverty.

Superficially, Miles would appear to be a shiftless, old, street alcoholic. His street living, however, originates in the housing policy which has greatly depleted the stock of affordable apartments and hotel rooms. (Indeed, a 1985 survey indicated that 55% of the elderly in New York City shelters had lived independently in their own apartments or in SRO hotels before entering the shelter system; a majority of them had been evicted because of inadequate funds [Human Resources Administration, 1987].) Miles's drinking problem is nurtured and exacerbated by fear and anxiety brought on by street living. Because of his overriding desire to secure an apartment he prefers to sleep on a park bench rather than pay even small amounts for the inhuman housing available for blacks on the Bowery. Miles's intelligence is reflected in his ability to maximize the meager resources available to men on the street.

Roland is a man who, due to his bad experiences in flophouses, has opted for a homeless existence which many would consider insane. His unusual speech and affective patterns amplify this image of a "crazy" person. If Roland were captured by the mental health system (and he has been at times), he might be labeled a chronic schizophrenic. But, in his element, on the streets, Roland is a successful entrepreneur who provides useful services to more needy Bowery men. He does not drink, use other drugs, or panhandle. Roland represents a rare type but he is hardly unique. He may be homeless but he is not a bum.

One of the principal purposes of this book is to explore the ways these men confront and adapt to their unrelenting crises. In order to fully comprehend their lives and their survival strategies we must explore the personal life paths as well as the socioenvironmental forces which shape their existence. In subsequent chapters we shall return to Ed, Miles, and Roland to illustrate the various biographical, psychosocial, health, and adaptive issues which confront skid row men. However, before addressing these topics we must consider some of the broader issues concerning the study itself and the historical forces that have spawned today's homeless population.

# CHAPTER TWO

# *An Orientation to the Study*

The classic triad of orientation is comprised of time, place, and person. We present these three components as a series of questions: Time: Why study aging Bowery men at this point in time? Place: What is the Bowery like in the mid-1980s? Person: Who are the men to be studied? Who are the researchers and what are their methods?

## WHY STUDY OLDER BOWERY MEN AT THIS TIME?

During the first three decades of this century the skid row man was one of the country's folk heroes. Rebellious, independent, and spirited by wanderlust, he was eulogized in word and song. Dr. Ben Reitman, so-called "King of the Hoboes," aptly described the lifestyle of skid row habitués in the following epigram: "The hobo works and wanders; the tramp dreams and wanders; and the bum drinks and wanders" (cited in Anderson, 1923, p. 87).

The Second World War, the ensuing economic prosperity, the elimination of railroad jobs and seasonal labor resulted in a diminution in the number of wandering homeless. The number of "homeguard" skid row men also declined in numbers. During the '50s and '60s the skid row man was studied as an interesting representation of deviancy—the person who refuses to conform to the American ideal. These men were labeled deviant not only for their alcoholism, their dishevelled appearance, and their lack of employment but also for the spilling of their private lives into public spaces. If the American ideal was a large private home to protect the family from public scrutiny, then the lowest form of degradation was to be a "bum on

15

the streets" (Kasinitz, 1986, p. 243). The last major studies of skid row were conducted during the 1960s (Bahr & Caplow, 1973; Blumberg, Shipley, & Shandler, 1973; Bogue, 1963).

By the late 1960s several authors were predicting the imminent demise of skid rows (Bahr, 1967; Rubington, 1971). For example, over a period of less than 20 years the population of New York City's Bowery had dropped by 10,000, falling to 5,406 men in 1966 (Bahr, 1967). However, by the early 1970s, researchers were reporting some stability in the size of skid rows (Levinson, 1974). Other reports out of Philadelphia and San Francisco indicated that the elimination of old skid rows resulted in the cropping-up of new ones in other sections of the city (Blumberg, Shipley, & Moor, 1971).

The economic downturns of the '70s and '80s, the retrenchment of social welfare programs, psychiatric deinstitutionalization programs, and the reduction of inexpensive housing stock in urban areas resulted in an increase in the number of skid-row dwellers living in the flophouses and on the streets. As one Bowery hotel manager put it, "The lodging houses are barometers of business; business down, you're up" (cited in Bahr, 1967, p. 43). Thus, skid rows began filling with an influx of new denizens comprised of ambulatory psychotics, "flower children," young unemployed blacks and Hispanics, and even some women. Wiseman (1979) observed:

Yet for all this influx of new types, the appearance and appointments of Skid Row and its satellite treatment areas have really changed little. It is as though this cluster of buildings, agencies, and services has a life and purpose of its own apart from the characteristics of its inhabitants. As a phenomenon, Skid Row seems able to resist the most concerted efforts by urban renewal experts, public officials, downtown merchant associations, and police to eradicate it. When the physical structures are razed, its elements coalesce and spring up mushroom-like in another susceptible part of the city. (p. xiii)

Not only has skid row resisted eradication, but the widely held notion that skid row was a phenomenon unique to the United States (Levinson, 1966; Wallace, 1965) was undermined by the "discovery" of skid rows in England, Scotland, and Canada. Thus, skid row has not only persevered but seems to be ubiquitous (Lodge Patch, 1970; Olin, 1966; Scott, Gaskell, & Morrell, 1966).

In the past few years there has been a burgeoning of interest in the homeless population. However, much attention has focused on the younger homeless ("the nouveau homeless"), and in particular, the mentally ill. We do not wish to minimize the plight of this younger group but our goal is to call attention to the aging homeless population.

In reading the scholarly and popular literature of the past few years, one would get the sense that the unattached homeless population is comprised solely of young psychotics with an occasional tragic case of an elderly bag woman and a few remaining old skid rowers. For instance, Leona Bachrach (1984a, pp. 14–15), a sociologist who has done extensive analyses on homelessness and the mentally ill, notes that the average age of the homeless is "dropping precipitously," and she largely attributes the rise in the homeless mentally ill to the postwar baby boom and the development of a young chronic mentally ill population. Similarly, two researchers from Bellevue Hospital in New York City contend that a significant proportion of the homeless mentally ill fall into the category of the "young adult chronic patient" (Lipton & Sabatini, 1984, p. 155). Most surveys of homeless populations or the homeless mentally ill have tended to emphasize the youthfulness of the sample. For example, investigators in Philadelphia found that nearly two thirds of the shelter population were younger than 50 years of age (Arce, Tadlock, Vergare, & Shapiro, 1983). A report by the Community Service Society summarizing surveys in New York City's municipal shelters estimated that the mean age "hovers around 40, with fully ¾ of the men being younger than 50" (Hopper, Baxter, Cox, & Klein, 1982, p. 7). A study of the New York City Women's Shelter found more than half of the clients to be under 40 years old (Vera Institute of Justice, 1981).

In emphasizing the youth of the homeless population, these surveys have ignored the older segment of the homeless, who still comprise a substantial proportion of the total. Moreover, by using shelters or psychiatric emergency rooms for surveys, the number of older homeless people are probably underestimated. Based primarily on shelter reports from eight cities, the Aging Health Policy Center (1985) estimated that the percentage of homeless people aged 50 and over ranged from between 14.5% to 28%, with the percentage of persons 60 and over ranging from 2.5% to 27.2%. However, many members of the older homeless population avoid public shelters because of fears of mugging, because the shelter staff are abrasive and insensitive to their needs, because they are fearful of being

institutionalized, and because they feel vulnerable since they may
have a regular source of income such as Social Security (Coalition for
the Homeless, 1984). Thus, the elderly are "crowded out" of the
municipal shelters. One elderly street man graphically described his
last encounter at New York City's Men's Shelter:

I was in the line and this guy said, "Hey, give me a cigarette." I said, "That's
all I got." The next thing I know, he stabbed me in my side and stole my
cigarette and he run like a demon. I finally got a security guard and they
called an ambulance, took me to the hospital, stitched me up and let me go
that same day.

The older homeless individual is commonly ignored by existing
senior programs. "Elderly persons who become homeless are not
typically reached through the network of services to the aged. It is
rare, for example, to find a senior center which serves the homeless"
(Coalition for the Homeless, 1984, p. 21). Thus, street outreach
programs report a much higher percentage of older persons: The
Midtown Outreach Program reported half their clients were age 47
or older (Coalition for the Homeless, 1984); Project Help reported
23% of their clients were in their 50s, and 20% were over 60 (Cohen,
Putnam, & Sullivan, 1984).

Finally, surveys of the homeless have tended to ignore men
living in skid row flophouses. In his classic study, Samuel Wallace
(1965) pointed to the historical links and common features between
the hobos, vagrants, paupers, rogues, and vagabonds of the past and
the skid row men of today. Thus, the skid rower has been traditionally considered "homeless" even though he no longer lives exclusively on the streets. Many of these men may periodically spend time
on the street, but more importantly, their alcohol abuse, physical
impairment, lack of traditional social relationships, and economic
deprivation are considered characteristics of "homelessness." Moreover, with extensive urban renewal and fires that have occurred in
recent years, many of these men teeter on the edge of becoming
undomiciled. For example, during the course of our study one of the
major Bowery hotels suffered a partial collapse and the owners
threatened not to reopen.

We have estimated that between three quarters and four fifths
of the men living in the Bowery flophouses are aged 50 and over (see
Table 2-1, below). Rough estimates suggest that about one fifth of

homeless people are skid row persons (Brickner, 1985); and, in many cities, since the recession of the early 1980s the skid row population has increased in depth (Erickson & Wilhelm, 1986).

Thus, it appears that the true number of older homeless persons must be revised upward. As the Aging Health Policy Center (1985) concluded, "Studies conducted on the homeless in recent years indicate that while the proportion of older persons has been declining, their absolute numbers have increased" (p. 5). Clearly, they are a group that cannot be easily ignored and, because of their age, they may require more specialized services. In this vein, Bachrach (1984a) pointed out, with respect to homeless mentally ill persons:

Finally service planners and providers must bear in mind that the homeless mentally ill population is very diverse in its composition. Individuals within the population differ widely with respect to demographic indicators, diagnoses, treatment histories, functional levels, residential histories, and prognoses. . . . Each local cluster of homeless mentally ill individuals has its own distinctive demography, epidemiology and history, as well as its own treatment needs. (p. 916)

Although older homeless persons can be found in other quarters of American cities, skid row remains one of the principal areas of concentration. Therefore, skid row can serve as an excellent laboratory for assessing a number of problems that have been largely neglected concerning the needs, adaptive strategies, physical health, and psychiatric problems of the aging homeless population. Moreover, previous research has pointed to various commonalities among skid rowers that render this study generalizable to other skid row populations (Bogue, 1963).

Another salient issue is whether the new young homeless will someday come to resemble their older counterparts. If there is support for this notion, then an examination of the older men of today may provide a projection of what the lives of the new homeless may be like in the future. Although the composition of the homeless population has changed over the past two decades, two important characteristics—maleness and substance abuse—still predominate. For example, a national survey by the U.S. Department of Housing and Urban Development (1984) found that approximately two thirds of the shelter populations are still single men; 13% are single women and 21% are family members. The majority of the homeless are still white (56%), but minorities—who comprised 20% of the national population—are overrepresented among the homeless. Over one half of the homeless have lived for over a year in the area where they are currently located. There are a few cities (e.g., Kansas City, Richmond, Phoenix, Las Vegas, Salt Lake City, Birmingham) that report a majority of recent arrivals and transients, but this reflects these cities locations on transportation routes or the perception that they are good places for obtaining employment. In some cities such as New York and Boston nearly half are chronic homeless (i.e., homeless for at least two years), whereas in other cities the figures were between 12% and 30%. The level of alcoholism remains high, varying from 27% to 63% in different regions of the country.

A survey of New York City shelters placed the percentage of problem drinkers at 49% and drug abuse at 26% (N.Y.S. Office of Mental Health, 1982). Moreover, one fifth of shelter managers believed that nonusers of shelters probably had more problems with alcohol and drug abuse than did users (U.S. Department of Housing and Urban Development, 1984). Finally, with respect to marital status, a New York City survey found that 64% of shelter persons had never married (N.Y.S. Office of Mental Health, 1982). Thus, it would not require a great leap of the imagination to predict that those new homeless who are now being placed in traditional skid rows will come to resemble the older long-term residents of these areas. We shall return to this theme later.

Last, we must consider and understand how these aged, often physically debilitated men have managed to cope with recent social upheavals in the downtown skid rows. Indeed, over the past two decades these men have witnessed a host of rapid changes in their traditional milieu: the urban renewal and gentrification of much of skid row; the consequent diminution of many of the traditional skid row institutions such as taverns, "slop joints," barber schools, used-clothing stores, and job agencies; the influx of the young, the non-white, and the deinstitutionalized; and a retrenchment in social service programs in the early 1980s that made the obtaining of entitlements more difficult. In addition, these men are often physically and emotionally ravaged by many years of heavy drinking, poor health care, a treacherous environment, abject poverty, public abuse, and feelings of powerlessness and hopelessness. The ability of these men to somehow garner enough resources to endure suggests an inner strength that is in marked contrast with popular images of these men as helpless, passive dregs of society. As one man put it, "I won't say I 'live' on the Bowery, I'd say 'survive.'" Such a perspective underscores the human qualities of these men and thwarts societal attempts to invalidate and discard them. Perforce it compels us to rethink the consequences of replacing a slop joint with a nouvelle cuisine bistro, a barber school with a beauty salon, or a flophouse with a condominium.

## WHAT IS THE BOWERY LIKE?

The site for our study is the world's most renowned skid row: The Bowery. As one former skid rower put it, "The Bowery of New York is the mecca, the hobo melting pot, the *sine qua non* in the travels of the professional derelict" (Parker, 1970, p. 3). Bowery Street is a two-way street running for 16 blocks in lower Manhattan, bounded by Chinatown on the south and East Greenwich Village on the north. The actual skid row section, "The Bowery," encompasses a somewhat larger area of side streets and avenues running parallel to Bowery Street.

The Bowery, once spelled "Bouwerij," is the Dutch word for farm (Bendiner, 1961). In the 17th and 18th centuries wealthy Dutch families owned large estates along Bowery Road, then a country road in Manhattan. Charles Dickens visited the Bowery in 1842 and noted that two of the city's principal theaters were located there, calling them "large, elegant, and handsome buildings" (Wray, 1984). One European visitor to the city described Bowery Road and Broadway as "two of the finest avenues in the City of New York" (cited in Wray, 1984, p. 6).

By most accounts the Bowery as a congregating place for the destitute had its beginnings around 1873, when the YMCA established a branch there (Wallace, 1965). In the following year the first lodging houses were established by various philanthropic organizations. In the 1890s the Salvation Army built four hotels on the Bowery and in 1909, a permanent municipal lodging house was opened by the City of New York, although this was situated north of the Bowery. Around the turn of the century there were some 100 lodging houses on the Bowery. During the first four decades of the century, it is estimated that some 26,000 to 75,000 people lived on the Bowery at any one time. However, in the period following World

War II, social and economic reforms resulted in a precipitous drop in the population. Hence in 1949, the Bowery population was 15,000, and by 1966 the number was down to almost 5,000 (Bahr, 1967). At the time of this study (1982–1983), there were approximately 3500 men living on the Bowery.

Until the early 1960s an elevated subway line (the "El") ran over the street, and it gave the area a dark, seedy appearance. Yet it was a frenetic environment with dozens of bars, "B-girls" (tavern prostitutes), bookies, slop joints and beaneries, "slave markets" (street corner employment sites) and "sharks" (employment agents), various commercial establishments, vaudeville houses, and movie theaters. It was a home for the down and out, but many "straights" would sojourn to the Bowery for a night of drinking and entertainment. One man recalled, "I can remember years ago when they had the El and I used to come down to the Bowery. They had beautiful bars. We were all working men. We would come down on the weekend and just party."

Perhaps, the area's most famous native son was Jimmy Durante, whose father owned a barbershop on the Bowery. Durante began his career playing the piano in a Bowery nightclub. In his 1931 book, *Night Club*, Durante describes his hometown:

What a street it was! Narrow and pathed with boards. Lined on both sides with saloons, music halls, night clubs, exhibition[s] of freaks, cootch dancers, Japanese ping pong stands, a thousand different kinds of catch penny and shake down places. It had the Coney Island smell ten times as strong as Surf Avenue. It was so noisy with the yelling of barkers, the harmony of singing waiters, the blare of bands, and the shouting of drunken men and women you couldn't hear yourself think.

The Bowery of the 1980s is considerably different. The El is gone and the street now has an open, bright appearance. Also gone are most of the lodging houses (flops) and traditional skid-row institutions. Only 12 flophouses and 3 missions are left. Incredibly, there remain only two taverns, a few used-clothing stores, and perhaps two or three classic slop joints (cheap restaurants). Replacing the more informal supports of taverns, bookie joints, restaurants, clothing stores, and the like are a variety of social service agencies such as the Bowery Residents' Committee, the Holy Name Mission, the Salvation Army, the Manhattan Bowery Project, and the Volunteers of America. Most of the buildings now house commercial establishments that specialize primarily in wholesale restaurant equipment and lighting accessories. The upper floors of many of these buildings are being converted to artist's lofts and residential cooperative apartments. Thus, outsiders driving along the Bowery might observe a few men lying on the sidewalks or find a dirty rag being wiped across their windshield as they pause for a traffic light, but most would probably be unaware that they are in the heart of New York's skid row.

The more perceptive passerby might observe the old signs hanging over the entrances of the remaining flophouses and missions that dot the area. Each flop shelters between 34 to 554 men on a given night, and the total men housed in these facilities is about 2,500. On entering the typical lodging house the visitor encounters a rather steep, dusty, dimly lit imitation marble staircase with wooden banisters on both sides. The prevailing notion is that these houses were built with precipitous stairs so that persons who were too inebriated to negotiate them would be excluded for the night.

On reaching the top of the stairs the visitor turns left into a large room with rows of etiolated wooden, torn vinyl, or threadbare upholstered chairs. Most of the chairs face a 21-inch television set which is perched on a stand six or seven feet above the splintered wooden floor. The room is lit by one, bare, oblong fluorescent light. These rooms are usually painted in a two-tone motif such as mahogany below the mid-wall paneling and bone white above the paneling, although the latter might be more appropriately characterized as dingy yellow. In one corner of the room is a vending machine filled with several varieties of canned soups and hot foods. On the wall adjacent to the entrance is the cage which encases the hotel manager. The cage, made out of fine metal wiring, is usually adorned with several notices, the most prominent being a warning to persons with daily tickets from the Muni that they must be "*In* by 11:00 PM and *Out* by 7:00 AM."

Off this large room is a narrow corridor with mottled walls and blue-black wooden floors. Every seven feet or so is a door. Along the top of the length of the walls is a two-foot wide strip of chicken wire. Behind each door is a 4-foot by 7-foot cubicle with a bed, a locker, a night table, and whatever personal possessions the occupant can squeeze into his space. Frequently one finds a hot plate with some pots, plates, cups, and utensils. Each cubicle is separated from the adjoining one by a thin wall that extends only part way to the ceiling, the resultant space being filled with a two-foot wide strip of chicken wire to foil "lush divers." These are neighbors who sometimes leap into a cubicle in the dead of night to rifle a man's pockets while he is in a drunken stupor or at the john. In addition, there are usually several large dormitories on various floors of the flop. The dormitories are dimly lit, smelly, dirty, crowded hovels consisting of several dozen cots, frequently covered with soiled sheets and not uncommonly infested with lice or chiggers. Many of the hotels are referred to as "bug-houses" or "scratch houses." One man observed that at several notorious hotels "you come out with a family." Room rates vary with the quality of the hotel. The cheapest flops charge about $20 per week whereas the better ones charge about twice as much.

Some flops have chosen floors and sections for the "better bums," who are long-term clients not like the "ticket men" sent from the Muni. The special sections are cleaner and quieter. Although some of the flops are better than others, all are substandard. Racial discrimination on the Bowery is most blatantly revealed in its housing arrangements. Some of the flops admit neither blacks nor Hispanics, and those that do seldom allow them on the better floors or in the nicer rooms.

The following lamentation by an older skid-row man aptly depicts the ticket hotel experience:

In the dormitories you're up all night. Then if you get a chance you lay down on one of the cots and you've got a chance of walkin' out all loused up. The last time I stayed in one of these places I woke up itchin'. I looked down on my pants and I saw these damn things crawling all over me. This was back in the 70s. I never went back to the Muni for no damn tickets. I'd rather fight the streets than go to one of them flophouses. If you go in by yourself and pay for it, you'll get a fairly nice room. On a Muni ticket you get a dormitory.

Another component of Bowery life, although considerably less prominent than the flophouses, are the tenement rooming houses that are found on streets contiguous to Bowery. Many of them are four- to six-story dilapidated tenement buildings in which larger apartments have been reduced to one or two rooms. They are a notch above the flophouses in that they usually include bathroom and cooking facilities. The rents are higher for these apartments ($150 to $250 per month), and two men will often share an apartment. Many of the apartment men teeter literally on the margins of skid row. Our interviewer's account of Mr. Louis illustrates the tenuous state of many apartment men:

Mr. John Louis is a 59-year-old cafeteria worker who is temporarily out of work because of a foot operation. He is a man who is on the verge of entering the flophouse circuit. He has a long history of drinking although he denies being an alcoholic or having a drinking problem. He has a cheap apartment and is currently eating his meals at the Men's Shelter. Mr. Louis is a friendly, likeable guy who was dressed nicely. He himself expressed a fear that he would end up in a flophouse and this fear seemed justifiable to the interviewer. In the past he has made a great deal of money waiting on tables but has blown it all—a self-classified "good time Charlie." Mr. Louis now works in a cafeteria where he makes about four dollars an hour. A gentle and quiet man who one hopes will be able to put his act together and keep from making that last tumble.

The parks comprise another component of the Bowery scene since they often serve as bedrooms for those men who are "carrying the stick." There are no parks physically located on the Bowery. There are, however, several parks located within three or four blocks of the Bowery. Some of these parks are merely a row of benches and dirt patches situated on a divider of a major avenue. Others are concrete surfaced with fence enclosures having no trees or grass. The crucial element is the availability of a bench, although many men will use cardboard boxes, especially in inclement weather. The second crucial element is its safety. That is, can a man sleep there at night and not get jack-rolled? Many of the older men select parks farther away from the center of the Bowery because these parks are less frequented by younger, more dangerous homeless men. The socially adept homeless men try to sleep in groups to fortress themselves: "We sleep on the bench, two on this bench and two on this other bench. That way we protect each other."

The service agency is the last skid row component we shall introduce at this point. Along the Bowery and its adjoining streets there are a host of agencies that provide social service, medical and psychiatric treatment, alcohol detoxification and counseling, meals, showers, and shelter. About half the agencies are under the auspices of religious organizations: the Holy Name Mission, the Salvation Army Booth House, and the Nativity Mission. The other agencies

are not-for-profit facilities supported by a combination of governmental, foundation, and individual donations. The agencies commonly have large rooms, furnished with rows of tables which are
used alternately for meals and recreational purposes (e.g., card playing, bingo). The group activities, support, and behavior inherent to
these settings not only serve to provide material sustenance for
these men but also serve to transform a new arrival into a "Bowery
Man." In subsequent chapters we shall more fully examine the roles
that flophouse, street, and agency play in the creation and maintenance of the Bowery Man.

## WHO ARE THE MEN TO BE STUDIED? WHO ARE THE RESEARCHERS AND WHAT ARE THEIR METHODS?

Our aim was to interview a cross-section of Bowery men aged 50 or
over. In the United States, 50 is not considered to be very old. But on
skid row, by 50 many of the men look and act like men 10 to 20 years
older (Bogue, 1963). Physically they are slowed by the accumulation
of conditions indigenous to skid rowers, such as poorly healed fractures, missing limbs, respiratory conditions, wine sores, and so on.
Psychologically, many view their lives as over, and they have little
sense of future. Our interviewers commonly encountered phenomena such as the following:

Mr. Dennis left his wife and newborn baby and hasn't had any contacts with
his siblings in 20 years. He departed home when he lost a job and the
pressure became too much. He lives in parks most of the time though right
now he resides in an abandoned automobile. His face and clothes were dirty,
he said he had a heart condition, and he looked old for 51. He kept referring
to his own shortcomings and calling himself "stupid." He tries to help
himself but when he seeks employment he is told that he is too old to work.
Although Mr. Dennis harbors thoughts of leaving the Bowery, he knows
time is running out; throughout the interview he kept interjecting, "Life
goes too fast."

In developing a cross-sectional sample of the population we
were struck by the multitude of taxonomies that have been devised
over the years to characterize these men. Some classification schema
seemed to identify the men by their most prominent features, al-

though such divisions often combined work roles, drinking behavior, age, and racial divisions. For example, Levinson's (1974a) typology of Bowery men in 1972 included six subdivisions: old pensioners, resident workers, alcoholics, transient workers, young black men, and drug addicts. While these were valid characterizations, it appeared as though Levinson was mixing peaches and plums. Although including alcoholism and drug addiction within the same schema would be logically correct, placing alcoholism and young black men in the same schema seemed to be a categorical error. Moreover, a schema of peaches and plums can often produce some nectarines. Thus, many of those classified as "old pensioners" and "transient workers" were also "alcoholics."

Our task was further complicated by the knowledge that the alcohol-centered skid row culture had spontaneously generated its own typology around drinking behavior. Jackson and Connor (1953) had identified no less than six subdivisions among alcoholics: older alcoholics, bums (who don't adhere to skid row rules), characters (those with erratic or bizarre behavior), winos (run-down alcoholics), rubbydubs (those who drink non-beverage alcohol such as rubbing alcohol), and lushes (the prestige group). Although we had estimated previously that at least one third to one half of the men were daily drinkers (Cohen & Sokolovsky, 1983), we did not wish to focus our analysis solely on alcoholism, because we would then neglect a large segment of the older men (approximately 40% to 50%) who were light drinkers or abstainers.

In the end we opted for a pragmatic solution in which we obtained a stratified sample based on the men's residential status (flophouse, apartment, street) and race (white and nonwhite). In general, the use of a sample size that is about one tenth as large as the parent population is recommended in order to obtain a representative segment of the overall population (Roscoe, 1969). Therefore, we hoped to interview a minimum of 10% of the men aged 50 or over. Based on data from the New York City Human Resource Administration, surveys of the managers or desk clerks of all Bowery flophouses, and interviews of service providers, we estimated that there were 3500 men living in the flophouses, in apartments, and on the surrounding streets, of whom 2700 were aged 50 or over. A breakdown of the sample by location and race is provided in Table 2-1. Roughly three fourths of these older men lived in flophouses, one sixth lived on the streets, and the remaining few lived in apartments. Approximately three fifths of the men were white.

Table 2-1. Estimated Population Breakdown of the Bowery (1982)

|  | Flophouse | Street (warmer months) | Apartment | Total |
|---|---|---|---|---|
| Total | 2500 | 750 | 250 | 3500 |
| Age 50+ | 2000 | 500 | 200 | 2700 |
| White | 1300 (65%) | 250 (50%) | 100 (50%) | 1650 (61%) |
| Nonwhite | 700 (35%) | 250 (50%) | 100 (50%) | 1050 (39%) |

Our strategy was to obtain a broad-based sample of 300 individuals aged 50 and over, proportionately divided by race and location according to the proportions obtained in Table 2-1. We concentrated our interviews in two flophouses (one relatively better hotel and one relatively inferior hotel), within several agencies that provided meals and service programs, and at various parks and street corners where men congregated. Interviews were conducted during various times of the day, on weekends, and in different seasons so as to encompass the widest array of men. For instance, it was not uncommon to find seasonal street persons. An interviewer notes, "Mr. Patrick had been sleeping on park benches and doorways. By using cardboard boxes he says that he can get pretty comfortable. When it gets colder he stays one night in one flop and one night in another flop."

The final sample consisted of 281 men (some interviews were not completed, and there were a few two-timers) of whom 195 were nonstreet dwellers (177 lived in flophouses, 18 in apartments), and 86 lived on the street. Two thirds of our sample was white. The final sample was not statistically different from our estimates of the overall Bowery population, although our sample did have a slight over-representation of street men and slight under-representation of flophouse men (Table 2-2). Although we concentrated our flophouse interviews within two hotels, the final sample was comprised of men living in all 12 flophouses and the three missions that still remained on the Bowery.

The final sample had a mean age of 62 years (range 50 to 80 years) and was 69% white. The nonstreet men were somewhat older and there were proportionately more whites than there were among the street men (63 years versus 59 years of age; 73% versus 59% white) which reflected our estimates of the actual demography of the area (Table 2-2). The stalwartness of some of the street men is illustrated by the fact that 14% were age 65 and above, 6% were age 70 and above, and one street man was 78 years old. Approximately two thirds of the men approached for an interview agreed to participate. There were occasions in which we were forced to terminate interviews because the respondent was too intoxicated or too psychotic to complete them. However, fewer than 10% of the men fell into the grossly psychotic category. The relatively high acceptance rate was a result of offering ten dollars to the respondent upon completion of the interview, which generally lasted about two hours. The ethics of offering cash remuneration for interviews has always been controversial, and perhaps even more so in a population in which the money might be used for dubious purposes. For example, one interviewer wrote, "Mr. George stays around with two to five guys all the time. They pool their money for food and drink. When we finished the interview Mr. George and five buddies all left together to go buy alcohol." On the other hand, the interviews were often long (some lasted four to five hours) and tedious, and there is strong justification for compensating these men for their time and patience. We tried to view the money in a more positive light, that is, as a half a week's room rent or a couple of days of good meals. Indeed, as this interviewer noted, for some men the monetary compensation was truly a godsend:

Mr. Gardner went to churches for help. Welfare won't give him any money. SSI said he is still able to work, so over the past few years he's tried to kill himself three times. Once he cut his throat; then he tried gas from the stove. Then just two weeks ago he tried to jump off a building. Each time he was stopped. He has no friends and no means of support and said [that the interviewer] was sent here from God to bring him ten dollars."

Table 2-2. Breakdown of Sample Used in Study

|  | Total | White | Nonwhite |
| --- | --- | --- | --- |
| Flophouse | 177 | 133 (75%) | 44 (25%) |
| Street | 86 | 51 (59%) | 35 (41%) |
| Apartment | 18 | 9 (50%) | 9 (50%) |
| Total | 281 | 193 (69%) | 88 (31%) |

Sometimes soliciting for interviews created an amusing exchange. As one interviewer approached an elderly panhandler to request his participation in the study the panhandler asked, "Can you spare a quarter?" The interviewer responded, "No. But do you want to make ten dollars?"

There was also a sense that most of the men liked the interview and some even found it therapeutic: "All in all, Mr. O'Connor seemed to enjoy the interview and said at the end that he felt better for talking to me. 'Words heal wounds,' he observed."

In recent years philosophers and historians of science have more or less undermined the notion of total neutrality to one's object of study, especially with respect to the way research questions are posed and data defended (Bhasker, 1978, 1979; Feyerabend, 1975; Kuhn, 1970; Popper, 1963). In the natural sciences the investigator has the advantage of studying an external phenomenon that is non-human, thus there is a *subject* (i.e., scientist)/*object* (i.e., entity being examined) interaction. In the social sciences, the focus of study has subjective human traits. Hence we have a *subject* (i.e., scientist)/*subject* (i.e., person being examined) interaction. This situation does not preclude obtaining replicable information about the persons being examined nor does it prevent the possibility of explaining previous behavior or suggesting behavioral tendencies for the future. Nevertheless, it creates many more variables and subtleties. It necessitates interpretation of the affectual tone in responses, the nuances of meanings, and evaluating the context of the interview, to name but a few examples. Moreover, in some social science research such as this one, the investigators may in a sense be part of the focus of study by dint of their work in the environmental niche under investigation. In this study, several of us worked as service providers and administrators.

Although we believe our findings are objective in the sense that other investigators would elicit similar data, our motives for undertaking this study and our response to the findings clearly cannot be neutral. What is crucial is that we be aware of our subjective role in the study and not let it vitiate the "truths" that we have elicited.

For one of the authors, Carl Cohen, this study was part of a 13-year clinical and investigative relationship with the Bowery. He began working on the Bowery in 1973 as a third-year resident in psychiatry at New York University/Bellevue Medical Center. At a meeting for agency directors supervising site visits for medical students, Carl was introduced to John Tusa, who was then the director of the Bowery Residents' Committee (BRC). At that time, the BRC was a small social service and lounge program located in a recently closed entertainment club, *Sammy's Bowery Follies*. John asked him if he would help provide clinical service to the members. Having been stimulated previously as a medical student toward community health, Carl had decided upon entering his residency that he wanted to work in social and community psychiatry. Therefore he readily accepted John Tusa's offer, although his only prior experience with the Bowery had been through the windows of the Third Avenue Bus.

Carl recalls his first day at the BRC:

I came expecting to cure people's psyches, but the first fellow that I saw pulled up his shirt and pointed to where he had felt a lump in his abdomen. After careful questioning and palpation of the mass, I concluded that the lump was probably a recurrence of his lymphoma. The next patient came in with a half-inch leg ulceration exuding a thick yellow discharge. The third patient was a street man who I had initially thought was obese. He then proceeded to remove six layers of shirts and pants and after 15 minutes he had withered away into a scraggy, undernourished figure with a severe case of dermatitis beneath all the garments.

Carl realized that he would have to be more than a psychiatrist on the Bowery. Over the years he eventually came to see more than his share of psychiatric patients as the number of homeless psychotics grew in number. He continued, however, to see an assortment of respiratory infections, leg ulcers, body lice, and heart disease.

During his first year at the BRC, Carl worked by himself in a small cubicle in the front of the agency. Gradually, more clinical space was provided and a full-time nurse was added. In the early years he accompanied a BRC staff member or the nurse into the flophouses to evaluate men who were unable or unwilling to come to the agency. He reported on his work at the BRC in an article that was one of the first papers to describe the influx of young schizophrenics to skid row (Cohen & Briggs, 1975).

Beginning in the mid-1970s, he joined with Jay Sokolovsky, an anthropologist, for a series of studies on the health, psychology, and social supports of various inner-city populations such as aging men on the Bowery and discharged mental patients and elderly persons living in SRO hotels. Each study evolved out of Carl's clinical work and reflected his desire to accurately depict these populations so as to debunk various myths that tended to devalue them. He argues, "By elucidating the viability of their culture it becomes difficult to negate and consequently dispose of them. Moreover, our studies identify people's strengths as well as their vulnerabilities and thereby provide clinicians, service providers, and urban planners with points for intervention."

For cultural anthropologist Jay Sokolovsky, his participation in the Bowery project developed out of a long standing collaboration with Carl Cohen in doing focused applied research among the poorer members of New York's inner-city population. His earliest professional research was in a Mexican Indian village where he lived with a family and studied how the traditional culture was being changed during the 1970s. While conducting research in mid-Manhattan, he was able to apply much of the standard anthropological approach which he had practiced in Mexico:

To the anthropologist a personal, prolonged contact with the people you are studying is considered a prerequisite to a realistic understanding of their lives. We assume that you cannot know the proper questions to ask and how to ask them without first being a participant observer in a particular social setting. When I first had contact as a researcher with the Bowery in 1976 I was initially deceived in thinking that gaining rapport with the residents would be easy. Arriving on a warm summer day dressed in dungarees and a New York Knicks tee shirt I had casually started talking with an older man outside of the Bowery Residents' Committee. Based on my reading of numerous books on skid row life I was able to sprinkle the conversation with words such as "flop" and "carrying the banner." He assumed I was a young down and outer and invited me to join him at a local tavern. However, after buying beers I got carried away by the ease with which I seemed to be accepted and began to ask simple questions such as how he had come to live on the Bowery. Abruptly he banged his fist on the table and shouted, "I wouldn't even tell my father that," and stormed out of the bar. It was not until a month later that this man would talk to me again, although I saw him almost every day. I soon learned that the norms of skid row admitted an easy surface conviviality but did not readily permit probing of another's history. Subsequently, I realized that any real penetration deeply into the lives of these men would require a good deal of quiet participation in daily activities.

To accomplish this Jay worked as a kitchen helper at the BRC, serving food, calling bingo, and going along with Roland to deliver meals to the homebound in the flophouses. "Although Roland would never let me stay with him in any of his secret sleeping places, I walked dozens of miles through his urban domain and during these times he began to slowly reveal the saga of his life." It was in simply spending time with Miles in the park where he slept or with Uncle Ed as he looked for a job that he learned their basic patterns of survival and life histories. It was only after several weeks of interaction with such men that semi-structured questions about their lives could be asked and then, only with great caution. The three profiles in Chapter 1 are drawn largely from Jay's anthropological fieldwork.

Interviewers were selected by placing advertisements on the bulletin boards at New York University. Four interviewers were selected—Hal Onserud, Stephen Moses, Jonathan Herman, and Scott Kellogg. All were college graduates. The former two were working part-time as musicians, and the latter two were applying to graduate school programs.

As in the case of Carl and Jay, the Bowery could not help but evoke strong affects within the interviewers. Even after months of talking to these men, the interviewers were often deeply moved by a particular biography. Here are some excerpts from their notes:

Mr. Roberts is a man of creativity who has never found an outlet; he is wracked with anxiety and his body is full of medical problems—bad leg and pacemaker. All in all, a life totally wasted by drinking. It made me sad to hear his story.

Mr. Thomas thinks he needs help, that there's something wrong with him. He wants to live in a nursing home. He wants to have nothing to do with the people around here. He has been in and out of the Palma Hotel and McCauley's Mission where he attends religious services in order to get a bed ticket. He doesn't feel right today—he can't see clearly and he rubs his eyes a hundred times per day. He wonders if it would be better if he were dead. I didn't know what to tell him.

Mr. Henry is a talkative, intelligent 53-year-old man who has no home at the moment and is shuttled up to the armory from the Men's Shelter everyday. He used to have a regular job in the garment industry and he had once attended the Fashion Institute of Technology. He misses the old days when he had his old apartment and good clothes. He minimized his drinking, but it was quite obvious that alcohol played a big role in contributing to his current state. He's a man on the way down and if something doesn't improve for him it will be one more life with some promises washed out.

The research project was directed on a daily basis by Eric Roth, who worked half of the time with the research team and the other half administering the senior lunch program at the Bowery Residents' Committee. Eric provided important descriptions of many of the men and their behavior. He was also instrumental in applying some of the research findings to develop an expanded service program for seniors at the BRC (see Chapter 10). Data analysis for the research project was provided by Jeanne Teresi and Douglas Holmes who had worked previously with the authors in their studies of older persons living in SRO hotels.

Several methodological pathways were used to develop a picture of Bowery life. One approach was to use a structured questionnaire that was comprised of two instruments: The Comprehensive Assessment and Referral Evaluation (CARE) and the Network Analysis Profile (NAP). The CARE was developed by Barry Gurland and his associates (1977) in the mid-1970s and was designed to assess the level of physical health, psychiatric symptoms, and social and economic needs of geriatric populations. It was the principal instrument used in the Cross-National Study of elderly persons living in New York City and London. Thus, its utility for the present study was that it enabled us to contrast older Bowery men with a general sample of older New York City men who were interviewed as part of the Cross-National Study.

The CARE is comprised of various contingency items that can potentially yield up to 1500 bits of information. In other words, an initial header question might inquire about a particular problem (e.g., "Do you have difficulty walking?"). If the response is affirmative, then additional questions follow to elicit more detail (e.g., "Do you have to have someone help you to walk?" "What is this difficulty or limitation due to?"). Depending on the number of symptoms that the respondent may have, the CARE takes between 30 minutes and 2 hours to be completed.

The CARE yielded 25 scales, and they generally had high internal consistency; that is, the items comprising the scale correlated well with each other (alpha values of .70 to .90). The interrater reliability for each scale ranged from .64 to .97. Thus, interviewers were consistent with each other. The CARE was particularly appropriate for use with Bowery men since it is comprised of simple items that focus on the here and now, and it avoids detailed questions about past events. Bahr and Caplow (1973) in their Bowery research of the mid-1960s found the men to be "no more likely to be consciously untruthful in replying to interviewers' questions than are members of most other disadvantaged populations" (p. 360). However, because of their age and their high rates of physical and mental illness, the accuracy of their responses (as corroborated by agency records) was especially sensitive to variations in the complexity of the information sought and the recency of the situation being recalled. Although respondents were influenced by social desirability considerations (e.g., they tended to inflate their educational levels), Bahr and Caplow concluded that the social desirability factor was no more influential in biasing the responses of these men than it was among other populations.

Measures of social interaction were obtained from the NAP, which had been developed in previous work with geriatric populations (Cohen & Sokolovsky, 1979; Sokolovsky & Cohen, 1981). Therefore data were available from other groups so as to permit comparisons with the Bowery men. The NAP evolved out of an effort to distill the best elements of the sociological and anthropological approaches to examining social networks. In general, the former approach employed less detailed sociometrics that were capable of yielding large samples, whereas the latter approach examined more complex measures of interaction but consequently studied fewer subjects. The NAP was also designed to elicit both objective (behavioral) and subjective (affectual) measures of social interaction.

The NAP is a semi-structured instrument that examines several fields of social interaction: respondent–hotel linkages, respondent–outside nonkin linkages, respondent–kin linkages, respondent–hotel staff linkages, respondent–agency staff linkages. Persons were included in the social network if they were in contact (i.e., through a material exchange, social activity, or 15-minute conversation) with the respondent over the three months prior to interview (12 months for outside nonkin and kin). Significant persons could be included if they had been in contact with the respondent in the previous 12 months. The NAP generates 20 social network variables, and 14 of these were used to create two social network scales. Scales for

network proclivity (i.e., who a respondent would turn to if confronted with a particular health or social problem) and institutional/
agency linkages were also constructed (see Appendices 1 and 2).
Institutional/agency linkages represented at least a monthly contact
with a particular place (e.g., churches, stores, missions) rather than
an individual. Any meaningful personal encounters in these places
were recorded within the appropriate field of interaction. The piv-
otal role that these social network variables played in helping us to
understand these men's behavior as well as their role in affecting
health and buffering against stress will be elucidated in subsequent
sections. As with the CARE, the interrater reliability of .77 was
within acceptable levels.

Both the CARE and the NAP were designed to be administered
by persons with no previous expertise in research, aging, health care,
or social services. In fact, we had found previously that specialization
sometimes created problems for interviewers who might inadvertently interject their professional styles into the interview. Thus, a
clinical psychologist might evoke an excessive emotional response or
a physician might elicit an excessive number of physical complaints.
Moreover, the professional demeanor can create a distancing and
wariness from a population that is suspicious and cynical about
experts and service providers.

The initial training sessions for the NAP and CARE were completed over two and four days, respectively. Training consisted of a
detailed review of the instruments followed by scoring of video- and
audiotapes, and the interviewing of each other. Once the project
began, the interviewers audiotaped every tenth interview, and these
were reviewed along with the completed questionnaire for accuracy.
In addition, the project staff reviewed all completed questionnaires
as they were returned.

A second methodological approach to studying this population
involved the use of more traditional anthropological techniques such
as participant observation and intensive interviewing of several men
representative of various Bowery types. This work involved the
collection of lengthy life histories often taking several weeks to
complete each one. The extensive discussion of the early lives of
Uncle Ed, Miles, and Roland are largely drawn from this type of
documentation. As Jay described earlier, he followed these three
men around the city for several days. Thus, he accompanied Roland
as he made meal deliveries into the flops, or Ed as he made the

rounds of various social service programs, played cards in a lounge program, went to AA meetings, and conversed with friends on the street. With Miles, it meant spending time in the park where he slept with his buddies, visiting the food lines, and buying a bottle.

Although somewhat less systematic in their technique, Eric Roth and Carl Cohen were able to contribute observations gained from many years of working within an agency that serviced these men. Hence, they were able to recall vignettes and anecdotes to elaborate on the data derived from the formal questionnaires.

From earlier studies, several groups were available for comparison with the Bowery men. One comparison group consisted of a subsample of 61 men aged 65–69 living in New York City who had been administered the CARE during 1974–75. These men were part of a larger sample of 445 men and women, aged 65 and over, living in New York City (Gurland, Copeland, Kuriansky, Kelleher, Sharp, & Dean, 1983). The mean age of this subsample was 67 years; 80% were white, 8% black, 10% hispanic, and 2% other. Their mean income was $11,000 per year; two-thirds had been blue-collar workers, and they had completed 10.5 years of schooling. Three-fourths of these men were still married. We used a second comparison group of 12 community-residing men who had been part of a larger study of 25 persons aged 55 and over who had been administered the NAP. Their mean age was 67 years; they were all white. They had completed nearly 16 years of education. Two-thirds were still married. Finally, a subsample of 58 men (mean age = 73 years) who had been administered both the CARE and NAP instruments were available from a larger study of 133 older persons living in Midtown Manhattan SRO hotels (Cohen, Sokolovsky, Teresi, & Holmes, 1986).

The agenda for this book is to provide answers to two questions. The first question is: What makes a skid row man? In addressing this issue we must first examine homelessness in its general historical context. We will then explore the individual historical pathways that our Bowery men have taken to skid row and the skills that they have acquired so as to survive once they have arrived. Such an analysis will focus especially on how they cope with physical, psychological, and social difficulties. The second question is: Who is the older skid row man? This question will perforce be answered in pursuing the first question. We will learn about their strengths and weaknesses, their needs and aspirations, their possibilities and limitations.

# CHAPTER THREE

# *The Homeless in History*

In 1984, Margaret Heckler, then Secretary of Health and Human Services, summarized the Reagan Administration's position on homelessness: "The problem of homelessness is not a new problem . . . the problem is as old as time . . ." (Heckler, 1984). The objective of such a statement was to allay the public's concern about homelessness and to displace blame for the problem onto some universal human condition or onto the homeless themselves. Ironically, however, the historical forces surrounding homelessness are embedded in the moral conscience of the public as evidenced by the public's intensely ambivalent feelings toward the homeless, falling everywhere between sympathy and harshness (Sexton, 1986). Although the Protestant Reformation and the rise of capitalism provided religious and economic justifications for the harsh treatment of the homeless and poor, much of pre-Christian and early Christian teachings sanctified the poor and exhorted charity toward them. Consequently, even within public consciousness it is not easy to dehistoricize the problem.

In this chapter we shall discuss several historical themes that have affected the size and the content of the ranks of the homeless:

1. The effect of changes in the overall economic system—precapitalist, capitalist, late capitalist—and of changes within a particular economic system;
2. The effect of changes in moral and religious codes;
3. The effect of government intervention;
4. The effect of socioeconomic and governmental forces on the personality and behavioral styles of the homeless.

## THE BEGINNINGS

John Gillin (1929) has pointed out that "early human societies had no beggars" (p. 424). Begging, he argued, is a phenomenon of "civil societies." As long as people lived in blood-bound small groups, the nearest analogue to begging was the hospitality afforded travelers away from their groups, or "kin-wrecked" men and women. Hence, in early societies each person had a role, and there was no possibility of being excluded from the group except under very unusual circumstances. Indeed, cross-cultural studies of peasant societies indicate that efforts are made to find some sort of role for even highly deviant persons. For example, some writers (e.g., Foulks, 1975) have suggested that the role of shaman might sometimes be accorded to the mentally ill as an activity which they are capable of performing. Where violence and agitation are present, restraints are used rather than displacement from the community.

In antiquity, begging and homelessness accompanied periods of social and economic disorganization. Major contributing factors were wars or economic systems that displaced persons from the land and from their traditional family groupings. For example, there is no record of begging in Israel until the eighth century BC when the growing commercial activity had disturbed the old pastoral and agricultural economy. In other words, the privatization and accumulation of land and the growth of towns in which individuals had to survive based on non-agricultural skills created a potential for an underclass.

Nonetheless, these early societies made various attempts to diminish beggary. First, family ties were still strong so that aged and disabled members could be cared for by their kin. Gillin (1929) observed that for several centuries the Israelites made efforts to prevent distress by providing for gleaners in the fields and vineyards. Athens provided for its needy citizens so that none of them had to beg. Other substitutes for charity included polygyny; the Code of Hammurabi (ca. 2200 BC) stipulated that when a woman was left behind by a soldier called into services she could marry another man if her husband had not provided her and her children with an abundant supply of the necessities of life. Other less desirable means for avoiding beggary included prostitution and slavery. In Rome and medieval Europe, hunchbacks, cripples, and the mentally ill often found a place in the entourages of the nobility.

As noted above, periods of economic or civil upheaval sometimes taxed the supportive system of most societies. For example, as can be seen from the later Hebrew writings and the New Testament, Israel under Roman rule had a substantial number of blind, lame, and leprous beggars. Similarly in Rome, beggary began to appear when foreign wars displaced the landed proprietors and sent them in hordes to the city.

Although state structures of early societies and familial succor tended to reduce beggary and homelessness, the breakdown of the Roman Empire and growth in the population (especially after 1000 AD) served to increase the number of these groups in Europe. Yet, prior to the Renaissance two overlapping philosophies tended to preserve the dignity of the homeless (Gilmore, 1940). First, folk customs found in European as well as in modern-day preliterate societies have generally afforded hospitality to strangers. In these societies, where mystery and magic are prominent elements in the world, the stranger is viewed as a mysterious person representing a magical, possibly threatening, force. Consequently, to protect themselves, customs evolved so that the stranger could be accorded the most royal hospitality which the household or tribe could afford. To protect themselves from abuse, a three-day limit was often set. A good illustration of such custom is found in the story of Ulysses, who, although dressed as a beggar, was treated as a guest and thereby able to gain admittance, incognito, into his palace to challenge his wife's suitors. In this early form of almsgiving, the givers feel that they are giving also for their own benefit and not solely for the benefit of the beggar.

As the population and number of strangers increased, people had to begin to distinguish between guests: Friends and guests of high esteem received lavish hospitality whereas those of more lowly station received reduced hospitality. Population growth probably enabled some persons to live on the hospitality of others. They invented stories or carried news from faraway places that enhanced their esteem in the eyes of the host. As cities grew, beggars could settle in one city without necessarily being known to everyone.

The second moral philosophy that built on and flourished concomitantly with the earlier philosophy was that of Catholicism. The sanctity of charity to the poor and assisting strangers is a prevalent theme of the New Testament:

[You] shall inherit the Kingdom prepared for you from the foundation of the world: For when I was an hungred, and ye gave me meat: I was thirsty, and ye gave me drink: I was a stranger, and ye took me in. (Matthew 25:34, 35)

And now abideth, faith, hope, and charity, three; but the greatest of these is charity. (I Corinthians 13:13)

And above all things have fervent charity among yourselves: for charity shall cover the multitude of sins. Use hospitality one to another without grudging. (I Peter 4:8, 9)

For the most part, the Catholic Church assumed the functions of relief that had been carried out by the Roman government. Monasteries cared for the physically and mentally handicapped, and they also served as a place of respite for wanderers. The rise of Monasticism with its forsaking of worldly possessions valorized poverty. The Franciscans, in particular, who had no monasteries, but adopted wandering and begging as a mode of living further helped to sanctify begging and vagabondage.

## THROUGH THE MIDDLE AGES

As with their earlier counterparts, the vagabonds of medieval England and Europe kept jokes, stories, tricks, and news of afar to prolong their welcome. Indeed, the arrival of any stranger probably broke up the monotony of life in the feudal manor. Finally, by the late Middle Ages, with the development of money and the growth of population and the consequent availability of cheap labor, the lords found it more economically sound to hire workers, who tended to be more efficient than the serfs. By the 14th century wandering and begging were well-established, generally tolerated, and perhaps even encouraged. This era marked the end of a Golden Age for mendicants and homeless wanderers.

A watershed year in Western civilization for the homeless was 1349. One year following the end of the Black Death in England, Edward III and his Council promulgated the Statute of Laborers (Gillin, 1929; Gilmore, 1940; Ribton-Turner, 1887; Wallace, 1965). The law, intended to suppress vagabondage, was actually one of the earliest attempts to regulate the workforce. Following the Black Death, there was a shortage rather than a surplus of workers. Many of the manors had been decimated, and those people who had survived the plague left the manors in search of better wages and conditions. So, ironically, the first governmental intervention against homelessness arose when workers had an economic advantage over employers and when there was a shortage as opposed to a surplus of workers. The Statute of Laborers set wages at the prevailing level before the Black Death; compelled those offered work at these wages to accept them or face imprisonment for refusal; penalized those accepting more than their specified wages; provided that food should be sold at "reasonable prices"; and outlawed the giving of alms to able-bodied beggars. Employers ran little risk of paying higher wages. Its principal effect was on workers. Thus, we find here one of the first confrontations between the state and the traditional Catholic and folk doctrines of charity.

As with many governmental responses that were to follow over the centuries, the statute not only failed to solve the problem but actually created a larger vagrant class, more crime, and civil unrest (Gilmore, 1940). This was because the wages were set so low *vis-à-vis* the cost of food and other necessities that many persons fled in order to prevent having jobs offered to them.

The law, being less enforced in towns, contributed to a large influx of country folk into urban areas. Because there were fewer jobs in towns, many of these immigrants turned to begging or crime. In response, in 1359, the authorities of London ordered that country laborers who flocked to the city leave on pain of being put in the stocks.

For the next two centuries, the laws dealing with vagrancy were repressive and severe, the prevailing notion being that the threat of punishment would reduce the problem. One of the most severe of the measures was promulgated during the reign of Edward VI. He ordered that any vagabond could be taken up before two justices by anyone who had offered him work and had been refused. The justices would mark the vagabond with a hot iron on the breast with the letter "V" (for vagabond) and hand him over to the person presenting him as a slave for two years. If he ran away, he was to be branded on the forehead or ball of the cheek with the letter "S." If he ran away a second time, he was to be put to death. Various other severe punishments were periodically experimented with such as whipping, placing in the stocks, burning the gristle of the ear, and banishment overseas.

The idea of providing workhouses (also called in various forms beggar houses, almshouses, or labor colonies) to deal with the homeless poor was the dominant policy from the 17th century onward. These facilities provided shelter and a small wage in exchange for work (industrial or agricultural). The quality of these facilities varied greatly, although most were harsh. Moreover, the refuges were offered as an alternative to the severe, punitive vagrancy laws that continued to exist. The Poor Law of Elizabeth (1602) stipulated that able-bodied vagrants were to be sent to workhouses and provided with work. Those who did not work were to be sent to the galleys or banished.

On the European continent, the attempts to deal with homeless persons were essentially the same as those in England. For example, in 1656 Louis XIV established the "Hôpital Général," which served as a workhouse for the able-bodied poor, the disabled, the infirm elderly, and the mentally ill (Foucault, 1965). Similarly, labor houses and colonies were flourishing in Holland, Belgium, Prussia, and Switzerland.

Although the major thrust of governmental anti-vagrancy laws throughout Europe was punitive (as it often is today), by the mid-16th century there were some modifications of the laws to provide relief. First, the impotent poor were often given licenses to beg, though the licenses might restrict begging to areas outside cities. Second, in England in 1536, as a consequence of civil unrest, the government initiated its first relief program directed at the poor. Each parish was to appoint an Overseer of the Poor to levy a tax for their care. It should be underscored, however, that the law was tied to a variety of harsh measures concerning enforced servitude of vagrants, regulation of maximum wages, and the like.

By this time increases in population had created a worker surplus, thereby aggravating the problem of vagrancy. It became impossible to place the able-bodied into bondage. As a result, many parishes attempted to alleviate the problem by diminishing relief to a minuscule amount, hoping that the poor would leave. Additional ordinances established a residency requirement which held that vagabonds were the responsibility of their community of origin. These laws left many in dire straits, and since many vagrants were without well-defined residences, they had no place to go. Once again, we find that laws designed to ameliorate the problem actually lead to its exacerbation.

During this period there was a need to discriminate between able-bodied beggars, who the government considered undeserving, and a variety of other beggar-types who might qualify for assistance and be exempted from bondage. Several classes of beggars existed in England and on the Continent during the late Middle Ages and Renaissance (Gillin, 1929):

*Gypsies* first attracted notice in Europe in the late Middle Ages, and they were so conspicuous by the 16th century that they are mentioned in the laws. They were dealt with as severely as sturdy vagabonds.

*Sturdy beggars*, as we have noted, began to be identified as a problem following the Black Death and the disintegration of feudal arrangements. A second wave of sturdy beggars arose in England in the 14th and 15th centuries because of forced deportation of persons from Ireland, Scotland, and Wales. Many wandered across England and the Continent using some craft or game as a cloak for begging and roguery. Palmists, physiognomists, fortune tellers, collectors for hospitals, fences, minstrels, and performers of interludes swelled the flood of vagrants wandering from place to place.

*Impotent beggars* received no special attention until the draconian laws against sturdy beggars had made people cognizant of the many disabled beggars incapable of working. At first they were given licenses, but apparently there may have been a tendency for sturdy beggars to feign weakness or infirmity to obtain a license. This forced cities—and eventually nations—to provide humane assistance.

*Mendicant friars* wandered over Euope from about the 13th century onward. The disestablishment of monasteries in England released many monks and nuns onto communities. As in the case of impotent beggars, some able-bodied beggars began posing as clergymen to obtain charity.

*University scholars*, in the late Middle Ages, often had to resort to beggary in order to pay their fees. Because many vagrants represented themselves as students, they had to have letters from the Chancellor giving them permission to solicit alms. Apparently this measure produced letters by the score for vagrants and practically none at all for students. By 1600, scholars were included with sturdy beggars on the list of vagabonds.

*Bands of thieves and robbers.* Some of these groups consisted of ex-soldiers or serving men who had left their masters who evolved from the order of sturdy beggars seeking employment into criminal bands of thieves, highwaymen, and robbers.

Finally, it should be emphasized that this rather large and heterogeneous group of homeless consisted of many women, children, and elderly, although adult men were the dominant group. For instance, of 60,000 vagrants in England in 1821, one fourth were under the age of 15.

Through the 16th century we find several trends affecting the homeless in England and on the Continent:

1. Central governments issuing extremely harsh measures to punish vagrancy;
2. Some early attempts to provide minimal relief, especially for the truly handicapped;
3. Attempts by towns to exclude vagrants from relief through residency requirements;
4. Continually increasing numbers of homeless persons because punishment, no matter how severe, left the fundamental causes of vagrancy untouched.

(Clearly, there are some interesting parallels here with responses to the homeless and poor found currently in Western industrialized countries.)

Despite the repressiveness of the laws directed against the homeless, however, they did not fare quite so badly as one might expect from the language of the law. For one thing, the Catholic ethos of charity still prevailed over much of Europe, so alms-giving continued despite condemnation from the central government. Second, central governments were still quite weak, so the force of their edicts was often diminished. Unfortunately for the homeless and poor, the 17th century, with the spread of the Reformation and the consolidation of central political power within Western nations, resulted in further deterioration in their condition.

The Protestant Reformation provided a religious and philosophical justification for the harsh treatment of the homeless and poor. Protestantism made work a religious duty. Persons working hard and living properly would be rewarded in this world and the next. If a person did not prosper it was either because he or she did not live properly or did not work hard, or both. In any case, the victim was to blame. Therefore, it was thought that the poor had only themselves to blame for their poverty. To give to an able-bodied beggar was to give to one who God himself would not favor. Only the maimed and the blind might be righteous and yet be dependent on others. Compelling people to work became a religious act of forcing them to do what they should want to do as God's will. Following this line of reasoning, relief of the able-bodied, if it should become necessary, was valid only for political, and never for religious, reasons. Consistent with this philosophy, in 1528 Martin Luther edited and wrote an introduction to a book ("Book of Vagabonds and Beggars") exposing the fakery of professional beggars (cited in Sexton, 1986). Although Protestantism did not stop alms-giving, it did become more difficult for the poor to rationalize their lot and to secure alms.

Although the combination of legislature edict and religious morality should have served to diminish the ranks of homeless, the underlying economic structure continued to increase their number. The growing industrial revolution with its requirement for the free movement of labor, its destruction of old occupations, and the growth of large cities resulted in the mass movement of people and a resultant rise in homelessness and beggary.

Thus, at this historical juncture we encounter several important trends that laid the groundwork for 20th century homelessness. The traditional rural-based medieval social structures had been torn asunder. People were no longer tied to a particular locale, social matrix, or occupation. The new marketplace required persons to sell their labor and purchase their basic necessities such as housing and food. However, the new economic order was anarchic—it demanded that laborers be in the right place at the right time to obtain work. Even in good economic periods, there were mismatches of available workers and available work. Such mismatches were compounded during periods of economic decline when jobs became scarce throughout the system. Hence unemployment and its resultant homelessness were part of the baggage of the new order.

Two groups fared particularly poorly under the new economic order—the mentally and physically disabled. In feudal and rural societies, these persons were more easily cared for by their families or the communities, and often less demanding roles were found for them (Cohen, 1984). However, the free marketplace required that they also compete in the workforce. Unable to compete with able-bodied workers, these persons were highly vulnerable to unemployment and homelessness. Failing to accommodate them within the workforce, society ultimately placed them in various institutions—initially poorhouses and later special hospitals and asylums—that provided them with housing, food, clothing, and a role, albeit a stigmatized one. The vast majority of disabled persons would remain confined to institutions until the second half of the the 20th century when the deinstitutionalization ethos gained sway.


## IN THE NEW WORLD

The causes of homelessness in the United States seem to be similar to those in Europe: various disasters (natural and man-made), economic forces, and migration. For example, crop failures, civil strife, old age, infirmity, returning soldiers, alcoholism, criminals, and itinerant farmers all filled the ranks of the homeless. In addition, the English policy of forcibly deporting vagrants to the colonies compelled the early settlers to come face-to-face with the problems of homelessness (Erickson & Wilhelm, 1986).

The early policies toward the homeless in the colonies were similar to those in England. Legal residency requirements were established in order for persons to obtain relief, and in 1735 an almshouse was established in New York City based on the realization that homelessness could not be legislated out of existence. The expansion of the American West presumably heped draw many potential vagrants away from the cities, and at the beginning of the 19th century, seamen constituted the greater proportion of the homeless (Wallace, 1965). After more than 30 years of litigation, the Sailors' Snug Harbor opened in New York City in 1833 as the city's first shelter (Hopper, personal communication; Wallace, 1965).

The first soup kitchens appeared briefly in New York City in 1802 and then reappeared during economic downturns in 1808, 1812, and 1817. By 1840, there were seven separate organizations devoted to sailors in New York City, as well as one each in Boston, Philadelphia, and New Orleans.

Samuel Wallace noted that during the first half of the 19th century the vagrant and pauper classes were literally homeless, though many were periodically confined to almshouses and prisons.

They also could find temporary shelter in hallways, basements, alleys, or commercial establishments such as stale beer dives, but there was no distinct ecological area in American cities for these people. There was no skid row.

Despite assertions by some authors that skid row is a uniquely American phenomenon, as we indicated above, skid rows exist in the United Kingdom and probably elsewhere as well. However, American skid rows are undoubtedly the largest, most notorious, and well-studied in the world. The traditional skid row is a run-down area of a city filled with a collection of saloons, pawnshops, cheap restaurants, second-hand clothing stores, missions, flophouses, barber colleges, all-night movies that cater primarily to the needs of the alcoholic drifter and down-and-outer who resides there.

The rise of skid row can be traced to the period following the Civil War. Enormous numbers of men and women were uprooted and rendered homeless and destitute by the war. For example, in 1866 the City of New York rented a building to shelter some of the "large number of entirely homeless men and women adrift in the streets" (Wallace, 1965, p. 14). Residency requirements were often waived so as to take into account the victims of the war, that is, disabled veterans, and soldiers' widows and children.

A second factor that contributed to the rise of homelessness during this period was the flood of European immigrants. For example, in 1854 alone 500,000 persons arrived in the United States.

A third powerful factor that contributed to homelessness and the rise of skid row was the economic panic of 1873 (popularly known as "Black September"). Unemployment rose to encompass 30% to 40% of the population. Bread lines, soup kitchens, and emergency shelters were ubiquitous: "Homelessness had turned into something short of a national way of life" (Wallace, 1965, p. 15).

The triad of the Civil War dislocation, immigration, and economic depression proved to be the key ingredients for the rise of homelessness and skid row. To appreciate the magnitude, for example, in the City of Brooklyn the number of persons receiving outdoor relief tripled in the decade following 1851 and then more than doubled again by 1877 to 50,000 persons.

By most accounts, skid rows were established in the early 1870s (e.g., Erickson & Wilhelm, 1986; Wallace, 1965). In 1873, the YMCA established a branch in New York City's Bowery. The following year, the first lodging houses of various philanthropic organizations were established. In 1875, the City of Boston provided 45,000 lodgings for vagrants. Between 1891 and 1903, the Salvation Army built four hotels on the Bowery. In 1886, a New York State ordinance called for the establishment of municipal lodging houses but none were provided until ten years later, when an aging barge was converted into a shelter (Bendiner, 1961). In 1909, a permanent structure was established costing $425,000 and housing 1,218 persons, with emergency shelter for another 1,300 (Whiting, 1915). At that time, the population of the Bowery was estimated at 5,000 during the summer and 8,000 during the winter.

Nationally, in 1873, it was estimated that there were 38,000 tramps (Wallace, 1965). The numbers decreased in the 1880s with economic prosperity but then edged upward to 45,000 in 1890. With the economic depression of the early 1890s the number doubled by 1893. Vagabonds placed a heavy load on American cities, and by the 1890s more than 20 states had "tramp laws" on the books. At the turn of the century, skid row had truly arrived. Estimates (Wallace, 1965) placed the number of lodging houses in various cities at

200 in Chicago
120 in Washington
113 in Baltimore
113 in Minneapolis
106 in Philadelphia
104 in New York City
 45 in Denver

Thus, the homeless now had an ecological area that they could call their own. And because of the rise of lodging houses, many of the men would have an alternative to sleeping in the rough. As Wallace (1965) noted, "The emergence of skid row meant that the vagrants at least had a place that could be called 'home' when they cared to live there" (p. 18).

Many of these ecological areas developed colorful and descriptive names such as "Lower Town," "The Square," "Madison Street," "The Tenderloin," "The Bowery," "The Mission District," "Chippie Town," and "The Red Light District." Seattle perhaps made the strongest impact on the nomenclature by providing the term "Skid Road" (Morgan, 1951). The name was first affixed to a trail down which logs were skidded to the sawmills and along which lumberjacks lived in a community of flophouses, saloons, and gambling halls.

Wallace (1965, 1968) further explains that the establishment of skid row meant that the term "homeless" became a generic term for single, unattached workers who lived in skid row between jobs. Whether the skid rower was a true vagrant or an unemployed migratory or casual laborer made little difference to the community at large. Neither worked much while living on skid row; neither had much family contact or resources; and both traveled a lot.

The first three decades of the 20th century were the heyday of the American skid rows. It was the era of the legendary folk-hero, the "hobo," a name derived from a slight corruption of "hoe boys" (Bendiner, 1961). The enormous industrial and agricultural expansion required men to lay railroad tracks, pick orchards, fell trees. These men were the gandy dancers, apple-knockers, splinter-bellies, dynos, skinners, muckers and woolies who became symbols of the open road and an expansive country. Chicago became the center of the labor exchange, with an estimated 40,000 to 60,000 men living on skid row. New York City's Bowery housed some 26,000 to 75,000 during this period. The traditional institutions arose at this time to serve the needs of transient and unattached men: rooms for as little as seven cents a night, cheap restaurants, employment offices, clothing stores, and saloons. One worker wrote of the Bowery in 1909, "from Chatham Square to Cooper Square about every other building on each side of the street is a lodging house, and there are more saloons than lodging houses" (cited in Schneider, 1986, pp. 169–170). These saloons were more than drinking establishments. They also served as places for tramping workers to eat, socialize, talk to prospective employers, and even spend the night. John Schneider (1986) explains that street life on skid row had a more positive quality than the often destitute and desperate condition of tramping workers would suggest. The crowded and bustling sidewalks—"swarming with migratory workers" as one hobo recalled—offered the men an exhilarating experience. Bendiner (1961) writes that at the turn of the century, the Bowery provided "more than a quarter of all the city's arrests, a sixth of its saloons, and a fifth of its pawnshops. To many it is the most attractive part of town" (p. 75). Of course there was a dark side to skid row, but the many robust workers tramping across American cities during this period belie the totally negativistic descriptions of this era. (Interestingly, the term "skid row" was not commonly used until the 1930s [Schneider, 1986]. Rather, men spoke of the "main stem.")

During this period the men were powerful in numbers, often had some money in their pockets, and were intent on transforming society to the needs of their class. They even had their own newspaper, *The Hobo News*, and their own annual convention in Brett, Iowa. They were rebellious, independent, and group-spirited. A variety of colorful figures enlivened the image of hobos in the early decades of the century (Anderson, 1923). Dr. James Eads How, "The Millionaire Hobo," was born to a wealthy St. Louis family but renounced the life of ease and comfort to share the lot of the hobos. He was a visionary who believed that the hobos were a "chosen people" who had been denied their due. To help the hobos, How established the International Brotherhood Welfare Association (IBWA). The program of the IBWA called for a coming together of all organized workers to create a society of collective ownership in production and distribution. An auxiliary institution to the IBWA was the Hobo College in Chicago which afforded the migrant an opportunity to discuss topics of practical and vital interest to him, and to attend lectures by professors, preachers, and freelance intellectuals. How also established cooperative "flops" for men as they traveled across the country. At its peak, these "Hotels de Bum" were operating in more than 20 cities. The management of these hotels was left to the men who selected a house committee to run the establishments and provide work assignments.

An equally colorful figure was Dr. Ben Reitman, the so-called "King of the Hobos," who was known to more migratory workers than any other man. The title was apparently well-earned for he spent more than 20 years on the road, including two or three tramps around the world. Reitman described himself as

an American by birth, a Jew by parentage, a Baptist by adoption, a physician and teacher by profession, cosmopolitan by choice, a Socialist by inclination, a celebrity by accident, a tramp by twenty years' experience, and a reformer by inspiration. (cited in Anderson, 1923, p. 173)

Reitman, like many other hobo leaders, was active in the Industrial Workers of the World (IWW, or as they were often called, the "Wobblies"). As compared to the IBWA, which never attracted more than 5,000 members, the IWW had as many as 100,000 in its ranks at times (Anderson, 1923). The IWW was begun in 1905 as an alternative to the American Federation of Labor. It organized workers by industry rather than particular skill. The great appeal of the IWW was a revolutionary call for working men to "take possession of the earth and machinery of production and abolish the wage system. . . . It is the historic mission of the working class to do away with capitalism" (Anderson, 1923, p. 233). The IWW was unique in that it concentrated its organizing among migratory and seasonal workers, construction camps, and lumbering camps. This militancy was reflected in riots and strikes that erupted along the West Coast. Changes in the composition of skid-row men and the government attacks on the Left resulted in the decline of the Wobblies.

Also synonymous with the early 20th-century hobo experience was a sense of wanderlust: "It is the yearning to see new places, to feel the thrill of new sensations, to encounter new situations, and to know the freedom and the exhilaration of being a stranger" (Anderson, 1923, p. 82). Popular literature has glorified this aspect of homelessness. At the turn of the century, Jack London wrote, "This employer worked me nearly to death. . . . Too much work sickened me. I did not wish ever to see work again. I fled from work. I became a tramp, begging my way from door to door, wandering over the United States and sweating blood sweats in slums and prisons" (London, 1905, p. 140). In the '30s, the folk songs of Woody Gutherie ("I ain't got no home, I'm just a ramblin' round, I go from town to town") and the country songs of Jimmy Rodgers, writing about riding the rails ("Everytime I see that lonesome railroad train makes me wish that I was back home again,") glamorized the image of the man of the road (Allsop, 1972). In the '50s, Jack Kerouac's book *On the Road*, and later, such films as *Easy Rider* in the '60s and '70s, continued to project the positive image of the "free," unshackled, adventurous person on the road. Unfortunately, the classic hobo had long since departed the scene. Although there are still some road men among skid rowers and the homeless, the vast majority are now "homeguards."

Anderson (1923) identified six factors that accounted for the men found among the homeless of the early 20th century:

1. Seasonal work and unemployment;
2. Industrial inadequateness, that is, feeble-mindedness, physical handicaps, alcoholism, old age;

3. Defects of personality, that is, feeble-mindedness, emotional instability, paranoia;
4. Life crises such as family conflicts, death in family, criminal offenses;
5. Racial or national discrimination against blacks, foreign-born, and so forth;
6. Wanderlust—the longing for new experiences, the yearning for new situations, the desire to see the world.

It is evident that many of the men fell into the categories that have always been associated with homelessness. However, one factor differentiated this period from other periods with respect to homelessness: The greater availability of work attracted more able-bodied men into their legions. Moreover, the idealization of the hobo by the public, the political and union organizing among their ranks, and the fact that they often had some money in their pockets created a group of homeless that was historically unique.

By the 1920s, however, subtle transformations were occurring. The tramping workers had begun to disappear in the wake of mechanization on the farm, in factories, and in the lumber industry that reduced the demand for semi-skilled and unskilled migrant workers (Schneider, 1986). Hence there was already a large "homeguard" that was replacing the wandering hobo. Prohibition also contributed to skid row's transformation. The changing composition of the skid row population along with Prohibition greatly altered the status of the saloon. Saloons were fewer in number and different in style. The alcohol they served had no "kick," and they doubled only rarely as employment agencies, dance halls, or living quarters. They no longer commanded the prestige that they had enjoyed in earlier years.

It was during the period of the Great Depression that the "main stem" finally transformed itself to "skid row." When wages plummeted after 1929, the ranks of the homeless swelled with men who had no work, no money, and little hope of employment. The Depression created an unprecedented number of homeless individuals (Wallace, 1965). For instance, during the one-year period of October 1, 1930 to September 30, 1931, Chicago provided over one million lodgings. As dramatic as this was, during a 12-month period from 1931 to 1932, the number increased to more than 3 million, and finally in the peak year from 1933 to 1934, when more than 4 million lodgings were provided in Chicago alone. In New York City, over 40 separate private and public agencies were sheltering the homeless. The 1933 census estimate the number of homeless at one to one and a quarter million in a total U.S. population that was slightly more than half of what it is today. However, this figure was considered conservative and other estimates ranged from 2 to 5 million.

During this period public and private shelters became the focus and symbol of skid row. John Schneider (1986) describes how the image of skid row became one of "hundreds of men, looking strangely alike in their overcoats, hats, and dazed expressions, [standing] in a long line stretching down the block around the corner from a soup kitchen" (p. 84).

The Recovery of 1936 reabsorbed some men into the workforce, but the true recovery occurred during the war years. By 1944, the New York City Municipal Lodging House sheltered only 550 men per day compared with an average of 19,000 daily in 1935.

The period following World War II marked the first time that the United States made a serious effort to avoid the heretofore repetitive problem of filling the ranks of homeless with returning veterans. The G.I. Bill of Rights, the Veteran's Administration, disability benefits, Social Security, better pension plans, and welfare, medical, and educational benefits enabled most veterans to reintegrate into civilian society. The proliferation of these programs reflected a temporary shift in posture by policy makers and the public toward viewing poverty as a structural (systems) problem rather than as one of individual breakdown (Stern, 1984).

The post-World War II skid row population was considerably smaller and substantively different than the pre-World War II population. Levinson (1974b) points out that the pre-World War II skid rows (1) had a large percentage of the population that was transient and employed, such as, seasonal and day laborers, migratory workers, or men of the road; (2) were individual skid rows that were part of a larger subcultural system, examples being union organizing, the newspapers, the common argot; and (3) was a subculture that was a positive reference group for its members, especially in providing labor organization, newspapers, songs, and employment, which helped enhance self-esteem. The economic and social changes beginning in the Depression and especially after World War II created a new group of men in the 1950s and 1960s. The transients were generally gone, especially in the East and Mid-West. Mechanization had taken away many of the agricultural and seasonal jobs, and despite the early efforts of the IWW, most homeless laborers had no organized unions to protect them (Wallace, 1965). As early as the Depression there was a transformation of the skid rower from "activist" to "retreatist" (Merton, 1949). Sutherland and Locke's (1936) study of homeless men in Chicago's shelters in 1930s detailed a "shelterization" process by which men began to exhibit dependency, apathy, and discouragement. An interesting sidelight to the diminution of political militarism among skid rowers was evident in a survey by Bahr and Caplow (1973) conducted with Bowery men in the early 1960s. When queried as to "what is the greatest problem facing the country—fighting communism or fighting poverty," 42% of the Bowery men thought it was communism. This response was substantially higher than that of upper-class Park Avenue men among whom 29% thought communism was more important. As Elmer Bendiner (1961) reflected about the Bowery: "It is sad to listen to noises of a street that had its spirit broken. It is pathetic to see beggars where rebels once shouted, sang, and whored" (p. 180).

Although earlier studies such as that of Nels Anderson had alluded to defective personality types among the homeless, the general description was that of a vibrant group. Beginning in the 1930s and especially in the post-war period, these men were universally characterized by negative personality descriptors such as "undersocialized," having "no ego strengths," or having "odd" traits (Bogue, 1963; Levinson, 1958; Pittman & Gordon, 1958; Strauss, 1946).

It is difficult to discern whether these researchers were seeing the detritus of the former skid row population of the early twentieth century or whether economic hardships and governmental suppression of radical activities served to transmogrify these men. In Chapter 9, we shall more fully address this issue. For now, let us leave open the possibility that socioeconomic and governmental forces may have also contributed to the personality traits found among these men.

As noted earlier, David Levinson (1974a) identified six types of men living on the Bowery in 1972: (1) *The old pensioners* who live on Social Security, pension, welfare, or a combination of the three; (2) *Resident workers*, who range in age from 20 to 60, who hold jobs such as kitchen helper, hotel clerk, truck loader, messenger, bartender, or cook; (3) *Alcoholics*, who drink wine, panhandle, eat irregularly, and stay in lodging houses where the city pays the daily rent; (4) *Transient workers*, who, although disappearing, are more commonly found in the Catskill Resort region in the summer; (5) *Young black men* who started coming to the Bowery in the late 1960s and tend to stay away from the more traditional Bowery groups; and (6) *Drug addicts,* who are the smallest group and also tend not to mix with the other groups, and may prey on the other men to obtain money for their habits.

In the early 1970s, the decline of the skid row population and efforts by social activists resulted in a Supreme Court decision that marked the first time in centuries that vagrancy was no longer a crime. Arrests for public drunkenness, disorderly conduct, and vagrancy had constituted nearly two fifths of all arrests nationally in 1968 and more than half in 1960. In James Spradley's study (1970) of Seattle in the 1960s, 72% of the men had been arrested for drinking in public. In Donald Bogue's (1963) study in Chicago in the 1950s, 80% of the heavy drinkers and 70% of the moderate drinkers had been arrested for drinking. The endless cycle of arrest, detention in the "drunk tank," arraignment, conviction, incarceration, release, and re-arrest became part of a revolving door syndrome that Spradley called "life sentences on the installment plan." Chief City Magistrate John Murtagh cogently expressed the sentiment that eventually led to the changes in the attitudes and laws against vagrancy and drunkenness: "There is no drearier example of the futility of using penal sanctions to solve a medical or social problem than the enforcement of the laws against drunkenness" (cited in Bendiner, 1961, p. 185).

At the time Levinson wrote his study most writers were predicting the demise of skid row. For example, Howard Bahr's (1967) survey of 28 American cities in 1966 found that 24 had decreasing populations, 34 were stable, and only one was showing an increase in size. Likewise, Earl Rubington (1971) used the Bowery as an illustration of the decline in skid row population. In 1900, the Bowery population had grown to 15,000. By 1919, the number had swelled to 75,000. By 1949, it had leveled off to 15,000 and in each subsequent year there was additional decreases, so that by the late '60s there were fewer than 5000 men.

Several factors were identified as accounting for the decreases in skid row populations. One factor, already noted, was the decline in transient workers. Another factor may have been the availability of welfare and other entitlements, although Levinson (1974b) felt welfare may also attract men to skid row. This is because the cheaper services on skid row enhance the buying power of the welfare check, and it is less embarrassing to accept welfare while living on skid row than in other sections of the city. A third factor was the arrival of young, generally minority, men who at times may have victimized the older men. Clearly, the older men believed that crime had dramatically risen on skid row; psychologically, the arrival of these younger men was perceived as upsetting the harmony and stability of Bowery life. The result has been that some of the older men left skid row for other sections of the city. The final key factor in the decline of skid rows during the 1960s and 1970s was the extensive urban renewal that was being undertaken by many cities. The elimination of skid row by site clearance led several authors of the period to caution that the decline in skid row population should not be construed as indicating a decrease in the absolute size of the homeless population (Bahr, 1967; Wiseman, 1979). They observed that the elimination of a skid row without adequate low-cost housing replacement would merely result in new skid rows arising elsewhere in the city. Experiences in San Francisco and Philadelphia, where new skid rows appeared after the eradication of the old skid rows, confirmed this assertion.

The late 1970s and 1980s have seen a resurgence of interest in the homeless. A crystallization of three forces (deinstitutionalization of the mentally ill, continuing economic decline of the lower classes, and the decline of low-cost housing) over the past decade has created the growth of a homeless population that has been estimated at as many as 2.5 million, of whom 40% may be living in families (Erickson & Wilhelm, 1986). (Importantly, women and children have re-emerged once again as prominent members of the homeless population—a situation that existed in early industrial Europe, in the United States after the Civil War, and to a lesser degree during the Depression, although the current level of homeless women and children may be greater than that of the Depression.)

The most publicized of these three factors is the deinstitutionalization of mental patients. "Deinstitutionalization" must be conceptualized as including not only those individuals who were actually discharged from psychiatric institutions but also those who might have been hospitalized had the earlier policies of institutionalization been in effect (Bachrach, 1978). With regard to the former, the number of psychiatric inpatients reached its national peak of 559,000 in 1955 and fell to below 150,000 in the late 1970s (Bassuk & Gerson,

1978). However, the latter category of the never hospitalized or briefly hospitalized mentally ill—the so-called "young chronics"— has been consuming an increasingly large share of mental health resources (Pepper, Kirshner, & Ryglewicz, 1981).

The deinstitutionalized and "young chronic" patients have been especially vulnerable to homelessness largely because neither the individual nor the system are easily able to coordinate the various components necessary for community survival. Whereas prior to deinstitutionalization all components were provided by the hospital—food, shelter, clothing, medical and dental care, psychiatric treatment, socialization, social and vocational training—these components now have to be provided for the nonhospitalized individuals by a variety of agencies and from a multitude of sources, including the Department of Social Service, Social Security, Medicaid, Medicare, local hospitals, psychiatric clinics, Office of Vocational Rehabilitation, Department of Health and Human Services, and so on. Admittedly, institutions often were inept at providing a full complement of services. Nonetheless, the probability of successfully coordinating all these components for the discharged patient is fraught with the potential for disaster. Thus, lost welfare checks, discontinuance of Supplemental Security Income, eviction from hotel rooms, missed psychiatric clinic appointments, and inadequate medical care are the ingredients that contributed to large numbers of the mentally ill joining the ranks of the homeless.

It should be underscored that the inclusion of the mentally ill among the legions of the homeless is not a new phenomenon. A characteristic group of wandering beggars of Tudor England were the Abram-men or Toms O'Bedlam (Rosen, 1968). As we described previously, mental patients such as those discharged from Bethlem Hospital ("Bedlam") were often given licenses to beg. It should be recalled that Nels Anderson's study of the hobo culture in the 1920s listed "personality defects" as one of the six principal etiologies of homelessness. Similarly, Donald Bogue's large-scale investigation of Chicago skid row in 1950s identified "poor mental health" as one of the four factors responsible for the existence of skid row.

Hence, the presence of the mentally ill among the homeless is not a new phenomenon. What is new is that proportionately more of the homeless are mentally ill, and their absolute numbers are consequently considerably greater. A review of shelter studies conducted in New York City from 1965 to 1982 indicated that the number of severe psychiatrically disabled persons (sometimes defined as "schizophrenics") ranged from 33% to 70% (Hopper *et al.*, 1982). However, a national survey by HUD (U.S. Department of Housing & Urban Development, 1984) estimated the percentage of homeless who were mentally ill at 22%. The conservative estimate in New York City is that one third to two fifths of the homeless population have been hospitalized for psychiatric illness and/or manifest overt severe psychopathology (Hopper *et al.*, 1982). It is thought that the percentage is generally higher among homeless women.

In studying the homeless mentally ill it has become important to distinguish between two different prospectives: (1) the homeless who have mental illness; (2) the mentally ill who are homeless (Bachrach, 1984a). The latter perspective, often adopted by psychiatrists working in emergency rooms, with outreach services, or in psychiatric clinics of shelters, obviously deals with a more select group of homeless: those persons who are either self-referred or identified and referred by others to a psychiatrist. Importantly, despite having a primary diagnosis of mental illness, many of these homeless have secondary alcohol or drug abuse problems. In Philadelphia, for example, two fifths of the shelter residents had an abuse problem.

Several writers (e.g., Fischer & Breakey, 1986; Snow, Baker, Anderson, & Martin, 1986) have suggested that deinstitutionalization per se has been over-emphasized as a casual factor of homelessness. Specifically, they point to the substantial time lag between the major waves of deinstitutionalization (1960s) and the appearance in large numbers of the psychiatrically disabled on the streets (late 1970s, early 1980s). Rather, other factors, particularly the dramatic decrease in inexpensive housing stock (see below), combined to promote a crisis for the psychiatrically disabled. Kim Hopper and his co-workers (1985) have argued that as long as low-cost housing was plentiful enough and applied norms were forgiving enough, severely disabled individuals with disturbing behavioral habits could be accommodated. Even when they were forced to move, replacement quarters were available in other poor-quality, inexpensive housing. But as housing resources became scarce, "undesirable" tenants became expendable.

Two components have contributed to the rise in homelessness in all segments of the population, mentally ill or not. One of these components has been economic. By the Federal Government's own conservative estimates (U.S. Department of Housing & Urban Development, 1984), two out of five homeless persons come to shelters because of recent unemployment (p. 27). Clearly, under-employment and chronic unemployment contribute further to this picture. During the period 1970 to 1980, nonfarm workers experienced a 7.4% decline in real wages (Hopper & Hamburg, 1984). This figure obscures the fact that the national income distribution curve has been altered—there is a shrinking middle with expansion at the top and bottom. Kim Hopper and Jill Hamburg (1984) outlined the principal reasons for this trend:

1. A deindustrialization process leading to job losses in high-paid unionized traditional manufacturing industries and replacement with low paying non-union jobs in service and retail sectors; between the period 1969 to 1977, inflation-adjusted median income for renter households declined 26% while rent burdens continued to increase (Hopper, Susser, & Conover, 1985).

2. A rising divorce rate and growth of female-headed households, that is, half of all female-headed households lived below the federally defined poverty level by the late 1970s.

3. Persistent high levels of unemployment in 1970s created special problems for minorities, for instance, in the early 1980s only 54% of black men had regular employment.

4. A decrease in the social service programs that have traditionally kept persons out of poverty, such that, in 1980, 42% of the 11 million families living under the poverty level received no welfare, no food stamps, no Medicaid, no public housing, no school lunches (U.S. Bureau of the Census, 1982, p. 320). The real value of Aid for Families with Dependent Children declined by 28% during the period of 1970 to 1980.

The final component that has contributed dramatically to the rise in homelessness has been the decline in low-cost housing stock. Based on household size and lower-level family budget, approximately one third of the nation's households were "shelter poor" in 1980 (Stone, 1983). In other words, they were unable to pay for nonhousing necessities and still cover their housing costs. Although most of the families did not become homeless, the rise in utility shut-offs and the long lines for free cheese suggest that many persons are in a precarious state (Hopper & Hamburg, 1984). Nationwide, approximately 500,000 low-rent housing units have disappeared annually as a consequence of urban renewal, abandonment, conversions, and fires (Hartman, 1983).

One of the most serious housing losses has been the precipitous decline in SRO housing. Such housing often provided acceptable and affordable housing to the elderly, the working poor, discharged mental patients, and welfare clients. Between 1970 and 1982, 1.1 million SRO units disappeared, or nearly half of the existing stock. For example, in 1975, New York City had over 50,000 rooms and 298 lower-priced hotels. Six years later the number had dropped to 19,619, or a loss of 61% of the available rooms. San Francisco lost 4,000 units in the early 1970s and an additional 6,000 at the end of the decade; Seattle has lost 2,200 units since 1974 and Portland has lost 450 since 1978 (Hopper & Hamburg, 1984).

Thus, the inability of persons to pay increased rents and the rise in illegal evictions contributed to the growth in homelessness. Indeed, a HUD national survey (1984) reported that 38% of persons arriving at shelters had come because of eviction. Overlooked in this study as well as most other surveys are the "hidden homeless"—the thousands or perhaps millions of persons who have lost their homes and must double up with friends or relatives (the so-called "Couch People"). The Governor of New York estimates that there are one-half million such homeless persons in his state alone (Erickson & Wilhelm, 1986). Despite these statistics, the federal government has made disproportionately high cuts in federal housing subsidies. For example, in 1979 there were 200,000 publicly subsidized housing starts and renovations. This was reduced to 55,000 by 1983 (Hopper & Hamburg, 1984). Hopper & Hamburg (1984) concluded that severe reductions in governmental allocations for low- and moderate-income housing, the deterioration in the quality and possible sell-off of some public housing units, and the steady erosion of rent subsidies "all mean that the poor will pay increasing portions of their incomes for an increasingly scarce commodity" (Hartman, 1983, p. 65).

The rise in the number of homeless has altered the stereotypical homeless person of the 1950s and 1960s. At that time, homelessness was usually associated with those on skid row: a high percentage of men, generally old (median age between 50 and 54), mostly white, about half having married previously, native born, and at least one third being problem drinkers (Bahr, 1973, p. 10). We have already described how skid row in the early 1970s began to attract young blacks and some drug users. Also during the 1970s the mentally ill began to join the ranks of the homeless. They drifted to skid row, but they were also noticed on the streets outside the traditional areas. Finally, during the late 1970s and 1980s, the homeless began to include more families, more women, more recently unemployed individuals, and those unable to secure adequate housing. Although some of these persons migrated to the traditional skid row area where most services for the homeless were located, others wandered around the streets or settled in the nooks and crannies of the urban environment. When the number of persons living outside the traditional skid row areas reached a critical mass, the news media and public began to demand a response to the problem. In 1981, this was further fueled by the national attention surrounding the successful resolution of *Callahan v. Carey*, which had been filed on behalf of homeless men in 1979 (cited in Hopper, Baxter, Cox, & Klein, 1982). The court mandated that the City of New York provide these men with shelter.

HUD's 1984 national survey of shelter populations indicated that the homeless are demographically different from the skid rowers of the 1950s and 1960s: The mean age had decreased to 34 and the percentage of minorities had risen to 46%. However, a substantial number still fit many of the old descriptions. Levels of alcoholism vary from 27% to 68% (Breakey & Fischer, 1987; U.S. Department of Housing & Urban Development, 1984), and 66% were still single men (the remainder are families and single women). Clinicians report that many of the severe mentally ill will take to drinking to quiet the voices that plague them in a desperate "self-medication" (Coleman, 1986a). Thus, although the composition of the homeless has changed over the past two decades, alcoholism and the large proportion of males still predominate. It is likely that many of those new homeless who are being placed in traditional skid rows and large public shelters may come to resemble the traditional residents of these areas. Julio Torres (1986), a counselor at a public shelter in the Bronx, reports the development of a "Homeless Syndrome" among the men. He believes that 90% of shelter residents are suffering from this condition which is characterized by depression, hopelessness, demoralization, powerlessness, and anxiety. This syndrome parallels the "shelterization" phenomenon found among the shelter residents of the 1930s and among men currently living on skid row. We shall describe this phenomenon in Chapter 7.

In this chapter we have illustrated why homelessness cannot be viewed as a static phenomenon. Rather, it has been dependent on a combination of economic, political, and moral forces. Increases in homelessness have been largely a product of economic downturns, but expansion of the numbers of homeless has occurred during periods of relative worker advantage as well. The ranks of the homeless have varied from a handful of travelers in antiquity to millions during the Great Depression and, once again, in the 1980s. The composition of the homeless have ranged from priests, scholars, and actors to alcoholics, mental patients, displaced elderly, and families. Governmental intervention has generally been harsh toward the homeless, but a period of benevolence following World War II was a major factor accounting for a substantial reduction in the problem during the 1950s. Moreover, public attitudes to the homeless have fluctuated from a charitable one in the pre-Christian and early Christian eras to more punitive attitudes with the rise of capitalism and Protestantism. Nevertheless, in late capitalism, the poor and homeless at times have been aided by progressive and liberal ideologies that have shaped much of Western politics in the twentieth century. Finally, we have observed how the behavioral styles of the homeless have altered over the years from an activist, independent spirit in the early part of the century to a more dependent, hopeless, and docile posture in the post-World War II era.

Changes are still occurring. Skid rows are not the same as they were in 1950s and 1960s. These changes affect the behavioral and coping styles of the residents. Older skid rowers and street men may be more vulnerable to change than their younger counterparts. The older men had undergone their enculturation into skid row when many more of the traditional institutions were available. How they have adapted to the skid row of the 1980s and the effect of skid row on their physical, psychological, and social well-being will be the principal focus of the remainder of this book.

# CHAPTER FOUR

# Pathways to Skid Row

Nobody's a bum all their life. [You] hada been somethin'
once.                                    —William Kennedy, *Ironweed*

## DISRUPTIVE EARLY FAMILY LIFE

Edwin Sutherland and Harvey Locke's (1936) classic study of 20,000
homeless men living in Chicago's shelters in the 1930s was one of
the first reports to place blame for the problem on the nature of
family life. They observed that many of the men were reared in
homes in which the standard of living was very low and that many
men were compelled to leave school at an early age in order to earn a
living at unskilled labor. Consequently, they had to forgo the opportunity to develop the training to work as better-paid skilled workers.

Two decades ago David Meyerson and Joseph Mayer (1966) examined the skid row alcoholics of Boston. They reported that the
family histories of these men showed a high degree of poverty and
family disruption. The families often had frequent contact with community agency groups such as welfare. The skid row man in his own
family of procreation tended to replicate his childhood experience:
"When these men married they created families that, like their own,
were supported by the community" (p. 420). More than two thirds of
the men were in semi-skilled occupations, and approximately four
fifths became residents of skid row when their wives left them. Similarly, Griffith Edwards and his co-workers (1966) studied London skid
rowers and concluded that "the inability of these men to find roots
seems to have been caused in the first instance not by their drinking,
but by their damaged personalities, and the origin of this damage could

often be seen in a childhood home where the benefits of human contact were scant indeed" (p. 252). The authors added that there was little to stop these men from getting to skid row—they came from "loosely knit working class families which would evince little concern for a deviant member and would readily let him drift out of contact. In contrast, the tendency of the middle class to rescue its distressed members most often obstructs progress to Skid Row" (p. 252).

Similarly, in our study, we found many men who had unstable childhoods. For example, both Uncle Ed and Miles lost one of their natural parents during the first few years of their lives, and the ensuing years were fraught with instability. For Ed, it was life with a sociopathic, alcoholic stepfather; for Miles, it was a physically ill, alcoholic father.

Ed was born in New Hampshire in 1929 to an American father and an Italian mother. He was one of three children. When Ed was four, his father, a railroad worker for the Lehigh and Lakawana line, slipped off a car and "went under the wheel." Shortly after his father's death, his mother remarried "a sonofabitch bricklayer from Massachusetts named Pat." Along with Pat came five stepsiblings and the family moved to Massachusetts. Ed said that the last he had heard, his stepfather had been committed to Bridgewater State Farm. "That's a coo-coo hatch. He had picked up this little colored girl who was hitchhiking and tried to rape her. He had been drinking. He was a helluva drinker, but he never admitted to being an alcoholic." This was not Pat's first rape attempt. Indeed, Ed recalls how his stepfather once tried to rape his sister:

We were in the woods, Pat and I. My sister Gail came out to get us for lunch. So Pat told me, "You go ahead and tell your mother I'll be right there." So, ten, fifteen minutes, still no Pat, and no Gail. When I went back I found the sonofabitch doing the damage. He had ripped her panties off already and was trying to have sexual intercourse with her. So I turned around and I grabbed an ax. Good thing I had enough sense. I grabbed the head of the ax and knocked him out with the handle, otherwise I would have killed him.

Miles was born in Alabama. The recital of the date of his birth encapsulates his perspective on life, "I was born in '22 and the Depression was in '29." His father and mother separated when he was three months old. His father was 19 and his mother was 15. "My mother didn't want to be bothered so she left." His father worked for the railroad and paid for his upkeep. For the first nine years he lived with his grandparents in the suburbs. His father lived in town. He recalls that his father drank heavily, but they got along well. Miles's grandfather died when he was nine and his grandmother got a sleep-in job. Miles went to live with his father and his father's girlfriend. Miles remembers going to work in a bake shop at that time, pulling loaves of bread out of the oven: "One dollar a night, believe it or not. Seven dollars a week, seven nights a week." Unfortunately, Miles's father continued to drink heavily. His health failed and he died of tuberculosis in 1935 when Miles was 13 years old.

## OTHER FACTORS: ALCOHOL, ECONOMICS, JOB OPPORTUNITIES

A crucial question emerges. Given that many of these men have disruptive family backgrounds, is this factor the cause of their homelessness? Although the pathological family may ultimately be a product of social forces, a family-focused etiological theory concentrates attention and ameliorative active on the family rather than on society. In responding to the family-centered theory of homelessness, critics have argued that many more men have come from similar family backgrounds and did not become homeless. Why did these particular men end up on skid row? Over a century ago, the English social analyst Henry Mayhew (1851) observed that vagrancy could not be explained by "drink," "ignorance," or "the poor situation of their early lives." Rather, a more complex process must be elicited.

The men in our sample had been living alone for 22 years and on the Bowery for 16 years. Thus there was an average of six years between the time they began living alone and the time they arrived on the Bowery. However, in examining the data more closely we find that for street men the period was quite short—only one and a half years—whereas nonstreet men had taken seven years to reach the Bowery. Therefore, street men's path to skid row was a more direct one. The men indicated that their primary or secondary reason for coming to the Bowery were economic reasons (66%), alcohol (18%), placed by welfare (8%), having friends on the Bowery (12%), to obtain work or for convenience (10%), after family problems such as divorce or death (5%), and it "just happened" (17%).

Uncle Ed's biography highlights three of the aforementioned factors—other than family background—alcohol, economics, and job opportunities (or the lack thereof): "So I stayed at home until I was 16 and then said to my mother, 'I'm leavin'.'" Ed went to Newark and hung around with the "bottle boys" and winos in Washington Square. One day he decided to enlist in the Air Force. He got as far as the air base where he was to do his basic training. During basic training he had a seizure. Realizing that he had had a previous problem with seizures and then discovering that he had also lied about his age, the Air Force gave him an honorable discharge without any rights to benefits. "So I came out and went back home. I did spot jobs around Massachusetts." He relied mostly on Louie's Employment, an agency on the East Side of Boston. He also lived on the East Side—Boston's skid row—in an apartment for which he paid $17 a month for rent. He finally secured a job in the kitchen of a restaurant on Boston's South End, and he held it for nearly five years. "That's about the most I worked at one job." Back then (in the late 1940s), Ed was drinking "a little heavier than moderately. . . . On Friday night we'd say, 'Ah the hell with it. Let's get drunk.' And then Sunday, I'd straighten myself up to go to work on Monday. I always made sure I never went to work with a drink in me." Regrettably, Ed was laid off from that job. "Then I got tired of Massachusetts and moved to New York. I heard so many people talkin' about the big city, the Big Apple and all that shit, so I figured I'd go. That was my downfall."

Ed recalls getting off at Grand Central, and then spending his first day in New York in one of the movie theaters around Times Square. He asked someone where he could get an inexpensive room and ended up in an SRO hotel in Midtown. Soon he was working regularly in a restaurant on 26th Street and was able to pay for a cheap apartment on East 2nd Street, an area just off the Bowery. When the restaurant closed, Ed had trouble finding work and began drinking heavily. He had to move back to an SRO hotel and eventually he worked his "way down to the Bowery. And this is where I've been ever since." Ed said that one of the reasons he came to the Bowery was for day labor:

I couldn't find no jobs uptown so I heard that you could get a job on Houston Street on the Bowery; pick-up trucks, a day of work here and there. I did this for quite a few years. I used to be picked up by trucks, and the trucks used to look for me because I was a good worker. And that's how I started to make my day-by-day pay. You just get picked up and go somewhere. On my first job I went out to a place in the Bronx that was like a factory building. I delivered stuff there and then picked up some stuff and delivered it to Long

Island. They were payin' moderate. They were payin' about a dollar and a half an hour. At least I'd make enough to pay for my flop.

Miles came North at age 16 (after his father's death) to work in the 1939 New York World's Fair. His initial exposure to the Bowery was in the '40s and '50s when he would hang out with his friends and "party" all weekend in the "beautiful" bars.

A series of events in the early 1970s—a heart attack, the closing of the restaurant where he had been working regularly for 20 years, and an increasing consumption of alcohol—resulted in his making a transition from a steady working-class existence (i.e., small apartment and regular work) into a skid row lifestyle (i.e., irregular work, no permanent housing). Miles's first stop was an employment agency on the Bowery: "I left the restaurant in 1972. There's an agency down here on the Bowery, Louis's, down in the basement, that got me the work at a hotel in the Catskills. You take your bag with two or three shirts and whatever, and you pay your way on the minibus or station wagon and go up to the hotel."

In between jobs, depending on his level of drinking and cash reserves, Miles lived in hotel rooms or on the streets. For many older men their first contact with the Bowery came between jobs or when they were looking for work. A former "gandy dancer" (railroad worker) recalls:

I just passed through in the late forties. In those years I didn't stay long. I was out on the railroad then and I could pick-up restaurant jobs when I needed them. At that time they still had the agencies on the Bowery but it wasn't long after that they began cuttin' down on them. Anyway, I didn't want to stay around the Bowery very long.

In casual observation of the older men on the Bowery one is struck by the large number of men with arms festooned with tatoos, many of them quite exotic. This is a symbolic legacy of the varied ports of call from their days of service in the merchant marine or stints in the armed forces. Some will directly attribute their current predicament to their military experience. Roland, for example, relates his present state of existence to his stay in England during World War II. Claiming not to have been a drinker before being drafted, he cites the "two years drunk waiting for D-Day in London" as the origin of his problems and his low status in life. This is not a unique story and the impact of military service seemed to leave a good number of men ill-equipped for civilian life. An interviewer described two such men:

Vincent seems to be lost in World War II. He says he sleeps in the park or "by the river" all year long. He had two wives—one before and one after "the big war." He tells war stories at length without being asked. He blames the war for his loss of both families. He says the "country wouldn't do right by him" so he "lost touch" of his wife in Philadelphia and came to the Bowery in 1955. Life seems to have gone downhill for him after World War II.

Max is a pretty alert, dirty, smelly street person. He has not lived indoors in years. He is proud of his ability to panhandle. He is a loner but denies being lonely. World War II seems to be the last fun he had.

For many of these men the all-male group activities and drinking of skid row replicate their military experience. Similarly, a study by Lodge Patch (1970) of London's homeless found a disproportionate number of old military veterans: "It was apparent . . . that many had seemed stable enough so long as they had been in the services— often for many years, and sometimes (they claimed) with commissions. Their social failure had become apparent only in civilian life" (p. 439).

Several men have used the Bowery as a place to hide from the law. As we were told by one of the men we interviewed, "Yeah, I've been on and off the Bowery for years. I came in 1955 when I ducked and hid from a parole officer. I had violated parole and I was hiding down on the Bowery."

The data from our study points to the conclusion that these men were generally low-skilled workers with relatively poor education. This is contrary to the persistent myth of the numerous "fallen professionals" said to dominate the skid row scene. One hears this repeated by residents of flea bag hotels as well as store owners. They take great satisfaction in detailing the plight of the former star of a 1950s television show or the former New York University professor who they claimed to have seen last week lining up for mission food or lying drunk on the street. As with most myths there is a kernel of reality contained within it. The destitute of the Bowery include an occasional former stock broker or an electrical engineer, yet less than 5% of our sample had careers even as "lower paid" professionals such as business managers, teachers, or small proprietors. The majority of men served as skilled (21%), semi-skilled (39%), or unskilled laborers (29%). There was little difference between street and non-street men with respect to previous occupations. The men worked an average of 20 years at these jobs. Approximately three fifths of the men considered themselves "retired" from their principal occupations, although only 39% of the nonstreet men and 19% of the street men had retired voluntarily. Two thirds of both groups of men reported some part-time job since leaving full-time employment, but the men averaged nearly four years since they had last held any type of job.

With respect to education there was no evidence to support the notion of ex-college graduates living a life of wanderlust. On the contrary, these men were relatively undereducated. Only 5% of the men claimed to have graduated college. The mean educational level for street and nonstreet men was approximately 10th grade; 28% of the men had graduated high school. This percentage of high school graduates was less than the national average, which was 39% for this age group.

The role that socioeconomic factors play in generating the skid row men has been debated for nearly a century. For example, Jack London at the turn of the century epigrammatically summarized the plight of homeless persons:

Go to work is preached to the tramp every day of his life. The judge on the bench, the pedestrian in the street, the housewife at the kitchen door, all unite in advising him to go to work. So what would happen tomorrow if one hundred thousand tramps acted upon this advice and strenuously and indomitably sought work? Why by the end of the week one hundred thousand workers, their places taken by the tramps, would receive their time and be "hitting the road" for a job. (1905, pp. 59–60)

London continued: "There being more men than there is work for men to do, a surplus labor army inevitably results. The surplus labor army is an economic necessity; without it, present society would fall to pieces" (p. 95).

London observed how the mediocre, the inefficient, the unfit (e.g., the mentally and physically ill), and those incapable of satisfying the needs of the industrial system are herded into this surplus army. The struggle tends to lead to discouragement, and one of the primary victims of this discouragement as London saw it was the tramp: "The tramp is not an economic necessity such as the surplus labor army, but he is the by-product of an economic necessity" (p. 96).

By mid-century, armed with empirical data, Donald Bogue (1963) more or less echoed London's analysis. Bogue contended that skid row was a regional collecting place for physically disabled common laborers who are in poor health and who are having difficulty getting work even though they may not drink. Bogue asserted,

The problem of Skid Row, therefore, is not simply one of alcoholism but is a matter of broad employment policy and a by-product of the functioning of the labor market. Almost any American citizen, if denied work opportunities for a span of time would end-up in the Skid Row soup line unless saved from this fate by a family or by some program of social legislation—irrespective of his drinking habits. (p. 197)

Bogue pointed to the validity of his assertion in the mushrooming of skid row that occurred during the depression of 1929–1939. A similar process continually operates on a smaller scale even during better economic periods because of the built-in unemployment present in our economic system.

Bogue further noted how in recent decades the nation has attempted to put a "floor" beneath the labor market in order to make it impossible for persons to be brutalized by the working of impersonal competitive processes. Minimum wage laws, public assistance, and unemployment compensation are intended to serve these functions, "but there are flaws and loopholes in the program" (p. 197). During the 1960s, various entitlements were added to plug up the loopholes. Most important were medical insurance, food stamps, public housing, and social security for the disabled, aged, and blind. By the 1970s and 1980s, many of these social service programs were being retrenched, and the rising number of homeless attested to the fact that many were falling through the "safety net," as the "floor" is now called.

London argued that the "road" was one way for society to rid itself of its excess "waste." Today, people do not take to the road, but they take to the urban sidewalks, alleyways, heating vents, or cots in the armory. The "luckier" ones find a cubicle in a skid row flophouse.

As with the pathological family theory, the economic factor may ultimately explain "homelessness," but it does not explain the individual case. As Wallace (1965) retorted to Bogue's presumption that under certain economic circumstances we would all end up on skid row, "Of course, this simply is not true. Other 'victims of economic circumstances' turn to friends, commit suicide, take to crime, leave the country, or suffer mental breakdowns" (p. 128).

## SKID ROW AS A CULTURAL REFUGE

For large numbers of these men the Bowery's major attraction is its function as a cultural zone of refuge, where they can either hide from their prior life or "rest" until restored psychological and economic resources permit an escape. The reluctance to reveal details of one's background or even a person's real name is reflective of the need to hide from one's own past. Roland exemplifies this phenomenon. Many questions about his life history are simply ignored or he will repeat a cycle of stories depicting an extreme reaction to simple mistakes. He will use a tale of estrangement from his sister as a form of closure when being questioned about his past. Yet these well-worn stories provide some clues as to what really pushed Roland onto the Bowery:

I was staying with my sister in Connecticut, after the War, and it was my job to do the lawn work. I was runnin' the tractor mower and I don't know, I must have not seen a rock or somethin', and the motor made a giant, loud sound and just stopped workin'. I tried to start it, I looked under it, but I didn't know how to fix it. I left. That was 18 years ago, and I've never spoken to her since. She doesn't even know I'm on the Bowery.

Whenever Roland makes a mistake he mentally flagellates himself. He knows its his fault and he leaves for good to avoid embarrassment. As he says, "I've been doin' it all my life."

Finally, marital turmoil, break-ups, and deaths are commonly implicated as part of the pathway to the Bowery. As one disheveled street man who we initially encountered panhandling on Delancey Street bemoaned, "Since my wife left me I've had no place to go but the bottle." Indeed, the Bowery with its virtually all single male environment is the ideal place for a person to go to forget about women and family.

On the average, the men reported living alone for 22 years, or since their late 30s. Fifty-seven percent had been married previously, and 45% of the men had children. Of those who had been married, 31% reported having begun living alone after a divorce or separation and 17% after the death of their spouse. Another 12% of our sample started to live alone after the death of their parents or another close relationship. One fourth merely moved out on their own during their early adulthood. An additional 29% reported miscellaneous reasons, the majority of which were because of "drinking" or that they "liked being independent."

Although neither Miles nor Ed had married, both had traumatic episodes with women that contributed to their current lifestyles. For example, Miles occasionally reminisces about his former girlfriend: "This was in the forties. I just started working for Con Edison and she was a bus girl there. We lived together roughly two and a half years and got along really well." Then one day she told him that she was pregnant, but wanted to have an abortion. Miles confronted her, "You tellin' me that you gonna kill the child? She said 'yes.' So that turned me off with females. I didn't live with any women before her or after her." Although he has had a few roommates, Miles repeatedly remarked, "I prefer to live by myself."

As we briefly described in the first chapter, Uncle Ed attributes one of his "downfalls" to a break-up with a girlfriend with whom he had been living in Philadelphia. "We were pretty close to each other, though not to the extent that we were thinkin' of marriage." However, his girlfriend was a heavy drinker. One day Ed exploded, "Lookit Marie, I can't stay here with you boozin' like you are. I find money of mine missin' and you always seem to have a fifth or two of gin." She angrily responded, "If you're accusin' me of stealin' you can get the hell out of my house." Then Ed, who had been struggling to remain sober at the time, retorted, "I've spoke to my two sponsors at AA and they told me it's best to get the hell away from you because you're goin' to drive me to drink." So that night he moved into the living room and slept on the couch. During the night, he awoke quite depressed, "I guess John Barleycorn talked to me. . . . I forgot all about AA. I poured myself a couple of good shots of gin 'cause I was depressed and didn't know where the hell to go. All I could think was to go back to the bottle." After he drank nearly a fifth of gin he left the house, got a bus to Penn Station, and came back to the Bowery.

In summarizing the pathways to skid row, it is not possible to identify any single pattern. However, several recurrent themes emerge:

1. A disruptive early family life.
2. Low-skilled employment with relatively poor education.
3. Occupations that resulted in earlier exposures to the Bowery for brief stays, such as merchant marines, day labor.
4. A history of moderate to heavy alcohol consumption.
5. Physical or psychological conditions that may have impaired work ability.
6. Psychological turmoil over the death of or separation from a spouse or girlfriend.

Perhaps one factor could be sufficently powerful in a particular individual to lead him to skid row. However, in most instances, several factors seemed to operate. Importantly, despite these contributing factors, these alone do not make a "Bowery Man." The Bowery culture and environment must be absorbed by each new arrival. In subsequent chapters we shall explore this environmental effect as well as further elaborate on several of the key contributing variables enumerated above such as alcoholism, and physical and psychological dysfunction.

# CHAPTER FIVE

# How Old Homeless Men Survive

What I would tell them is that if they've never been on a Bowery before, of course do their utmost to stay off because it's really no life to live. With the trials and tribulations you're not livin'; you're just existin'. And existence is very hard. All I'm livin' for is today.

—Uncle Ed

During an interview with Miles on a late summer afternoon, he spots a policeman who yesterday had given an old man a summons for public urination in this same park. A gleam came to Miles's eye on noticing the cop. He whispered, "Watch this, I'm going to teach you about life in the streets." In full view of the cop who was about 50 feet away, he casually strolled over to a cluster of garbage cans at the entrance to the park. With his stomach flushed against the cans he leaned over them. With his right hand he rummaged through the debris, while with his left hand he opened his zipper. Miles then urinated invisibly into the garbage as both hands seemingly moved over the can as if in quest of a treasure. Displaying a weak smile, he returned to the bench: "Nobody's gonna get me for peein' in the park."

## DAILY ROUTINES

Once a man arrives on the Bowery he must develop the requisite skills to survive in this frequently treacherous environment. Those men who previously had even brief exposures to Bowery life may possess much more of the wherewithal to survive than those men with no skid row experience. Our sample consisted largely of veteran skid rowers. The men averaged more than 16 years on the Bowery. The flophouse and apartment men had spent five years at their current address, suggesting some degree of stability. Approximately half the street men had been living on the streets for three years, and three men claimed to be on the streets for 25 or more years. With more persons receiving Social Security and other entitlements such as Supplemental Security Income, Medicare, and Medicaid, Bowery men have achieved somewhat greater stability over the past two decades. As one 73-year-old man stated, "With my monthly check I can now pay the rent in advance and whatever happens I know it's gonna be hard to put me in the street." By contrast to their 1960s Bowery counterparts, who were studied by Bahr and Caplow (1973), nearly nine of ten had been at the same address for one year (versus two thirds in the past) and one in five had been at the same residence for ten or more years (versus one in six in the past).

While life for most Americans has a linear quality—an orientation toward the future and a sense of progression toward something—life for skid rowers is largely cyclical (Murray, 1986). Their cyclical schedules are molded by the agencies and institutions on which they depend for daily meals, monthly checks, or daily room tickets. Often they must be in and out of their flops by a certain time. Some are regulated by the season, living on the streets during the warm months and in the flops when the weather turns cold. "Weekends" do not exist for these men, except for the fact that many of the agencies are closed on Sundays. National holidays often mean little, and their real holiday is "Mother's Day"—the first of the month when the Supplemental Security Income (SSI), Veteran's Administration (V.A.), and welfare checks arrive in the mail (Murray, 1986). This is the time when men pay off their debts, make needed purchases, or go on a drunk. At the beginning of each month meal programs experience a dramatic decline in clientele, but by midmonth the number of men begins to rise rapidly. The twin themes of repetition and waiting is reflected in the commonly heard lament, "Oh, I'm just killin' time 'till. . . ."

One ex-Bowery man encapsulated the plight of the skid rower, "whatever else might be amiss, his primary problem is a physical problem. He needs food, clothing, shelter, and probably medical attention" (Parker, 1970, p. 10). To what extent a skid rower's daily existence will be devoted to taking care of his basic needs will depend on his financial status, which is extremely low for the majority of the men. Overall, half the men earned less than $3900 per year, and one fifth earned less than $1000 per year. On the other side, 3 of the 281 men indicated that they had earned $10,500 or more over the past year. Importantly, two fifths of street men reported annual incomes of less than $1000, and half of the street men earned under $1300 per year. Thus, income for these men approached levels found in third world countries. Overall, only one in six Bowery men earned above the 1983 poverty level of $5061 for a single individual.

To Miles, a street person with minimum income from Social Security, his life revolves around ensuring that he has food, a few cigarette butts, some wine, a bench to sleep on, some semblance of hygiene, and a relative degree of safety. Typically, Miles gets up at 5:30 every morning. He leaves his park on 23rd Street and walks uptown to the St. Francis of Assisi Church on 31st Street where he waits on line for half an hour to an hour to get two sandwiches and coffee. He'll then go to the park on 16th Street where he'll eat one of the sandwiches. He likes this park because it has a fountain in which he can wash his hands and face. Miles points out, "I keep soap and towel in my bag. I even clean my teeth and my dentures." Then, several times a week he will walk downtown to the public bath house on the Lower East Side where he can get a free shower. However, as he interjects, "It's now dangerous there because there are guys goin' there and shootin' drugs. They could reach over and take your clothes or bag." His shower usually takes about 40 minutes.

After the shower, Miles walks several blocks to the Bowery Residents' Committee where he can get a hot lunch. After lunch, he walks back to the park on 23rd Street. "Most of the day I'm usually by myself or I meet the guys at the park." Sometimes he'll go with a friend to cash in empty cans, but the lines are long and the machines are often broken. They might use the money to buy a pint of wine. Often he'll sit in the park and read magazines or talk to other homeless men he knows. "People come by and they call it bum's row and make derogatory remarks. You just learn to accept the insults." Sometimes Miles will start to doze off, but the police patrolling the park don't permit sleeping on benches during the daytime, "They tell you bedtime is midnight." So Miles must sit up and take catnaps.

Around 8:30 PM, he goes with his friend Jake up to Grand Central Station for sandwiches. "It's a long walk. It takes 45 minutes.

I pick up cigarette butts and put them in my pocket, smoke a couple, and then get on line 'til the guy comes out and gives you a ticket." The lines overflow with tension. Miles recalls how one night he was ticket number 3 but wound up being the 40th person to pick up a sandwich. "That's because the young fellas jump the line, there's no respect. I saw one guy move through the line four different times. There's no control by the staff."

Miles usually brings his sandwiches back to the park, where he arrives around 11:00. At midnight, he goes to sleep on a bench with three friends. On cold nights or if it rains, they run across the street and spend a sleepless night standing under a scaffold.

After reciting his daily routine, Miles lamented:

I'm really tired, I'm worn out. You sit in the park, you eat, then you have a drink, you smoke a cigarette. If you can, you sit there, drop your head and sleep. Then you get up in the mornin' to go to one of the sandwich lines for coffee and sandwiches. You walk back and forth from 23rd Street Madison Square park to 42nd Street to the Bowery. I must walk 30 miles a day.

Despite the rigors of this existence, the Bowery and its environs do provide the down-and-outer with the opportunity to survive on very little. Indeed, the low cost of living is one of the prime motivating factors for coming to the Bowery. For example, Roland bragged, "I didn't have any money a long time ago. Sometimes I didn't even have five dollars a month. I'm not kidding you. Sometimes I lived on two bucks a month. There were soup lines. A guy can go to soup lines or somethin' like that. There's always a place to live with a ticket from the Muni or on a bench, and there's always a place to eat."

For Uncle Ed, who lives off SSI, daily life is a little less exhausting than for Miles. Although he must constantly watch expenses, he is not so impoverished that he must be constantly on the move to make the next food line. Moreover, despite the noise and squalor, the flophouse affords Ed a few more conveniences such as toilet and shower facilities, a hot plate, and the absence of harassment from police and passers-by.

Ed is an early riser, usually waking between 5:00 and 5:30. Sleeping is a problem for him in the summer since he lives right under the roof, "They're up there partying all night so I have damn little sleep in this joint." After waking, he'll light up a cigarette and sit and think, "I meditate and try to figure what I'm gonna do for the day that will not only be financial but to my benefit. I've just recently got over a heck of a chest cold. So yesterday I just meditated that I was gonna take it easy, not overexert myself because I have a bad heart." Next Ed goes to the bathroom, and if the showers aren't locked, he can take a quick shower. He usually leaves his room by 6:30, and if he has some money he buys some coffee from the machine and sits in the hotel lobby "shootin' the breeze" until about 8:30. At that time he'll head toward the Bowery Residents' Committee. Ed's life revolves around the senior program at the BRC, much like an elderly suburbanite's life might revolve around the country club. The BRC opens at nine, and Ed has breakfast there.

After breakfast he hangs around the BRC playing cards and waiting for the noontime lunch. After lunch, Ed returns to his hotel. Sometimes he'll catch up on his laundry; he brings his clothes to a Chinese laundry several blocks from his house. Other days, he'll take a nap or watch television in the hotel lobby. Then, he'll head back to the BRC for the four o'clock snack, and sit around with his pals for a while.

During the early part of the evening he returns to the lobby for some more televison. Around 8:30 he'll meander back to his room, eventually lying down with a book. Recently, he had been reading *Gone with the Wind*, "I'm about two thirds of the way into the book. There's about 1200 pages." Other days, he might go uptown to Greenwich Village to attend an AA meeting. Although there are AA meetings on the Bowery, Ed is cynical about the men attending Bowery AA meetings, believing that most of them lack motivation or because they are required to attend a treatment program in order to receive public assistance checks. Around 10:30 Ed puts out the lights and, as "I always do at night, I say my prayers and think about my loved ones."

Uncle Ed's daily routine, compared to the more frenetic and treacherous pace of Miles's day, might be considered humdrum. But the regularity and security of this routine is a blessing for Ed, who had spent many years on and off the streets alternately fighting and succumbing to alcohol.

At the other side of the continuum is Bill, who represents a small, but interesting minority of Bowery men. Bill is 71 years old, intelligent, well-spoken, neatly dressed, and spanking clean. A small man, of obvious Irish heritage, he is clean shaven, opinionated, and birdlike with energy and alertness. He is never without a library book, well-versed in current events, up on modern nutritional theory, and participating in a self-designed exercise program. Inevitably, after a few weeks, the average helper on the Bowery starts to think of Bill less as an elderly unfortunate, and more as a prospective mate for the helper's widowed aunt or mother.

Bill lives in a fairly large room with a window and sink in one of the less-dangerous and infested SROs, but still one that is a far cry from any senior retirement centers. His income is derived from Social Security and a small pension from one of many clerical positions he held prior to his retirement 10 years ago. He utilizes some services and eschews others available to the elderly on the Bowery. He belongs to a regular free-meal program but avoids the missions, bars, street hangouts, and parks that so many men weave into a rhythm of daily existence. Instead Bill behaves much like a retired middle-class New York gentleman. He takes long walks to various sections of the city. He has a routine of library visitation encompassing all of southern Manhattan which he says serves the dual purpose of enabling him to maintain a current mini-library in his room of both fiction and nonfiction and gives him the exercise and rest stops he requires in his physical fitness regimen. He carries a copy of the New York Times everywhere he goes, primarily to drape over fire hydrants to create an emergency seat when he becomes winded during these aerobic sprints from library to library. In the late afternoon he returns home, takes a nap and reads for awhile, then watches television on the set that he has in his room.

Clearly, income is a crucial element in the quality of life of these men. Principal sources of income for these men were pension (19%), Social Security or SSI (57%), supplemental welfare benefits (14%), money from friends or relatives (10%) and other sources such as panhandling, "hustling," odd jobs, and the like (20%). Only 6% (2% full-time) had any regular employment; however, four-fifths of the men expressed a desire to work more and in half the cases it was in order to earn more money. Fifty-six percent of the men attempted to look for work, apparently without much success. Given their age and lack of skills it is not surprising that they had failed to find employment. Many of the men do occasional odd jobs or "runs" for other men. It should be underscored that these men's work histories and current desire to work tend to refute the presumption that these men as part of their lifestyle reject work, a point echoed in a recent study of a somewhat younger sample (mean age: 38 years) of mission users in Baltimore:

A signal finding was that, like domiciled men, virtually all of the homeless had worked at some point in their lives. Although their recent work history was poor, a substantial number reported having worked for some part of the year prior to the interview, suggesting a re-evaluation of the stereotype of the homeless as work shirkers. (Fischer, Breakey, Shapiro, & Kramer, 1986, p. 61)

Ed recounts his frustration in finding work:

Many a days I'll stay away from here for the whole day and the guys wonder where the hell I've been. I've been walkin' around tryin' to see if restaurants uptown need a busboy or a dishwasher, which I know I'm capable of doin'. Or I'd do porter work, that'd be adequate. If I could work myself into a doorman's job, that'd be more than adequate. This year, forget about it. I can walk 'till I'm blue in the face, and I still haven't accomplished nothin'. And these employment agencies, they're not sendin' out much 'cause people are holding on to their jobs. Let's face it. You give up your job today, you're on your ass trying to find another one. No matter what it is. I'm callin' up a lot of messenger places through the [New York] Post. They tell me, "Have you got a bike? No? Sorry, can't give you anything." I know there used to be one place on Greene Street, going into the Village, where you could meet in the mornin' and they'd send so many men out to a certain neighborhood to work. But that place is closed up.

Finally, despite their prior work record that might have qualified them for Social Security disability and the fact that nearly three-fourths of the street men had annual incomes that should entitle them to some minimal form of social service aid (i.e., they earned under $3900 per year), only 45% of the men were receiving such assistance. Nonstreet men did considerably better in that 67% of the men reported receiving some form of social service aid. Nevertheless, the 42% of nonstreet men who earned $3900 or less were presumably eligible for more assistance, since most subsidies should bring them at least up to that $3900 level. As might be expected, street men fared even more poorly in being able to obtain various entitlements.

Other surveys of homeless men have substantiated the severity of the problem in obtaining entitlements (Fischer, Shapiro, Breakey,

Anthony, & Kramer, 1986). For example, among the Baltimore mission users cited above, only one third had any form of health care coverage or received public support. We have already noted how only 45% of the Bowery men were receiving social service assistance. Worse still, only one fourth of the men had Medicaid and 30% had Medicare. According to the cut-off level at the time of the study, approximately half of all men and three fourths of street men should have qualified for Medicaid. Similarly, only 22% of men received food stamps despite at least half being eligible. Finally, although three fifths of the flophouse and apartment men should have qualified for senior citizen reduced rent exemption (i.e., for those 62 and over), only 1% believed that they were receiving such an exemption.

Obtaining entitlements can be a frustrating experience. Uncle Ed has been having trouble obtaining food stamps. As noted in Chapter 1, he went to the welfare office to find out what the problem was:

"Like I say, I was just ready to knock some sonofabitch in the head because I'm still livin' on only $277.58 a month." [Ed usually borrows from the hotel manager at 40% interest per month.] "A couple of times I'd get so much in the hole that by the time I paid my rent, the loans, and a few other bills, I'd be starting the month with thirty or forty dollars and no food stamps. That would make anybody kinda pissed off."

As might be expected, two thirds of the men worried regularly about finances (three fourths of the street men). Specifically, 57% of men claimed that they were unable to pay for essential expenses (87% of the street men) such as food (55% overall, 83% street men), rent (43% overall), transportation (48% overall, 83% street men), and medical bills (49% overall, 56% street men). Among those receiving social service aid, 42% said it did not overcome their financial problems. Concretely, these hardships were manifested by one third of the men reporting that they had lost ten or more pounds in the past three months. In approximately two thirds of these cases the men stated that it was due to their inability to afford food.

Now that we have introduced the problem of survival in a general sense, we shall examine some of the specific ways in which skid row and the broader urban milieu provide opportunities for these men to obtain money, odd jobs, food, and shelter.

## MONEY

Although a majority of men are obtaining some form of entitlement, most are receiving inadequate amounts. Among those men living on the street, half live on approximately $100 per month. Consequently, the Bowery man must devote a considerable proportion of his time looking for alternative sources of income. While extra money may be used for basic survival, often the money goes toward alcohol as well, though alcohol is usually perceived by the men as part of their basic survival. (We shall discuss the pivotal role of alcohol in more detail in Chapter 8.)

The most ancient of extant methods of obtaining money is begging. Uncle Ed describes the art of panhandling:

I'd usually go down to Houston Street, there's a good light there, and I'd bum a card [panhandle]. I go up to the cars, and I tell 'em. "Excuse me, sir. Could you pardon me. I'm thirty-five cents short on a drink. Could you help me out?" I found out that they think more of you if you were man enough to ask them towards a drink instead of coming up with the old bullshit you need a quarter for a cup of coffee. Sometimes I'd grab a hold of a piece of rag and wipe their windshield and wipe their mirrors and then put out my hand and usually they see at least you're tryin' to do a little work to help them and they give you a quarter or a dime or a half dollar. I go to every car I come to. Nor do I pick any special person to panhandle. But I never panhandle a woman if she was in the car by herself since you may scare the woman. And you can never tell if she may holler, "Help," and then the next thing I know my ass is in trouble, even though I wouldn't have touched her. First of all, I look at his appearance. If he looks pretty raggedy, unshaven, I figure he's probably on a bum too so I leave him alone. If I see a gentleman well-dressed with a suit, wristwatch, or a ring, I say, "That might be good for a quarter."

Uncle Ed smiles as he recalls the best hit he ever made.

Well, one time I was on Christie Street and Delancey. I hit [approached] this convertible with a party of four young fellas. The driver gave me a dollar and then the fella next to him said, "Well, I ain't gonna be cheap neither," so he gave me a dollar so I ended up with four dollars out of the four guys. For me that was sensational. And right away I went right to the One Mile House, which used to be open on the corner of Bowery and Rivington, threw the four dollars down, got a couple of bottles. I was all set for the night.

Although hitting cars for money can usually generate some quick cash, the yield varies considerably with the season: "In the winter time it's a bitch. They all got the windows up . . . 'course now all the cars are air conditioned so it's tough in the summer, too" (cited in Zettler, 1975, p. 6). Sometimes their take may not be in cash. One older man smiled, "The other day someone just gave me a box of cookies. Then one guy rolled down his window and said he had no change, but he held out a can of beer."

Another way to "hustle" for money is to become a runner. One of the Bowery's premier runners is Roland. Runners are the lifeline for many of the older men who are sick, who go on drinking binges, or who are simply too depressed to leave their room. The runner goes out for food, cigarettes, or booze for either a set fee (usually from a quarter to a dollar), or they will be allowed to keep the change.

Another odd job available especially to flophouse men is porter work or bedmaking in the hotels. For example, Uncle Ed often substituted for an absent helper as well as working as a runner:

Once in a while, the manager sends me out to make a run for his coffee and he always tips me. He usually gives me a dollar. Sometimes the porter or bedmaker may be drunk and he might ask me, "Hey, Uncle Ed would you clean the bathrooms for me? And check to see who needs linen, et cetera, et cetera." It would take about an hour. Then he'd throw me a couple of dollars.

Many of the men used to be able to get odd jobs through employment agencies or in taverns. Ed recalls the old days and contrasts it with today's Bowery:

Those trucks don't pick up guys anymore. They stopped a long time ago. Because the bosses of the trucks only give the drivers so much expense money and they'll tell you, "I don't get enough expense money to hire nobody." So they usually have a regular driver and a helper from the company. Once in a while, if you're lucky, you might pick up a truck, but very seldom. There used to be a helluva gang on Houston Street, all four corners, waiting for trucks. You'd be out there about five o'clock in the mornin'. If you didn't get a truck by eleven o'clock, you could forget about it. Oh, a truck would come along and you'd ask them if they need help. Sometimes you'd make one truck for three or four hours in the mornin' and if you're lucky, you might be able to make another one in the afternoon for three or four hours. Six hours was about the most you could make on any trucks. So you make yourself roughly about eight dollars plus they feed you. There ain't no more employment agencies here no more either. Louie's shipped upstate, and I don't want to go upstate. Sophie's used to be on the corner. She used to send me out everyday, you know, spot jobs, dishwashin' or shit like that. Now, if you go to an employment office, you've got to put down money before they send you out. And, as you can see, financially, I've got no money to put down for a job. So, my hands are tied as far as work.

When men are eager to work and there is little available in the city, some of the men can still obtain jobs in the kitchens or doing maintenance work in the Catskills resort hotels. Miles recollects his time there:

I worked at one hotel and shared a room with two other people. We had to pay for our board and lodging. At another hotel the guy caught me comin' up the hill one day with a six-pack. He says from now on you can buy your beer, cigarettes, and whiskey from me. So I borrow on my salary, and when payday comes the pay is very slim 'cause I done drunk most of it up 'cause there's nothin' else to do except eat, drink, and sleep. It's a very lonely life you know. I'd worked there six, sometimes nine months. I'd come back to the city for a while and then go to another place. I've been around the Catskills like a cyclone.

Another traditional option for men is to go to a pawn or "buy and sell" shop. There's only one left on the Bowery now, but several are near its perimeter. Miles describes how the pawnshop works: "I had one of those digital watches. He gave me four dollars for my watch and then I gave him six dollars to get it back."

Other men who have no possessions to pawn or fear that they won't be able to pay for its return, sell their foodstamps to other men. For instance, for ten dollars worth of foodstamps, they usually get five dollars in cash. Commonly, men will make the round of missions in order to obtain second-hand clothes, only to sell it as soon as possible. Although like Miles, many men feel degraded by scavaging though litter baskets for returnable cans and bottles, cash redemption of these cans and bottles is one of the popular ways to make a few dollars. A by-product of this has been to make cans and bottles a kind of "currency of the streets" (e.g., one cigarette for three cans).

When desperate, men turn to loansharks who are frequently the desk clerks or managers of their hotel. The loansharks are selective as to whom they lend money, "They don't lend it to any guy who comes to them from the street. They're in business, they're not giving money away. They gotta know you." With men in the hotel, they know that he is receiving a check, the amount of the check, and that he has to pay his rent—usually to the desk clerk or manager who lent him money. As one man summed it up, "They're not gonna lose."

For many years one of the most popular ways to earn money was by selling blood. However, the blood banks that used to dot skid row are gone. One older man recalled how some blood banks would even pick them up when they were in short supply and he could make "an easy five dollars for a pint of blood." But, with increasing government regulations the local blood banks closed. Now the blood banks are located in the hospitals. The men find the hospitals less receptive, and they are skittish about going. As this man reflected, "I haven't been to one of them in a real long time."

Other men steal items uptown and bring them to the second-hand stores on the Bowery: One former shoplifter remarked:

You'd go uptown and clip some transistors, or little TVs, or clothes if you're lucky enough. You go into some man's clothing store and pretend to be checking out some suits and put a suit under your suit, and then you go down to the Bowery. You can go to Pete, Tony, Lou, and Bill down there, they're all second-hand stores and they'll buy anything for a price. Of course you get very little, so they can resell it.

Finally, probably the most common way men obtain a few dollars is through loans from other men or pooling money together, usually for booze but sometimes for food as well. Some of the men keep a "crying sheet" or "sob sheet" which lists the names of people to whom they owe money. But lending other men money can be a problem, especially if they are drunk. As Ed rationalized:

When I lend a person any type of money while they're drinkin', I forget about it. 'Cause chances are when they're sobered-up they'll come up and say, "What the hell do you mean that you gave me a dollar? You didn't give me no goddamn dollar," 'cause they don't remember who gives them what when they're under the influence of alcohol.

## FOOD

Nearly two fifths of the men reported that they weren't eating well. As noted previously, one third of them believed that they had lost 10 or more pounds in the past three months, and in roughly two thirds of these cases it was due to their inability to buy food. Nearly half the men said that they sometimes go without meals. Among street men, two thirds reported that they sometimes go without meals.

The nonstreet men were considerably more likely to obtain a daily hot meal than the street men (61% versus 41%). This reflected the fact that 26% of nonstreet men had access to hotplates or stoves, and 17% had access to a refrigerator. The nonstreet men also had higher income, and therefore 38% were able to go daily to restaurants or cafeterias, and another 34% ate in these facilities at least once a week. On the other hand, fewer than one in ten street men ate daily in restaurants or cafeterias, although two of five street men went to these facilities at least once a week. One means to cope with the problem of obtaining food was to rely on one's social support network. Uncle Ed recounts an episode involving food exchange within his hotel:

Ted would come down to the lobby and he'd say, "Did you eat tonight?" I'll say, "No." "Come on up to the room in about a half hour; I'll have somethin' cooked." Half an hour later I'll knock on the door. "Who is it?" and he'd give me a little plate all fixed up for me. When he was drinkin' he'd always have a bottle of wine too so I could have a shot of wine with my food. He told me, "Before you eat, have a drink." I'd sit on the bed with him and we'd turn on the TV. Then I'd take the dishes and wash them for him. Then I'd say, "'Bout time for me to go to bed." I stand there until he locks the door and then I'd go downstairs. Usually he's out for the rest of the night.

Another primary source for obtaining hot meals was the local social service agency meal program. Both street and nonstreet men made equal use of agency meal programs, roughly half of the men went to such programs daily, and an additional one fourth went there at least weekly. Clearly, such programs were the bulwark of nutritional survival for these men. One older man describes the experience of waiting for breakfast at the Muni. He would awake about 7:00, dress, wash, get out of the hotel and rush over to the Muni: "If I get there early I can maybe beat the line." On the other nand, some days he'll go late, around 8:00 since you can sometimes beat the line that way as well. A typical breakfast might consist of juice, bread, oatmeal, and coffee. The lines are long for what this man described as a "joke breakfast." Men often wait a half hour to get downstairs into the dining hall, and they then encounter a room teeming with men, the old man continues.

You get in that hall, you start suffocating from the stink. Some guys don't believe in washing. And there's these weisenheimers, they're all pushing to get ahead. Those young punks are really obnoxious. They think it's a crime to be older than them. I come in and get out as fast as I can. I don't associate.

Because of the violence and aggressiveness on some of the food lines, the most popular places among the older men for meals are the St. Francis of Assisi morning bread line where the line is supervised by staff, and the Bowery Residents' Committee, the publicly funded senior lunch program that provides over 100 hot lunches six days per week. More recently, the BRC has begun to provide breakfasts and a late afternoon snack. The BRC program is especially popular with the seniors because it is open only to men 55 and over, thereby excluding young men who evoke fear among the older men.

Another alternative for meals is the mission. However, the "price of a meal is a 90-minute Bible Meeting." Other men, however, have been able to rationalize the mission routine: "They do not make you go to mass. They do not put no gun, knife, pistol, or stick on you, and say you gotta go in there. Your stomach might make you go in there."

There are still some men who use another time-honored method for procuring food: the hand-out. For example, John, a tall, fairly well-built 60-year-old man, leaves his hotel at 4 AM, and he begins his half-hour trek to the Fulton Fish Market: "They'd be unloadin' fish, and they drop a whole lot on the ground. Very seldom do they pick it up since they ain't gonna put it out for merchants. So they give it to me." Sometimes he will sell the fish to men in the hotel after he has skinned it. But most of the fish he cooks for himself. John also goes to two or three different restaurants for food. One of his favorites is on Fulton Street: "Somebody found out about it and told me. You know how it is with poor people, one lives off the other one." John usually heads for the restaurant around 3:00 in the afternoon: "Usually about five or six of us go there. It all depends on the time of the month. Guys always run short at the end of the month. I usually bring my food back to the hotel, I don't know where they eat their food."

Last, there are still a few "bums" on the Bowery who, because of their suspiciousness and fears, lack of initiative, or physical disabilities will not regularly use formal agencies. For example, the following interviewer's narrative is illustrative of this type of man:

Frank Ronald (which I have a hunch is his first and middle name and not his full name, though it's only a hunch and I couldn't get any other name from him) is a true "bum." I found him going through garbage cans just off the Bowery in Chinatown. He says he lives in various places, sometimes in a box in the Chinese park, or near the Brooklyn or Manhattan Bridge. He gets food from garbage or from people at a Chinese restaurant who give him scraps. He occasionally finds money or panhandles. He wasn't that interested in doing this interview, even for ten dollars. I had to talk him into it. He showed me his feet which had been frostbitten during the winter. They looked sore, but healing (miraculously, under these conditions). He hates doctors and other authorities (police, park attendants, etc.) and generally has adopted a reclusive lifestyle in Manhattan.

How nutritious are the foods that these men eat? In our questionnaire we attempted to assay their daily level of nutritional intake. With respect to specified food categories eaten on the day prior to the interview, the street and nonstreet men appeared to eat approximately the same proportion from each food category except for dairy products. Overall, 72% of the men had milk, cheese, or other dairy products (other than eggs); among street men 59% had at least one dairy product. Eighty percent of the men had some kind of meat or poultry; 62% had green or yellow vegetables; 66% had consumed some citrus fruits; and 96% had eaten some bread or high carbohydrate food product. The findings suggest that nutrition for these men may be one of quantity. In other words, a substantial number of the men seem to be able to obtain many items from the essential food categories. However, the quantity of food may be small and there are times when, due to drinking, illness, or lack of cash, they are unable to obtain food.

Michael Zettler, in his photojournalist account, The Bowery, interviewed a man who pointedly encapsulated the contrast between the gross waste that routinely occurs in the general society and the extremes that homeless men must go to conserve enough to survive until the next day:

You see them guys on the news talking about the people wasting land and all the ecology stuff. They ought to come down here and talk to some of us about that. We don't waste nothing. You can't afford to waste nothing. It takes too much to get it together enough to get something done to waste none of it. (p. 26)

## SHELTER

We observed that for money and food procurement there was considerable heterogeneity in the ways the men fulfilled these needs. Similarly, with respect to shelter, depending on economic circumstances and individual styles, there is a continuum of range of refuges used by these men. Although to the outsider, apartments and flophouses would certainly seem preferable to street living, to some men the street seems to be a better value. For example, one interviewer writes: "Mr. Peterson is a tough old man. He's been living on the streets of New York in the summer and takes a bus or hitchhikes down to Florida in the winter. He gets $500 per month so it's not as if he can't afford to pay rent. He just can't see paying so much for so little so he stays on the street."

In previous sections we have described flophouse and apartment conditions. For street and flophouse men, an apartment even in the Bowery area is often considered a significant step toward returning to respectability. Unfortunately, the men's ability to obtain an apartment is markedly curtailed by the limitation of having to provide both rent and security. Miles, who longs to return to apartment living, bemoans his dilemma:

You must have the right amount of money 'cause landlords know you're poor so they ask for a month's rent and two months security. If the place is $200 a month, you have to have $600 to move in. There are very few people that can draw straight up a $600 check.

In rating the quality of life in the flops it was not unexpected, given the close quarters of cubicles and dormitories, to find that half the men complained of high noise level, and two fifths of them complained of disturbed sleep during the night due to noise. Surprisingly, only one sixth of the men complained of inadequate heat during the winter. Also, only one in ten men complained about the steep stairs that must be negotiated to get to the main floor of most of the flophouses. Given the relatively poor quality of the hotels, only 6% of the men complained of problems getting repairs done, and only 5% claimed to have any problems with the hotel manager. This was nearly 10% lower than the general New York City sample. On the other hand, many of the men are passive and predisposed to resignation. For instance, nearly two thirds of the men reported mice or roaches in their dwelling; however, only one in five men considered it a problem.

Their response to problems in the hotel reflects their sense of powerlessness and fear. Particularly vulnerable to being abused by hotel clerks, the old men have learned through bitter experience that complaints about even irrational violence yield little satisfaction. For example, a 62-year-old man, with a mild heart condition and living in one of the medium quality flophouses related this incident:

Last month I was lying in my room and someone knocks on the door and says "Open up." I ask, "Who is it?" He said, "Charley the clerk" and I thought I might have a telephone call as I was waitin' for one. As soon as I opened the door he punched me in the mouth, knocking off my glasses and breaking them. He gave me another shot to the eye. He was quite drunk, and I was able to push him out of the room. When I complained to the manager he told me, "Well ya know when Charley gets drunk ain't no telling what the hell he'll do but as far as I'm concerned he's a good worker and does a good job with the books. That's just the way it is." And so I let it drop as I usually have to borrow some money from the manager and clerk every month.

Often older men who live on the street will justify their residential situation by alluding to stories such as the one above. Yet, while some will almost wax poetic about the freedom of "carrying the banner" or "sleeping in Bush 13," and talk with disdain about "mission stiffs" who have sold out to religion, virtually all the men recognize the extreme dangers of flopping in the street. As was seen with Roland, his "healthy" paranoia about skid row slashers and bizarre deaths of Bowery men has enabled him to survive for over ten years without suffering any major beatings. Roland, like most men in his situation, will have in their minds a series of street flops which are perceived in relative degrees of safety from the weather and from harassment. In the winter, places with solid enclosures such as abandoned buildings, empty trucks, all-night movies, railway stations, or the subway are preferred places. Lucky individuals will be befriended by a doorman who will let them sleep in a storage room or behind stairs. Most of these indoor free flops have different types of risks. In public buildings one risks persecution by workers or the police. To sleep all night in the subway invites being mugged. Many men will stay awake while riding the subway, and during the day try to get some sleep in crowded public buildings where they are less likely to be noticed than at 3 AM. Places such as abandoned buildings and trucks offer little chance of escape if muggers appear, and the high rate of arson in New York City makes the former locale a possible site for a fiery demise. While Roland seldom sleeps in abandoned buildings anymore he described the precautions he took the last time he did:

About five years ago I was living in an abandoned building on the West Side and although I tend to wake up at the slightest noise, I don't take no chances. I took up half the floor near me and covered it [the holes] with paper so that if anyone snuck up on me they'd go right down to the basement. Eventually someone set the place on fire and I had to leave.

Other alternatives for street living include finding places such as park benches or the high grass under the Brooklyn Bridge where one can fade into the urban environment. Most habitual street men will have several such possible flops in mind for a given night and make a choice based on their perception of its safety for that night. Typically, in checking out one of their nonpark sleeping sites, they will not get to the designated spot until late at night when nobody would normally be around. If any young men are spotted nearby they will go to their next spot. In the dead of winter, the cold can be more lethal than thugs since each year several dozen street men die from hypothermia. Survival depends on finding several layers of warm clothing at a mission and a thick packing crate.

Parks are easier to define as a sleeping place. How well lit is it? What type of people hang out there? How often do police patrol the park, and are they particularly brutal? These factors can change precipitously. Much of the conversation people like Miles have with other street people concerns ferreting out whether there have been any changes in the safety of a particular park.

As has been noted by various authors, especially Spradley (1970, 1972), an important component of the skid row cultural scene is a colorful, specialized lexicon which centers most importantly on types of men one is likely to encounter, strategies for survival, and the variety of places where a person can secure a place to rest or sleep. In constructing and using this argot, these men are creating an urban version of reality that is related to their marginal economic position and the general condition of homelessness. In Chapter 1 we encountered some of this slang when Uncle Ed talked about the last time he was living on the street, "holding (or carrying) the banner," or when Miles lamented about having to scavenge in the street for cigarette butts, "pickin' shit with the pigeons." Some differences existed between blacks and whites in the terms they used for flopping. Some distinctions were relatively minor and involved substitution of a single word in a broader phrase such as when Miles, who is black, used the expression "carrying the stick" (instead of "banner") to describe his living on the streets. Similarly, although white men would say "I've been flopping in the weeds," to describe sleeping in some type of grassy area, blacks would say, "I've been flopping in Bush 13," to convey the same basic idea. There were some entire expressions which seemed to be used exclusively by blacks in this area such as "pickin' shit with the pigeons" or to "cat in the flick"—to sleep in a movie theatre.

With the decline of many skid row institutions and certain types of life-styles, such as frequent tramping across the country, significant portions of the specialized vocabulary are no longer used or even known. While terms such as "flop" (either a place to sleep or the act of finding a place) or "stiff" (tramp) were known by virtually everyone we interviewed, few knew more than a very small number of the numerous modifiers or linked words which were being more widely used by skid row men in the 1960s. For example, most men understood that a "bug house" was a cheap hotel with poor hygienic conditions and that a "mission stiff" was a mission-dwelling tramp, but only a handful knew that a "crummy" is a type of flop related to railroads or that an "airdale stiff" is a tramp who carried his "home" with him in the form of a pack and bedroll.

Despite the public image of the street man as being a lone, psychotic individual, most of the older street men that we encountered were neither isolates nor psychotic. (This will be discussed further in Chapters 6 and 7.) Many of the men in order to attain some degree of security would sleep in pairs or groups. As Miles observed, "It's dangerous by yourself. So it's better to sleep with a couple of other people." Thus, Miles now regularly sleeps with three other men. Another street man told us he shared an abandoned car with another man: one in the front seat and one in the back seat. Although group sleeping provides some security Miles still finds that life on the street can be intensively anxiety-provoking:

I can stretch out, but I can't relax my body, lay down, and sleep. It's no joke sitting up in a hard bench sleepin'. Everytime somebody passes and scrapes their feet, you jump up. My nerves is on edge 'cause I've seen people attacked in the park. I was sitting in Central Park, day was just breaking, and a guy picked up a wire basket and beat another man to death.

A final consideration must be protection from the elements. On nights that it rains, Miles and his friends must run across the street and stand under some scaffolding. Other men will will find a warm doorway, one that has a radiator. Or they might try to get into a cellar. Some men bundle themselves inside of a big cardboard box. In *Ironweed*, William Kennedy (1984) graphically depicted these men's preoccupation with the elements: "I was thinkin' about how many old bums I know died in the weeds. Wake up covered with snow and some of 'em layin' there dead as hell, froze stiff. . . . Pocono Pete, he died in Denver, froze like a brick. And Poocher Felton . . . pissed his pants and froze tight to the sidewalk" (p. 77).

Uncle Ed recalled his strategy for braving the elements during his time on the streets:

Sometimes you can try a building or an apartment house but in the winter they know the guys are out on the street and they keep pretty well secured with the locks. Many of the guys don't consider that, they'll turn around and piss in the hallways and shit in the hallways, and leave their wine bottles and newpapers there and then some poor bastard's got to clean up after them. Once I had a nice place in a business building and I got acquainted with the night watchman. He used to leave the door unlocked long enough for me to get in. There was a nice radiator there for me. And in the morning he'd send me out for coffee and throw me a buck for my "eye opener" plus a cup of coffee. One night I got drunk and I brought this other guy. He relieved himself by the elevator and took off. So the night man woke me up in the morning and said, "Look, who'd you have in here last night? He put wine shits all over the elevator." I had to use a cleaner. I didn't like the idea of cleanin' up after this other bastard. And then he told me, he says, "Never mind the coffee; I'll get coffee later. Here's a buck. The door will be locked tonight. You won't come back here." So I fucked myself up tryin' to help another guy. After that, whenever I find myself a hideaway or a flop, any doorways, I never tell nobody about it. People come up to you and say, "Hey, where you holdin' the banner," and I'd say, "Oh, I landed some doorway on the West Side. I don't remember the number." Of course I do, but I'm not about to take another sonofabitch in and fuck myself up. That's how it happens when you're tryin' to be a good guy.

Other places to go in inclement weather include subways, railroad stations, movie theaters, missions, and places "upstate." (In his book, *Subways Are for Sleeping*, Edmund Love (1956) provided a good illustration of how a means of transportation becomes redefined as sleeping quarters.) Uncle Ed used to ride the subways, especially when the weather was bad. He'd get on the train around 10:00 when the shift changed. Usually when the night man was talking to the clerk who was leaving, Ed would slip past the gate. "Generally I'd go to the end of the line, Coney Island, and then ride it back." Occasionally a policeman would wake him and ask where he was going. "I'm goin' nowhere. I'm just goin' to the end of the line and then I'm goin' right back. They'd say all right, be careful." Ed would try to stay near the conductor where it was relatively safe. "I was riding about two and a half months and I never got hassled." At about 6:00 in the morning he would "get the hell off the train" and go panhandling.

Grand Central and Penn stations are also popular shelters for these men, although the opportunities for sleeping are practically nil. One street man told an interviewer: "At Penn Station every second hour or so the cops come around and tell you if you ain't got a ticket to take a walk. And when they'd leave the waiting room then you'd come back in."

Although police can no longer officially arrest men for vagrancy and only rarely will they arrest someone for public intoxication, it is not uncommon for police to harass men out of certain areas. In areas around the Bowery, which fall under the jurisdiction of four different police precincts, policemen may prod an unruly man across the street into another precinct. In more gentrified quarters of the city, a man's appearance rather than any untoward behavior may be sufficient to elicit a belligerent response from the police. In extended discussions with the older men of the Bowery we did not obtain tales

of widespread severe police abuse as did anthropologist James Spradley (1970) in his study of Seattle skid row dwellers during the period
prior to the decriminalization of public vagrancy. Nonetheless, the
combination of police and public abuse can make even the simple
activities of daily living an ordeal. Miles related to us a scene from a
street drama he had recently witnessed in which a policeman had
stopped a ragged old man in the park. The policeman was pointing
his finger in the man's face and telling him to get out of the park.
"When the old man got down to the garbage cans at the end of the
park the officer grabbed the man and started to shake him. The old
man held onto the can to keep from fallin'. He took the man some-
place and he came back 20 minutes later covered with blood." The
next day, the same old man was back in the park. A little girl came
over and kicked him. Miles ran over to her and said, "Don't do that.
This man is old enough to be your grandfather. Would you want
anybody to kick you like that?" The old man profusely thanked him.
Miles lamented, "People find a way to pick on other people. It's not
fair."

Things that most people take for granted become foci for con-
frontation. For example, Miles talked of the problem of not having
any toilets in the park open to the public:

Now the toilets are only for the employees. So one day this man goes behind
this building to take a leak. The officer said to him. "Why did you pick this
park to urinate?" He said, "When you have to go you have to go." He says
the toilet over there should be open. It's closed and if a man wants to move
his bowels or take a leak where can he go 'cause everything is closed? And
the officer gave him a summons. This morning I had to go to the bathroom
very bad, the bathhouses were closed on Sunday and Monday, the toilet
down at Delancey and Allen Street is closed, BRC don't open til nine o'clock.
It's rough all over.

Besides learning about how these men cope with their elemental
needs, many interviews included tales of momentary transformations. Probably every street man has a story of some Cinderella-like
episode that enabled him to escape his world for a brief instance.
Uncle Ed reflected on such an episode during his life on the streets:

One time I just come out of Selix Bar and I got under this long doorway. I'm
layin' there and this elderly woman comes out of the door and almost fell

over me. She said, "What are you doin' here?" I said, "Stayin' out of the weather, ma'am" because it was rainin' like a sonofabitch. She said, "What are you shakin' for?" I says, "I'm cold," I had nothin' on but a shirt. She says, "Come on inside." I said, "All right." She made me a hot cup of coffee, and put a double shot of brandy in it to warm me up. She says, "Now stay here," and she went into her little kitchen and she came back with a pile of clothes. Nice heavy woolen suit, shirt, pants. She says, "You're about the size of my late husband. Now go in the bathroom, take a nice shower, shave, and put on these clean clothes. See if they fit." They fit me better than your glasses fit you. So then she says, "That cup of coffee isn't much of a breakfast, would you like a couple of ham and eggs?" I said, "Love it." She notices that I'm lookin' up at her buffet, she's got a pack of cigarettes there and I'm lookin' at the damn things and I'm sayin' under my breath, "Aren't you gonna offer me a cigarette, dammit?" but I don't want to be forward enough to bump her since she's so good to me. God love her. So she says to me, "Do you smoke?" I says, "When I have them." So she says, "All right, put that pack in your pocket." The whole one. So now I had a smoke and I was all set. So she said to me, "Do you know how to do housework?" I said, "Yes, ma'am." I said, "When I was out in Jersey years ago I used to go out for these couple of families and do housework, beat rugs, clean the living room, et cetera." She says, "Can you do any paintin'?" I said, "Yes, ma'am. I've done it in the past. I'm a jack of all trades." She says, "I'd like to have my kitchen painted. I'll pay you." "Ma'am, as far as I'm concerned you've paid already. This beautiful suit; you fed me." So she says, "Go down through that stairway and you'll find some paint brushes and all the material to paint at the bottom of the stairs. Take your time. Don't worry, you'll have lunch. Don't rush yourself. Paint my kitchen for me." So I found the drop cloths, paint brushes and rollers, and about three hours later she had a brand new kitchen. She says, "You know, last time I had this painted I paid over a hundred dollars to paint it, and they didn't do half as good a job as that. I'll tell you what you need right now. Have a cup of coffee?" I said, "Yes, a cup of coffee would be good." So she made a fabulous roast beef dinner. We ate and she says, "Now would you do me one more favor before I pay you?" I said, "Yes, of course." "Stay with me for the afternoon, I'd like to have company. You're such a wonderful gentleman. Will you stay with me?" I said, "Yes, of course." So we sat there, watched TV and I left her about seven o'clock that night. She gave me thirty dollars, three ten dollar bills. I said, "No, I can't take this. Look you dressed me up, my God Almighty." She said, "Where my husband is, he can't wear them. They were in the closet collecting moth balls." So I left there, thirty bucks in my pocket and all dressed up. I went back to the Pacific Hotel that night and I told the night clerk, "Billy, put me in for a week." "Who the hell did you rob?" he said. I said, "None of your damn business." He put me in for a week.

Mission living as an alternative to street living has never been looked on favorably by the skid row culture. As Samuel Wallace (1965) commented more than two decades ago,

It is all right to attend mission services now and then when one is really desperate or perhaps simply in need of some diversion. To make such attendance a regular habit, however, to take active part in the services, or even worse, to take up regular lodging in a mission—to become a mission stiff—makes one an outcast on skid row, possibly the lowest stage imaginable. (p. 62)

Phil Parker (1970) describes the true mission stiff as being "generally quiet and tractable; he likes orderliness and takes pride in fulfilling his duty in the system of things. He does not function best on his own" (p. 7). On the other hand, for those who must go to the mission to avoid freezing or starving to death, the humiliation that these men experience as the price for their lodging evokes considerable rage.

Ed considers the missions "a place to sleep and a place to eat." His first exposure to a mission was in 1959. He was sitting on a park bench, hungry and tired, and the fellow on the bench beside him "bummed him" for a cigarette. After he gave him the cigarette he asked, "I'm new in town and not too acquainted with any of the flops." The man responded, "Right up the street is McCauley's Mission. Go there around three o'clock. They have a little service and they'll give you a ticket for a bed. Only 30 men get a bed, so get there early. If you need clean clothes, tell the man when you sign up and they'll give you some clothes."

So at 2:30 PM, Ed went to the front door and a man came out and said, "All right guys. Start linin' up here. Don't crowd the sidewalks." About 15 minutes later they were marched inside to attend a Bible meeting: "I didn't pay no attention to it. I didn't really hear the damn thing. I was just there to get a ticket. My ticket was number seven." After the Bible meeting the men left and were told to return at 5:00. Upon returning, they attended a second Bible meeting, and after about a half-hour, they ate their supper and went upstairs to the dormitories. They were told to turn in their clothes, and in exchange they were given a metal tag with a number and a Mother Hubbard gown. In the morning "you shave and shower, put on your clothes, have breakfast, and then you're back on the street."

This initial experience with the missions was a relatively positive one for Ed, but he gradually came to share the feeling of many Bowery men that sitting through the long hell-fire and brimstone sermons was too much to bear in exchange for a simple meal and a bed. His last experience was five years ago:

I'd hit the Bowery Mission where you'd get an hour and a half of "ear bendin'" [a sermon]. And then they give you a bowl of slop, colored water which they call tea and some day-old bread or week-old rolls and shit like that. But I didn't care for all that damn ear bendin' just for a bowl of slop. Hell, if I could panhandle money and buy myself a sandwich, it would have been better than that.

The antipathy towards missions and church-based organizations has remained remarkably consistent during this century. George Orwell, captured these feelings among London tramps in the 1930s:

"Well," said somebody as soon as we were out of hearing, "the trouble's over. I thought them ——— prayers was never goin' to end." "You 'ad you bun," said another, "you got to pay for it." "Pray for it, you mean. Ah, you don't get much for nothing. They can't even give you a twopenny cup of tea without you go down on you ——— knees for it" (1933, p. 142).

As we shall discuss in Chapter 6, the anger toward missions is part of a broader negativity toward all institutions in the "miseries business" (Wiseman, 1979, p. 252).

The skid row of New York may be unique in its ability to provide shelter for men outside the urban squalor by way of a "camp" for the down and outer. Camp LaGuardia was established by the New York City Welfare Department in 1934 using buildings that were formerly part of a prison for women. It is still operated by the City of New York and it is located in Chester, about 60 miles north of Manhattan. The ethos of Camp LaGuardia centers on the therapeutic value of rural life. In the healthy rural life debilitated men can be given adequate health care, good food, some light work, kept off alcohol, and thus be able to return to the urban community better able to help themselves. In reality, the staff have come to believe that the regimen is only temporarily beneficial since most of the men resume their old patterns when they leave. The staff rationalize that the outside world is a bad place for most of these men—the men are prey for muggers and rip-off artists—so the camp affords them protection from the predators on the Bowery. In fact, the staff encourages the Men's Shelter to send them older men. Four out of five of the camp residents have been there before, with many coming for the winter and leaving in the spring. In 1986, the camp housed 1150 men and had a staff of 150. Men are expected to do some light work for which they are not paid, but for more important jobs men may receive remuneration. All men receive a few dollars to buy personal items, and those that receive outside income must turn part of it over to the camp as reimbursement for their room and board.

Despite this pastoral description, the men view the camp in an entirely different light. Uncle Ed is one of those who excoriated it:

I couldn't understand the damn place. You'd go up there to rehabilitate yourself, get off the booze, and they're putting it right in front of you. Anybody could buy it. The first three days though, you can't buy it. You're bounded to the building. Then the third day, you should see that room, it's full. You can't find a chair to sit on. I can't see no use to a place like that. A guy goes there drunk and the beer's right there to be had. You know he's gonna drink it. He don't even have a chance to sober up. Man, you see the truck come with those goddamn big barrels everyday. Big mugs of beer for a quarter. They give you tokens and you go to the dispensary. For two dollars you get ten tokens. For a dollar you got only four. For one token, you get a big mug of beer. You'd sit in there until eleven o'clock at night until security comes and says, "Okay, boys, come on. We're closin' up." My work routine was the first shift in the kitchen. In other words, at five o'clock I'd wake up and by six o'clock I'm in the kitchen. From six to quarter of twelve was our shift, breakfast and half of the lunch. Then we got relieved by another shift who got half the lunch and supper. That's all I did for seven days a week; I worked in the kitchen. They have a pool room, a big TV room, and they have a tap room where the guys drink beer all night.

Miles disliked the regimentation and the deprecation that he experienced at Camp LaGuardia. He angrily recalls a contemptuous woman who was in charge of the kitchen and who was particularly demeaning toward the men. One night they served peanut butter and jelly for the main course and stringbeans and peas for dessert. "The guys got so pissed off that they surrounded her and were ready to throw her down a flight of steps."

There is another country retreat that has become an interesting exception to the general antipathy toward religious institutions. It is

Graymoor Manor, which the men call "The Holy Mountains." Located in upstate New York in Garrison, 55 miles north of New York City, it currently houses 94 men and has 20 to 25 employees. Graymoor was started in 1909 in a converted chicken coop by Father Paul Wattson who founded the Franciscan Friars of Atonement. He believed that he should share his food and lodging with wayfaring men just as the legendary St. Christopher had borne the baby Jesus. The program funded by private contributions now shelters some 4000 men each year. Some are referred by city agencies but most scrounge the six dollars for the bus trip or find their way to the Atonement Residence in Manhattan for a free bus ticket.

Virtually all the men seem to have respect for Graymoor and view it as a positive experience. Uncle Ed contrasted Graymoor with Camp LaGuardia:

Graymoor is different. It's run by Gregory, a beautiful person. But at Gregory's you can't go up there drunk. No way. 'Cause if you go up there drunk, they won't throw you off right away. They let you sleep in Calvert Hall for the night and in the morning you take a bus back to town. You go up there like on a retreat to rest up. That's the ideal place in the world. The food is fabulous. The dormitories you sleep in are double deckers. Man, that's the best place in the world to get yourself better. Then from there, if you're a veteran, you've got a chance to go up to the V.A. Hospital in Montrose. It's an alcoholic hospital. If you go there you can get in a program, and then you can get a job and a place to live.

When you go into Calvert Hall there's a sign on the door that hits you right in the eyes: "One year from today, you may return." In other words, it's once a year. At Camp LaGuardia, you could go there every fuckin' day since they send buses there from the Muni five days a week. I could go there right now. It goes up there and whoever's comin' back to the city, they bring him back and leave him in front of the Muni. That's it. You're on your own.

For Miles, Graymoor is a place to treat his nerves as well as his alcoholism. It also can serve as a vehicle for helping to fulfill his dream of getting an apartment:

I could go up there and stay forever. I've been there three times. They have a program there and you don't necessarily have to be an alcoholic. You go there and get your nerves together and give yourself time to think. You stay in this program for 90 days. They give you fifty dollars weekly; forty goes in the bank and ten goes in your pocket. That's for spendin' money. After your 90 days is up, all that money has been addin' up. You can come back to the city and get yourself a halfway decent place 'cause you have that money.

## HYGIENE

For hotel and apartment men, keeping clean is relatively easy because of the availability of toilet and shower facilities in their residences. More of a problem in the hotels is lice or bedbug infestation. In the better hotels, the managers try to stay on top of the problem. As one manager told us:

I check my linen everytime we change them, which is twice a week here, Wednesday and Saturday. Sometimes you'll catch a sheet with bed bug spots on it. Men crush 'em and then you see the blood stains. Occasionally you will find somebody and you gotta track down which room it is because if a guy doesn't complain about it you're not gonna find it. I can tell from my sheets whether they're stained and what the stains are. And the same thing with lice. Occasionally, we do get somebody who destroys us. I mean we get a sheet or a guy brings down a towel they use and it's just loaded with lice. We look to find out who it was and then we take all the bedding out of the room and spray it, put in fresh linens, and make him get rid of the clothing he has on. Because if he doesn't do that and take a shower, forget about it. He's just messin' up a room. If they refuse, we'll get rid of them eventually. When the guy tries to pay the rent again I say, "Either ya get clean or you're out." Most of them will do it since they have no place to go. They can go to the Holy Name Mission or to the City to get deloused and for a change of clothing. It's just motivation. If they want to stay here they'll usually go.

For street men, keeping clean, as with most things in their lives, demands considerably more effort than it does for the average person. For Miles, it entails a two mile walk down to the bath house on Allen Street, although he can usually wash his hands and face in the park fountain. However, virtually all of the public baths and toilets in the city have been closed, and some of the street men we studied have abandoned any attempt at personal hygiene. The typical result is matted hair, filthy clothes, skin crawling with lice, and an odor so offensive that some of the men brag that it is strong enough to ward-off would-be muggers.

Many men make use of several of the local agencies for showers, especially the Holy Name Mission. The Holy Name affords considerably more safety than the bath house which Miles described as "very dangerous." Uncle Ed used the Holy Name during the time he was living on the subway. He would get off the train about quarter to six and go to the Holy Name to take a bath, shower, and shave. Even now living in a flop, Ed still regularly cleans up at the Holy Name: "I think the Holy Name is practically my second place to shave and wash up."

As for laundering, most men use either coin-coperated or Chinese laundries just off the Bowery. Ed points out the economy of the Chinese laundry in that a relatively heavy bag costs him only $2.35.

Whether a man has one suit or two suits of clothing is often crucial in determining his level of hygiene. Those men with two suits have an obvious advantage in that they can wear the second suit when the first becomes soiled and requires laundering. The one-suit man must either wash his clothes in parts, find a place where he can simultaneously disrobe and wash his clothes, or wear his clothes until their stench or their shabbiness necessitate the procurement of new clothes.

In our questionnaire we attempted to elicit some broad measures of personal hygiene. For example, we found that half of the street men, but only 18% of the nonstreet men had problems getting their laundry done. Moreover, 37% of street men reported not always being groomed but only 21% of the nonstreet men reported problems with grooming. Our interviewers observed that 57% of the street men and 21% of nonstreet men were wearing "dirty" clothes; 31% of the street men and 11% of the nonstreet men had matted hair, unshaven or smudged faces; and 26% of the street men but just 2% of the nonstreet men smelled of "excretion" or other unpleasant odors. Thus, in general, nonstreet men were relatively well groomed whereas one fourth of the street men were extremely poorly groomed and perhaps another fourth were moderately poorly groomed. Conversely though, half the street men were reasonably well kempt, thus undermining in part the popular image of homeless men as invariably fetid and tattered.

## CRIME

And now it's a real animal kingdom down here and I don't like it.
                                                                        —Miles

Crime is far and away the major fear of older Bowery men, whether they live in a flophouse or on the street. Two thirds of men felt afraid of crime (about equal between street and nonstreet men) and nine of ten felt that the Bowery had a high rate of crime. A startling 59% of the street men and 51% of the nonstreet men were crime victims during the previous year (e.g., mugging, assault, robbery). Moreover, 37% of street men and 33% of the nonstreet men reported having been involved in a crime in which they sustained personal injury during the previous year. By contrast, 4% of the New York City community elderly reported a crime to self and 2% reported a crime-induced personal injury during the previous year. This was reflected in the significantly higher scores that the Bowery men obtained on the Fear of Crime Scale when contrasted with elderly community men. There was no difference between street and nonstreet men on this scale. For most men the danger is in the streets; only 18% felt their room to be unsafe, 14% are afraid of burglary when they are out, and 6% are afraid of someone breaking in when they are at home.

Although "jackrollers" (men who rob other men, usually when the latter are intoxicated) have been associated with skid rows since their origins, the general opinion is that the quantity and viciousness of muggings are substantially higher than in the past. Phil Parker (1970) describes jackrollers who travel in pairs, trios, or even quintets (one notorious group was called the "Filthy Five") who prowl the streets and dayrooms of the Muni around the 1st and 16th of each month when welfare checks arrive: "The jackrollers are notorious for inflicting pain. They brutalize their victims as a point of example to any who might be tempted to resist them, yet many men are hurt pitifully because of the sadistic sickness of the jackroller and his frequent rage at not finding enough money. . . . These men roll people in broad daylight. . . . They rob the old, weak, the drunk" (Parker, 1970, pp. 9–10). One elderly black man told us, "I get mugged nearly every month. This month I lost my entire check right after I cashed it."

Miles described the terrifying experience of a mugging he had six weeks prior to the interview: "I was going to the Muni at night and two black dudes snatched me and threw me to the ground. I had a case with some toilet articles and a pair of jeans and they took 'em. The guy hit me in the eye. I ended up in Beth Israel Hospital with ice packs on my eyes for nine hours."

Such unprovoked, irrational violence finds everyday expression on the Bowery. Scars from knifings are a common sight on the bodies of older men. In the worst of the flophouses, assault on older men is a common occurrence and is especially likely in the squalid dormitory rooms. This is one of the reasons why these sections of hotels are being closed down by the city. Workers at such places sit behind wire barriers and have baseball bats or police billy clubs nearby for protection. Sometimes even this is not sufficient. For example, the head clerk at one such place explained why he had just spent several months in a hospital:

There was a young guy, here just a short time, arguing and pushing with some regulars over which football game to watch on the TV in the lobby. I'm not afraid of no one. I used to be a tunnel rat in Vietnam [a soldier who went after the North Vietnamese in their elaborate tunnel system]. So I go out there to calm the situation down. This new guy turns on me with a knife and stabs me about four or five times in the chest and arms before he could be stopped. I probably should be dead.

To men sleeping on the streets at night, being jackrolled is a way of life. Hopefully, they will not be physically harmed. Ed recounts that during his time on the streets he not infrequently awoke to find someone going through his pockets: "I'm usually broke so I figure the best thing to do is to keep quiet and make believe I'm sleepin' and they find nothin' in my pockets and go away."

Worse than losing some money can be the loss of the ID cards that help these men secure medical assistance, foodstamps, and the like. One man described being drunk when "they cut out my pockets" and took all of his IDs. He told us that he was still trying to get them back after almost a year.

The fear of streets after dark is reflected in the fact that 56% of the nonstreet men did not go out in evening. Indeed, Parker (1970) observed that "At night no one is safe from them [jackrollers] unless he wears a police uniform or travels in a group" (p. 10).

We have described previously the violence older men encounter at the Men's Shelter or waiting on food lines. The fury and aggressiveness on food lines sometimes evokes a feeling in the observer of wanton, irrational savagery. One older man described such a scenario:

I remember one time there was a guy, a white fellow, he had his camera and he started taking pictures of guys. He was just a man taking a picture of people on the breadline at St. Francis. And one big guy comes running out, grabbed the guy and throws him down, breaking his camera and beating his head on the sidewalk 'til the people had to come and break them up. I don't know why he did that. You know a nut. That's the most disgusting thing I ever seen. No reason. I guess he's mad cause he got to be on this line. Some of them guys got attitudes down here you know.

Interestingly, despite the high level of crime victimization, only 13% of street men and 20% of the nonstreet men believed that crime had affected or changed their ways of life. Yet this assertion is belied by the fact that three fifths of the nonstreet men avoided going out at night and half of the nonstreet men and one third of the street men avoided carrying money when they could help it. On the positive side, only one in seven men thought that crime affected their visits to social activities or stopped them from going out alone.

Although violent street crime is the most pronounced problem for these men, they are also victimized through various "white collar" crimes. We have already alluded to the loansharks, many of whom work in the hotels or taverns. One such man who worked the Bowery was known as "Big Man." He was a large individual who shylocked in most of the flops and physically intimidated the men into timely payments. As we reported above, the usual loan rate was $14 back for every $10 borrowed (480% annual interest). Even more insidious is that most of these loansharks often have the men's checks turned over to them. So they extract the amount owed, and then he is already short for that month and then has to borrow again. It is like the sharecropper "owing the man" out of the check for the next period. Sometimes the men leave their money with these persons when they start drinking. Usually they are cheated, but "these persons of trust" justify their "collections" by arguing that the "rollers will get it if they don't and at least they don't hurt the men" (Parker, 1970, p. 10).

In citing a cause for crime, the vast majority of older men placed the blame on the influx of younger men, especially minorities, ex-mental patients, and addicts. Four out of five men believed that the

Bowery was "deteriorating" because of changes in the population, and two thirds of the men talked about there being too many young men on the Bowery. Although historically the Bowery has been notorious for its low-life, many of the men portray an almost idyllic picture of the old Bowery versus that of today. In most cases there are code words or even overt racial epithets with respect to the new Bowery denizens:

Years ago there was a lot more of a fraternity because they're all the same type. Workin' men from the railroads and stuff. They worked the summers and came and lived for the winters on unemployment insurance and whatever else they had. Certainly there were some muggings but not like you have now. In my opinion the men had respect for each other and they didn't go around beatin' up and muggin' each other and breakin' each others heads like now. Now they beat you to death for a nickel. Now you can't come up the stairway at night. It was a lot different, there's no doubt about it. Talk to the oldtimers. There was no trend like you have now of constantly being hurt. It's the element they let in that comes from all over the gosh darn country.

## RECREATIONAL ACTIVITIES

When homeless men are not just trying to survive, what are their favorite pastimes? Casual conversation was virtually a universal form of activity. Many men, however, spoke disparagingly of these interactions in which most of the talk is "the usual garbage about what this guy is doing, what that guy is doing, what's happening on the Bowery and all that." Once in a while, the men get into "a really semi-intellectual conversation about something. Some good topics are about health or about history and all that."

Other common activities in which both street and nonstreet men engaged on at least a monthly basis included reading newspapers or books (78%), watching TV/listening to the radio (82%), going for walks (82%), or playing cards (47%). Only about one in ten men reported going to a movie in the past month. Despite the hardships of street living, 69% of the street men regularly read a newspaper and 72% managed to watch TV or listen to a radio. Some of the less active flophouse men will spend virtually all their waking hours in their cubicles connected to tiny televisions through an earphone. Many of these men never leave their hotel for months at a time. The level of depression among these men was reflected by the fact that 23% of them reported that there was nothing that they had enjoyed doing in the past month.

Although many men frequent "OTB" (Off-Track Betting parlors), occasionally visit a bookie, or gamble small sums of money in card games, there is a small, but not insubstantial number of men who are addicted to gambling. Whereas most of the addicted old men on the Bowery are hooked on alcohol, gambling is the second potential monkey on the back that leads men to skid row. In the '30s, Sutherland and Locke (1936) identified gambling as one of the four principal vices of homeless men (the other vices were alcohol, begging, and the use of prostitutes).

Brian is illustrative of one of the perhaps 10% of the men interviewed who were "sober but addicted." Brian was a frequently hospitalized mental patient in his younger years. As a 65-year-old he is unmedicated, but seems to have "outgrown" his illness. He does focus on certain topics excessively, rambling on about them in the characteristic and repetitive pattern of the mentally ill. The "luxuries of the past" is his favorite. Each point in a story may be repeated 10 or 12 times. Eye contact is non-existent and he carries a shopping bag full of knickknacks which he hands out wherever he goes. Magazines, post cards, and calendars are his most frequent gifts. His weight shifts from one foot to the other as he pauses to see if you'll accept his offering. As Brian got to know us better he would, on occasion, tell us he "struck it big" yesterday. Or, that he "won a ton of money last night." On these occasions he would give a dollar or two instead of the usual 25-cent donation for lunch at the BRC. We skeptically questioned him about this, and perhaps the third time we did, he proved his story by displaying his wealth. Brian removed the safety pin from his front right pocket and pulled out a fist-sized roll of hundreds that he said he had won at the track. Two days later he gloomily asked to eat for free for he had lost it all. This pattern repeats itself a few times a year. He ebulliently displays his money to us. We warn him about muggers and try to intervene and help him open a bank account. He gambles again and loses it all. His original stake can only be his monthly social security check (around $400). While a few of the men we encountered had Brian's winning days, many of them are obsessed with the state lottery and the track. Pouring over the racing form is a major form of recreation at the BRC, and stories of near wins are rife.

How well do the Bowery men meet their daily needs? On our Activity Limitation Scale, which is a measure of a person's physical ability to perform activities of daily living, the Bowery men did not score significantly worse than the community men (Table 5-1). (There was no difference between street and nonstreet men scores on this scale.) This may be because those who are physically unable to negotiate the Bowery find it difficult to remain. When we looked at actual ability to meet various specific material needs, as might be expected, Bowery men were substantially worse off than their community counterparts. For example, on the Service Needs Scale, the Bowery street men scored five times higher than the community sample and the nonstreet men scored nearly four times higher than the community men (Tables 5-1 and 5-2). Similarly, with respect to financial needs, the street men scored six times higher than the community men and the nonstreet men scored four times higher than the community men.

## MODEL OF ADAPTATION

Although the preceding narrative provides a sense of the daily struggles that these men face, it would be useful to service providers and policy makers to set priorities with respect to those factors that most affect the ability of the homeless to survive. Using the Need Fulfillment Scale as an approximate measure of adaptation, zero-order correlations were generated between need fulfillment and the other 14 variables described in Appendix 1. Seven variables correlated significantly with inability to fulfill needs (see Appendix 1 Table 1, column 1). The two factors most powerfully associated with inability to meet daily needs were poor health and mental depression. Depression and physical symptoms frequently occurred together, their intercorrelation being very high (.57). The five remaining variables that correlated significantly with inability to fulfill needs were stressful life events, living on the street, more institutional or agency contacts, alcohol abuse, and being among the relatively younger group of men. Street men were more at risk in part because they encountered significantly more stressful life events and had fewer institutional contacts. The younger men may have been more at risk partly because they had significantly more physical symptoms, the oldest men generally being healthier "survivors." A modified stepwise regression analysis in which all 14 independent

Table 5-1. Comparison between Bowery Men and New York City
Community Men on Various Physical Health, Psychological, and
Social Variables

| | | Mean Scores on CARE Scales | | |
|---|---|---|---|---|
| | Maximum Score | N.Y.C. Men N = 61 (age 65–69) | Bowery Men N =281 (mean age, 61.5 yrs.) | t values (df = 340) |
| *Physical Health/Activity Scales* | | | | |
| Somatic Symptoms | 29 | 2.56 | 6.73 | 6.26** |
| Activity Limitation | 30 | 2.62 | 2.99 | 0.72 |
| Ambulation | 29 | 1.75 | 2.70 | 2.14* |
| Hearing Disorder | 13 | 0.34 | 0.89 | 2.27* |
| Visual Disorder | 11 | 0.59 | 0.77 | 0.67 |
| Heart Disorder | 11 | 1.64 | 1.84 | 0.63 |
| Hypertension | 4 | 0.72 | 1.13 | 2.26* |
| Edema | 9 | 0.54 | 1.58 | 3.69** |
| Respiratory Disorder | 6 | 0.97 | 2.17 | 5.42** |
| Arthritis | 7 | 2.39 | 2.68 | 0.88 |
| Sleep Disorder | 8 | 1.23 | 1.64 | 1.60 |
| Stroke Effects | 6 | 0.30 | 0.37 | 0.50 |
| Cancer | 4 | 0.16 | 0.21 | 0.57 |
| *Psychological Scales* | | | | |
| Depression | 23 | 3.48 | 7.44 | 7.25** |
| Organic Mental Symptoms | 10 | 0.67 | 1.48 | 4.32** |
| Subjective Memory Problems | 9 | 0.85 | 2.27 | 4.50** |
| *Social Scales* | | | | |
| Service Needs | 16 | 1.16 | 4.76 | 11.45** |
| Financial Needs | 6 | 0.82 | 3.82 | 9.48** |
| Utilization of Family Help | 8 | 1.46 | 0.05 | 14.34** |
| Total Service Utilization | 11 | 0.21 | 0.33 | 1.45 |
| Housing Problems | 9 | 0.84 | 0.89 | 0.23 |
| Dissatisfaction with Neighborhood | 6 | 1.02 | 2.70 | 8.21** |
| Fear of Crime | 10 | 1.62 | 3.70 | 6.89** |

*$p < .05$
**$p < .01$

Table 5-2. Comparison between Street and Nonstreet Bowery Men on Various Physical Health, Psychological, and Social Variables

| | | Mean Scores on CARE Scales | | |
|---|---|---|---|---|
| | Maximum Score | Nonstreet Bowery Men N = 195 (mean age, 63 yrs.) | Street Bowery Men N =86 (mean age, 59 yrs.) | t values (df = 279) |
| *Physical Health/Activity Scales* | | | | |
| Somatic Symptoms | 29 | 6.42 | 7.45 | 1.60 |
| Activity Limitation | 30 | 2.98 | 3.01 | 0.07 |
| Ambulation | 29 | 2.59 | 2.95 | 0.89 |
| Hearing Disorder | 13 | 0.83 | 1.04 | 0.90 |
| Visual Disorder | 11 | 0.80 | 0.69 | 1.06 |
| Heart Disorder | 11 | 1.71 | 1.90 | 0.68 |
| Hypertension | 4 | 1.15 | 1.07 | 0.48 |
| Edema | 9 | 1.55 | 1.65 | 0.36 |
| Respiratory Disorder | 6 | 2.14 | 2.26 | 0.57 |
| Arthritis | 7 | 2.55 | 3.95 | 2.44* |
| Sleep Disorder | 8 | 1.52 | 1.92 | 1.33 |
| Stroke Effects | 6 | 0.38 | 0.34 | −0.35 |
| Cancer | 4 | 0.19 | 0.11 | 1.02 |
| *Psychological Scales* | | | | |
| Depression | 23 | 6.98 | 8.48 | 5.67** |
| Organic Mental Symptoms | 10 | 1.49 | 1.44 | 0.28 |
| Subjective Memory Problems | 9 | 2.39 | 2.00 | 1.30 |
| *Social Scales* | | | | |
| Service Needs | 16 | 4.38 | 5.63 | 4.37** |
| Financial Needs | 6 | 3.17 | 5.27 | 7.58 |
| Utilization of Family Help | 8 | 0.05 | 0.04 | 0.37 |
| Total Service Utilization | 11 | 0.40 | 0.19 | 2.81** |
| Dissatisfaction with Neighborhood | 6 | 3.02 | 1.97 | 5.68** |
| Fear of Crime | 10 | 3.94 | 3.83 | 0.68 |

*p < .05
**p < .01

variables were entered in concert indicated that four of the seven variables (physical health, depression, institutional or agency contacts, and stress) contributed significantly to explaining the variance in need fulfillment. Together they accounted for 19% of the explained variance. In Chapter 10 we shall return to these findings to discuss their implications for service providers and planners.

# CHAPTER SIX

# *Social Supports*

"S'pose you had to sit out here an' read books. Sure you could play horseshoes till it got dark, but then you got to read books. Books ain't no good. A guy needs somebody —to be near him." He whined, "A guy goes nuts if he ain't got nobody. Don't make no difference who the guy is, long's he's with you. I tell ya," he cried. "I tell ya a guy gets too lonely an' he gets sick."

—John Steinbeck, *Of Mice and Men*

## INFORMAL SOCIAL SUPPORTS

Informal social supports—that is, support from acquaintances, "associates," friends, and family members—are a crucial element in the survival formula of the homeless. Interestingly, many earlier researchers have tended to minimize the role of such supports. Moreover, these researchers have suggested that skid row men are lifelong isolates and that their inept sociability is one of the principal factors in accounting for their presence on skid row.

Analysts of skid row life have been divided into two camps: In the first are those theorists who contend that the skid rower is "undersocialized" (Pittman & Gordon, 1958; Strauss, 1946), "incompletely socialized" (Dunham, 1953), "disaffiliated" (Bahr, 1973; Bahr & Caplow, 1973), "unable to empathize" (Levinson, 1958), "retreatist" (Bendiner, 1961; Merton, 1949), or "lacking a need for attachments" (Vexliard, 1956). Characteristic of the statements from this camp are these two observations:

Skid Row seems to be composed largely of discontented individuals who live in semi-isolation, who have few if any close friends, and who survive by being suspicious of everybody. (Bogue, 1963, pp. 169–170)

In general the shelter man is a homeless and friendless person, isolated from all social contacts of intimate and personal nature and this unattachment has been characteristic of his life since he left the parental home. (Sutherland & Locke, 1936, p. 37)

More recently, a medical component—mental illness—has been added to this characterization. Nevertheless, the homeless of the 1980s are still portrayed as social nomads: "To talk with homeless people is to be struck by how alone most of them are. The isolation is most severe for the mentally ill" (Bassuk, 1984, p. 43).

On the other side of those writers who argue that skid row men replace former relations with new relations as they become progressively enculturated into the "skid row way of life" (Wallace, 1965). James Rooney (1976), for instance, has empirically confirmed this replacement hypothesis, and he concluded that his findings "run counter to Vexliard's postulate of loss of need for meaningful personal relationships with increased exposure to the life of an outcast" (p. 87). Other investigators have observed that the men frequently coalesced into small groups, some permanent, most in flux, whose main focus was the procurement and consumption of alcohol (Jackson & Connor, 1953; Peterson & Maxwell, 1958; Rooney, 1961; Rubington, 1968; Wallace, 1968; Wiseman, 1979). These groups also served as a source of emotional and material support such as money, clothes, food, medical aid, and even intimate support. For example, Jacqueline Wiseman (1979) notes that, "Athough many of the studies . . . have referred to the Skid Row man as lonesome and undersocialized, any observer who spends any period of time on Skid Row will be struck by the general air of open conviviality there" (p. 38). Wiseman further reflects,

In other parts of the city, the sidewalk is used by adults as a pathway between a point of origin and a point of destination so that it presents areas of continual, on-going movement. On Skid Row, however, the sidewalks are used as areas for conversing, drinking, watching traffic, and panhandling. As a result, the purposeful pedestrian gets a feeling of moving through a private outdoor area. . . . It is more comparable to some of the characteristic use of outdoor space that might be found on a college campus. (p. 38)

Several authors, however, have maintained that these groups were chiefly materially oriented and usually devoid of intimacy (Blumberg *et al.*, 1971; Jackson & O'Connor, 1953). Others viewed group phenomena as part of a superficial gregariousness, "but without bonds of friendship" (Caplow, cited in Bahr, 1973, p. 163).

Partisans of both camps have generally agreed that skid rowers lack family ties. For instance, Wallace (1965) stated that by definition a skid rower is "kin-less." Still, a few have quarreled with this position. Bahr (1973) maintained, "It is an exaggeration to say that they [skid row men] lack contact with their families. On the contrary, some of them see their relatives fairly often" (p. 88). Similarly, in an earlier study (Cohen & Sokolovsky, 1981) we found that nearly half the men reported interaction with a relative, and one fifth had contact with at least three relatives.

The origins of these seemingly divergent viewpoints have stemmed in part from the rise of nonspecific terminology such as "isolate" or "disaffiliate." Thus, for example, although Bogue (1963) and Rooney (1976) found virtually equivalent levels of friendship among two skid row populations, the former characterized them as "semi-isolates" whereas the latter asserted that skid row was "clearly . . . not a population of isolates" (p. 85). Most researchers, by failing to provide any nonskid row groups for comparison, are especially predisposed toward such vague categorizations.

In our earlier research we suggested that some of the confusion among investigators might be a result of their disparate methodologies. Most techniques have involved either participant-observation or a "limited-choice" sociometric questionnaire. In an attempt to resolve this dichotomy we have employed an instrument (the Network Analysis Profile), which combines elements of an anthropological and sociological approach to measuring sociability along with traditional participant observation and intensive interviewing. (See Sokolovsky, 1986 for use of the instrument.) As we shall demonstrate shortly, we believe that our methods have provided a resolution to the discord.

We shall now examine the Bowery social world in order to tease apart the myths and realities. First, we believe that the notion that these men are total isolates or loners is patently false. Although the notion of isolation is untrue, Bowery men were relatively isolated versus our comparison group of elderly middle-class community men: 8.5 overall contacts versus 11.1 among the community men

Table 6-1. Comparison between Bowery Men and New York City
Community Men on Social Network Variables

| Variables | New York City Men[a] | Bowery Men[b] | t values[c] |
|---|---|---|---|
| Numplex | 2.98 | 2.88 | 0.23 |
| Proportion of sustenance links | 0.06 | 0.62 | 6.24** |
| Proportion of "very important" links | 0.41 | 0.37 | 0.32 |
| Frequency of interaction | 2.38 | 3.57 | 2.17* |
| Directionality | 2.17 | 2.11 | 0.30 |
| Proportion of multiplex links | 1.00 | 0.80 | 2.47* |
| Proportion of intimate links | 0.76 | 0.42 | 3.51** |
| Proportion of understanding links | —[d] | 0.73 | —[d] |
| Proportion available for help | —[d] | 0.69 | —[d] |
| Length of linkage (yrs.) | 29.09 | 7.06 | 11.82** |
| Total network size | 11.08 | 8.47 | 1.45 |
| Total informal links | 10.83 | 6.43 | 2.91** |
| Total formal links | 0.25 | 2.03 | 3.21** |
| Degree | 1.68 | 2.28 | 0.81 |
| Density | 0.23 | 0.41 | 1.62 |
| Clusters | 2.75 | 1.41 | 4.64** |
| Large clusters | 0.42 | 0.62 | 0.87 |
| Proportion same sex links | 0.46 | 0.77 | 3.76** |
| Proportion same age links | 0.63 | 0.68 | 0.54 |

Note. See Appendix 2 for description of variables
[a]$N = 12$. [b]$N = 281$. [c]$df = 291$. [d]Item was not included.
*$p < .05$;**$p < .01$.

(Table 6-1). Although the difference in the total number of contacts
was not statistically significant, the difference between the two
populations in the number of informal linkages (kin and nonkin) was
significant. Bowery men had 6.4 informal ties versus 10.8 among the
community men. Also, within our sample the street men had one
third fewer overall contacts than did the nonstreet men (6.0 versus
9.6 linkages); they also had one third fewer informal contacts (4.8
versus 7.2 linkages) (Table 6-2). Although small, the Bowery man's
social world is a highly active one. The Bowery men tended to see
their contacts one-and-a-half times more frequently than did the
community men (i.e., the Bowery men saw their contacts 3.6 times
per week). The flophouse men were especially apt to interact socially, perhaps because the lodging house, with its communal spaces,

Table 6-2. Comparison between Nonstreet and Street Bowery Men on
Social Network Variables

| Variables | Nonstreet Men N = 195 | Street Men N = 86 | t values (df = 279) |
|---|---|---|---|
| Numplex | 2.74 | 3.21 | 2.46* |
| Proportion of sustenance links | 0.59 | 0.70 | 2.79** |
| Proportion of "very important" links | 0.35 | 0.41 | 1.45 |
| Frequency of interaction | 3.82 | 2.99 | 3.45** |
| Directionality | 2.13 | 2.06 | 0.30 |
| Proportion of multiplex links | 0.77 | 0.87 | 2.69** |
| Proportion of intimate links | 0.39 | 0.45 | 1.42 |
| Proportion of understanding links | 0.73 | 0.72 | 0.25 |
| Proportion available for help | 0.68 | 0.72 | 0.99 |
| Length of linkage (yrs.) | 6.77 | 7.71 | 1.22 |
| Total network size | 9.55 | 6.01 | 4.64** |
| Total informal links | 7.15 | 4.81 | 3.64** |
| Total formal links | 2.40 | 1.20 | 5.03** |
| Degree | 2.56 | 1.64 | 2.84** |
| Density | 0.43 | 0.39 | 0.74 |
| Clusters | 1.51 | 1.16 | 2.92** |
| Large clusters | 0.69 | 0.45 | 2.38* |
| Proportion same sex links | 0.76 | 0.78 | 0.56 |
| Proportion same age links | 0.67 | 0.70 | 0.75 |

*Note.* See Appendix 2 for description of variables.
$*p < .05; **p < .01.$

serves as a focal point to conviviality. Nonetheless, street men also saw their contacts quite often (about three times per week).

Despite a modest degree of socialization, a few of the men were nearly complete loners: 5% had only one linkage and an additional 7% had only two ties. Relative isolation was more common on the street: 9% of the street men had only one linkage and an additional 11% had only two. Among those who are most isolated, their stated reasons for their social withdrawal came from negative experiences in the past such as failed loan repayments, theft of one's belongings. One Bowery resident told us "People are more trouble than they're worth. Ya think they're your friends then next thing ya know your shoes are gone. Living on the street is easier because you can stay away from everyone if ya want to." Another man remarked, "I stay alone because other men are trouble. They could be your friend one minute and your enemy the next." Given the frequency of untoward social encounters it is surprising that more men are not isolates.

For some men their isolation is a result of psychosis or depression. Our interviewers described two such men:

John has psychiatric problems and has been in and out of psychiatric hospitals for 20 years. He lives in a Wards Island shelter, and he drinks heavily. He talked incoherently half the time, saying that "he went with Hitler in '39 and stayed away from everybody." He talked of Hitler and Russia a lot. I believe he has very few contacts with anyone except his bookie and the package goods store proprietor who loans him money. He says he can still work (though I doubt it) but that he hasn't worked in some time (a truck ran over his hand). Though he sleeps at Ward's Island his life is centered on the Bowery where he can wander around relatively freely in his condition.

Mr. Thomas was an obviously depressed man struggling with his alcoholism and his slowly descending life. He is on welfare and has a hard time meeting necessary expenses. He has a badly arthritic back that causes him pain and discomfort and prevents him from working. He was rather somber and introverted during the interview. He hasn't had a drink for two weeks and is in the AA program at the BRC. He is an isolated man who, when he drinks, drinks alone in his room "until the walls start to close in" and he has to get out no matter what. In his depressions he often spends days at a time in his room eating out of cans and sleeping. It doesn't seem that he has anyone he can count on and he is pessimistic about the future.

Ironically, although we found several depressed alcoholics such as Mr. Thomas who drank alone and tended to be loners, those men who didn't drink at all were also apt to be more isolated. As one respondent remarked, "I think I have trouble making friends because I don't drink."

As an interviewer noted, physical impairment can also stifle socialization:

Mr. Andrews is 72 years old and has been living on the Bowery for 40 years. Twenty years ago he had an operation which resulted in the loss of his vocal cords. He has learned to speak esophageally. Many of his friends have died and his handicap has made it difficult for him to make new contacts.

Finally, a few men did appear to be true lifelong isolates. One man contended: "Being alone is my natural state, how can I be lonely?"

The Bowery man's social world reflects an adaptation to the needs of his environment. When comparing Bowery men with elderly community men who rarely use formal agencies or rarely have any personal relationships that involve exchange of "sustenance" items (e.g., food, money, medical aid), more than three out of five of the Bowery men's relationships involve exchange of sustenance items, and two thirds of the men use formal agencies (see Table 6-1).

Uncle Ed recalled several instances when his hotel buddies helped him during an illness. For example, after he returned from the hospital following a heart attack, he wasn't feeling well and a friend, Ted, walked into his room: "What's the matter, Uncle Ed?" "I need somethin' to eat real bad. Don't go out special for me, but when you go out bring me back a coffee and donut." When Ted returned with the food, Ed offered him a quarter tip. He said, "I got my own money. Don't be silly. You've done me errands and don't look for a tip. You don't get enough money out of your damn check."

Reciprocity was the hallmark of nearly all Bowery relationships. Failure to reciprocate can quickly terminate a relationship. Indeed, Spradley (1970) has pointed out that "friends" are defined not only as persons with whom one travels, flops, or shares a jug, but also by the kind of reciprocity that is involved in doing favors rather than hustling. Reciprocity was especially keen among street men who had a mean directionality score of 2.06 (helping = 1; reciprocal = 2; dependency = 3); the nonstreet showed some tendency toward increased dependency on others with a mean directionality score of 2.13. General community elderly men who likewise viewed themselves as quite independent had mean scores of 2.17. By contrast, older men living in SRO hotels evidenced the most dependency with their mean directionality score being 2.36.

Therefore it was not surprising to learn that Ed had soon returned the favor to Ted who wanted someone to accompany him to the Delancey Street Medical Center. He said to Ed, "I want to go get my eyes tested for glasses." Ed responded, "All right. I'll walk you." So Ed walked him there, and after Ted took his eye test and as they were leaving Ted asked, "You hungry? Come on. We'll go across the street to Blimpy's. We'll have a sandwich and coffee if you want." So Ted bought Ed a sandwich and a cup of coffee, and then Ed walked him back to the hotel. Ed added, "And he's got glasses now."

For men who are drinkers, a common element of an important social relation is counting on that person to watch out for you when you are drunk. Many men know they will drink themselves into senselessness and sometimes end up sprawled out in the street. Consequently, they try to find someone whom they trust and who will not take advantage of such a situation. Ted and Uncle Ed have slowly developed such a relationship over the last few years. Ed recalls several episodes when he "literally carried Teddy back to his room when he was too drunk. I'd take him home and put him to bed. Then I'd take his pants off, hang them up." Ed would tell him, "Here's your wallet and your money. It's in your pants. Make sure you lock that damn door when I leave." And he'd stand there to make sure he'd click the lock. And then Ed would say, "Okay, Teddy. I'm goin' downstairs." "Good-night Ed," Ted would whisper.

Except among very close associates, a quick material return was often expected for many types of helping behavior. This attitude was expressed in several terse aphorisms such as "money talks and bullshit walks," "the only friend ya got is in ya pocket." The marginality of the hotel men is further exploited by many of the hotel clerks and managers who will demand payment for even the most meager of services. One of the reasons Roland gave for not wanting to live in Bowery hotels was this not so subtle form of blackmail:

If you need a new blanket or clean sheet ya have to give 'em a few bucks. Or let's say you go to pay your month's rent at the desk and your mattress is full of holes and you can't sleep on it. The owner is a crook and sometimes will say "I'll give you a new mattress for $40."

## SOCIAL GROUPS

Group formations were a common part of Bowery life; five out of six men were enmeshed in at least one group formation (i.e., three or more men who knew each other). During our interviews we encountered various structures and different functions of group activities. Some were small groupings of two, three, or four men who might sleep together. In recent years with the escalation of violence perpetrated on older skid row men, more groups were forming as protective units, coming together largely at night. Remember that this was the case for Miles who, due to his growing fear of street crime, had linked up to several men to sleep with in the park. There also were larger groups of five or six men who panhandled together, drank together, fed and cared for each other.

Although "bottle gangs" are usually transient, many street groups were composed of men who knew each other for many years. Whereas relationships oscillated over the years, the overall mean length of acquaintance among street men was nearly eight years. Such groups often provided the men with some emotional and material support in addition to alcohol. In a few instances, group formation revolved around "father-figures" who provided assistance to street men. For example, "Roscoe" is a 75-year-old former street person who had come to have his own place and served as the superintendent of the building. He would allow men to sleep in the building's basement in inclement weather.

Several empirical measures of group formation were employed. First, we looked at the number of clusters (i.e., respondent plus two other men) in which each man was engaged (Table 6-1). Bowery men averaged 1.4 clusters; 83% of the men were enmeshed in at least one cluster, and 44% were engaged in two or more clusters. Moreover, 46% of the men were engaged in clusters of five or more men, which reflected the large groups formed around drinking, food programs, and hotel lobbies. By contrast, community men were engaged in twice as many clusters, but only one third were engaged in large clusters of five or more men. Thus, we find the community man's social world consisting of two to three small clusters whereas the Bowery man's social world consisted of one to two clusters, with one cluster usually being quite large and involving a substantial portion of their social network. This finding was also evident in our empirical measures of overall network interconnectivity (density and degree). Bowery men had approximately twice the number of interconnections among their network members as compared to the community men.

It can be seen that the lodging house setting, bottle gangs, communal lunches, and other activities tends to promote considerable group behavior among men that apparently may endure into long-lasting associations.

The importance of informal social supports is illustrated by the fact that 68% of linkages could be "counted on for help." Moreover, when queried regarding whom they would turn to if they needed help with a small amount of cash, shopping, illness, or food, 54%, 49%, 35%, and 25% of the men, respectively, would go initially to

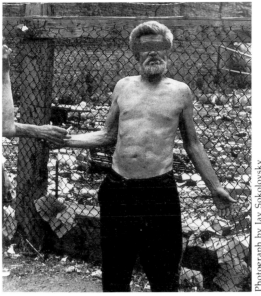

Early morning exchange of cigarettes with associates. Notice abdominal scars from fights.

A mission in the area.

Photograph by Jay Sokolovsky

Man sitting in his tiny wooden cubicle in one of the Bowery's worst flophouses.

Photograph by Jay Sokolovsky

An older homeless man collecting cans for resale in midtown Manhattan.

Photograph by Jay Sokolovsky

Morning scene, the Bowery.

Photograph by Jay Sokolovsky

Manager's cage in a flophouse. Sign indicates that those men sent there by the city—"ticket men"—can use the beds but must leave the establishment early in the morning.

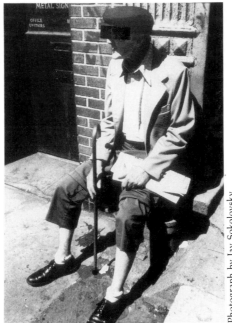

Sunning a skin ulceration outside the Bowery Residents' Committee.

Men getting ready to enter a mission for the evening.

their informal network system (e.g., hotel nonkin, outside nonkin, kin). Indeed as we noted above, three of five relationships among these men involved an exchange of sustenance items such as food, money, or medical assistance. Our findings correspond to that of anthropologist Anne Lovell. In her recent study (1984) of the general homeless population in New York City, she used the term "marginality without isolation" to summarize the fact that although networks were typically small, lacked substantial resources, and were highly changeable, virtually none of the street people she worked with were truly bereft of support relationships.

## FRIENDSHIP AND INTIMACY

Many writers, although acknowledging that considerable social interaction occurs among skid rowers, contend that most social ties are devoid of intimacy and emotionality. They maintain that relationships are solely for the purpose of material exchanges and tend to be rather transient. There can be found verbal evidence for this assumption in such street postulates as, "Ya got one dollar, ya got one friend." Such overt attitudes are born out of a socioeconomic environment in which one must sometimes exploit the meager resources of acquaintances as a simple matter of survival. However, we have found a considerably more complex social world than these writers have depicted. First, we have found that men generally have a hierarchy of categorizations of relationships. For example, relationships are strictly divided between "acquaintance," "associate," and "friend": An "associate" is someone that is more than just a casual acquaintance. It is someone with whom you sit and talk. A "casual acquaintance" is someone to whom you say "hello" and then may not see for another week. A "friend" goes out of his way to help you, and is capable of and willing to share intimacies. As Ed encapsulated it, "There's limitations to what you'd say and do with an associate where you'd go all out to help a friend."

Another man based friendship on how he was treated when he was sick:

Well they are the only ones who ever come to the hospital and ever done anything for me. They came twice. They gave me two packs of cigarettes, some money, and a small bottle of gin. If people come and see ya I figure they must like ya 'cause why waste your time going to the hospital to see somebody if you don't like 'em? So I got some good friends, that's all.

Often men will deny the possibility of real friends existing on the Bowery and encompass all relationships with the term "associate," while differentiating the importance of a tie with phrases such as "casual associate" versus "close associate." It is as if those who are no longer capable of having friends but only associates perceive themselves living outside of the normal world of "regular" human relationships and communities. For the most part, older Bowery men represent a classic case of "spoiled identity." They are regarded by the public as worthless bums, and to a large extent they have internalized this societal evaluation. In this respect many of the older men see themselves as socially terminal. This was expressed clearly by a 71-year-old retired painter who stated what to him is an axiom of the street: "Here, you can't have friends when you're old, old people don't have friends, you only have real friends from your childhood. If they are lost, friends are gone, and you just have some associates."

In contrasting the Bowery men with aging community men we found that two fifths (44%) of the Bowery men categorized their contacts as "very good" or "best" friends whereas nearly two thirds (64%) of the community men's linkages were considered as such. Similarly, four fifths of the community men's relationships were regarded as intimates whereas two fifths of the Bowery men's linkages were so rated. And although 77% of the Bowery men claimed to have at least one intimate, they were not necessarily persons to whom one could unburden their problems—47% of the men claimed to have no one to talk to about their problems. Two thirds said that they usually kept problems to themselves. By contrast, only one in eight community men lacked someone with whom they could unburden their problems or reported keeping problems to themselves. One elderly hotel man described his interaction with his "best friend":

We rarely talk about deep stuff or confide in each other. Most is just run of the mill conversation in the flophouse. We really never have anything that's really intelligent. I don't go to anybody to talk about deep things. I solve my own problems. I solve my problems myself or live with 'em.

On the other hand, the men felt that nearly three fourths of their contacts "understood their problems." Therefore, we propose that Bowery men have an *intermediate level of intimacy*. In other words, their levels of intimacy are not as intense as community men but their relationships are not devoid of feeling and empathy.

The resistance to forming very close human relationships belies a seemingly easy conviviality that many writers have commented on and which is still observable. Someone arriving on the Bowery with a week's growth of facial hair and wearing old jeans and a tee shirt is readily accepted as a member of the society of down and outers. This instant camaraderie, however, is very shallow with regard to the degree of interpersonal exchange that it readily permits. Buying a bottle of Thunderbird wine for a group of three men you have just met might entitle you to share in the next bottle bought by someone else but it will not mean you can inquire as to their actual names or what they were doing before landing on the Bowery. The men here accept the idea of skid row being a refuge area where normative expectations of the outside society toward family and work obligations do not obtain. Having failed in their non-Bowery lives, any probing into this other part of their past involves a violation of a sacred cultural norm. It will usually evoke an angry response which will assure the ostracism of the transgressor. In *Ironweed*, William Kennedy (1984) vividly depicted the ambiguity of these men's relationships:

By their talk to each other they understood that they shared a belief in the brotherhood of the desolate; yet in the scars of their eyes they confirmed that no such fraternity had ever existed, that the only brotherhood they belonged to was the one that asked that enduring question: How do I get through the next twenty minutes? (pp. 23–24)

Interestingly, neither intimacy nor being rated as a "very important" contact were statistically related to length of acquaintance. There was a modest significant association between length of acquaintance and mean proportion of sustenance ties (food, money, medical exchange). Therefore, long-term linkages may help with material support, but they may not necessarily engender trust or intimacy. Although the overall length of the informal linkages that Bowery men had was somewhat longer than expected (seven years), it was substantially shorter than the community men had who had mean length of acquaintance of 29 years. The transience of relationships was reflected by the fact that nearly one fifth of the men reported that a close friend had died or moved away in the past year. Nonetheless, as with most of our findings, there were numerous exceptions. Such was the case with Miles. Within his social network were two men with whom he had been friendly for over 40 years, and these were the men to whom he turned after he had been robbed of all his money.

## STREET VERSUS NONSTREET NETWORKS

What were the differences in the social interaction between street and nonstreet men? First, networks of street men were one third smaller than that of the nonstreet men (6.0 versus 9.6 linkages) (Table 6-2). Although street men had an average of one more person in their "outside" nonkin network and the same number of agency contacts as did the nonstreet men, they were unable to generate the additional informal and formal linkages available through hotel living. For example, informal hotel linkages (i.e., to friends and acquaintances) accounted for an additional 2.4 contacts, and formal hotel linkages (i.e., to hotel staff) accounted for another 1.0 contacts among nonstreet men. Moreover, the stability (and perhaps somewhat higher "prestige") of living in a flophouse versus street living resulted in more kin contacts for the nonstreet men (2.3 versus 1.4).

Despite having a relatively small social network the street men made the most of what they had. They had significantly more exchanges per network member and a significantly greater proportion of "sustenance" linkages than did the nonstreet men. Fully 70% of all their linkages involved the exchange of at least one sustenance category such as money, food, or medical assistance. Perhaps for this reason street men rated a somewhat greater percentage of their linkages as very important. Indeed, there seemed to be a higher level of subjective closeness reported among street men than for nonstreet men. The percentage of the network considered intimates, very good friends, or persons that could be counted on for help were all higher among the street men. It should be cautioned, however, this may represent merely a subjective bias of street men rather than any absolute difference in trust or warmth that they have generated within their network ties.

Ironically, while the street men are more in need of help from others because of their lack of economic resources, the vulnerability of living out on the street often leads to exceptional caution before entering into anything but the most fleeting, casual relationships. This attitude is borne out of bitter experiences which men frequently related to us. For example, Roland, who slept on the street for ten years, explained why he always sleeps by himself:

In 1979 I met this guy and we got to talkin'. He looked real pathetic and he asked me where the soup line was, so I tell him. Later that day I'm sittin' in the park and this guy comes back and says where you sleepin' tonight? So I told him and took him there to sleep; while I'm sleepin' he robs me. I didn't lose too much money but the sonofabitch he took all my papers. That's why my papers are still screwed up. It's like this, if I have money and you don't, you always want it and you're gonna kill me for it. Yeah, that's why I ain't got no close friends.

Street men were enmeshed in fewer clusters than the nonstreet men, although as a proportion of their network the number of clusters was not different from the nonstreet men (Table 6-2). Approximately one half were engaged in one cluster and an additional one third were engaged in two or more clusters. Also, fewer of the street men were engaged in a large cluster of five or more men (37% street versus 51% nonstreet).

Thus it can be seen that the street men were more likely to have a network of one (sometimes two) small clusters than the one small/ one large cluster pattern of the nonstreet men. One of the probable explanations for a greater number of larger clusters among the nonstreet men is the tendency to form group linkages within the flophouses. Obviously, the stability (men lived an average of five years in their flophouses) and the common spaces of the flophouses (e.g., lounge area, wash area, dormitories) provide a context for group formations. Indeed, the hotel served as an important differentiating variable in the social world of these men: Nearly two fifths of the nonstreet men's linkages evolved from hotel life (informal ties and hotel staff); nine out of ten nonstreet men had at least one such hotel linkage.

## KIN CONTACTS

Are Bowery men really "kinless," as some investigators have argued? In actuality, approximately one fourth of the social networks of street and nonstreet men were comprised of kin contacts; 65% of the nonstreet men and 55% of the street men had at least one kin contact. In absolute numbers, the nonstreet men have approximately one more kin contact than street men. As suggested above, being in a hotel perhaps fosters a stability that allows for more contact (e.g., letters, telephone in lobby, etc.). For example, Ed writes to his brother "about every second week, and his brother calls the other week." Of course, it should be underscored that the 62% of Bowery men who reported having at least one current kin contact is far below the 92% having such contacts among the older community men. Moreover, in absolute numbers, community men had more than twice the number of kin contacts (4.5 versus 2.0).

For skid row men, there is little expectation that relatives will provide any material support. As opposed to community men, who indicated roughly 50% of the time that they would go to kin if they needed cash, food, medication, were ill, or needed shopping done, fewer than 1 in 30 Bowery men would rely on kin for addressing these problems. The one exception was needing cash, where one in eight men indicated that they would contact kin. For most of these problems, nonkin or agencies were the common responses.

Despite the lack of material support from kin members, emotionally, for a substantial number of these men "family still comes first." Affect regarding family members remains strong as illustrated by this interviewer's notes:

Mr. Daniels is a very depressed and tearful 63-year-old black man who is currently homeless and sleeping on the streets. His wife died in May and the situation with his stepdaughter and stepgrandson is so bad that he would rather be on the street than with them. He is currently very depressed and occasionally hears the voice of his dead wife.

Other men were quite defensive and sensitive about their family life:

RC: I got a wife here in New York.
JS: Really? When was the last time you saw her?

RC: You know, I'm gonna answer your question just like you asked me. None of your damn business. I'm being brave now.

JS: It's your right to say that.

In spite of such emotional conflict, one fourth of the men expressed a desire to get in contact with one or more of their relatives whom they had not seen in the past year. Three fifths of the men who had children indicated that they did not see them as much as they would like, and 46% of the men were upset by not seeing their children as much as they would have wanted. Reasons for not seeing them included distance (33%), physical incapacity (36%), and indifference or hostility of their children (30%). Similarly, 57% and 53% of the men, respectively, did not see or hear from their siblings and other close relatives as much as they would like. Principal reasons included distance (42%), physical incapacity (29%), and hostility of siblings or relatives (22%).

One of the most poignant ironies is that between the Bowery man and his estranged family. He has perhaps made a few gestures at reconciliation or harbors the fantasy that someday he might be able to rejoin them. But the family seldom responds or shows any interest. Sometimes it is only after the man dies that the family shows "interest." One hotel manager reconstructs the scenario:

We have men in here who've never seen their kids or their wives for years. They might still be married but they're never in touch. Invariably when a man dies and the family hears about it they all rush down to get all his assets. "We heard he had a lot of money and where's all his belongings?" I said "You want his belongings, lady? I'll pack 'em up for ya and mail 'em to ya." I put the dirtiest, shittiest, crummiest clothes I can find and mail 'em to her. They eventually realize that they are just pissin' on a rope.

## CONTACT WITH WOMEN

George Orwell (1933) observed that the second great evil of these men's lives (after hunger) is that they are cut off from contact with women. First, because there are few women at their level of society, and second, because "women never, or hardly ever, condescend to men who are much poorer than themselves. A tramp, therefore, is a celibate from the moment when he takes to the road" (p. 204).

Is it true that these men are womanless and celibate?

The notion that Bowery men are "womanless" clearly is not true. Although there are virtually no women on the Bowery, approximately one fourth of the men's informal linkages were with women. For the most part, these were linkages to kin. This was substantially less, however, than the older community men who reported that slightly more than half of their informal linkages were with women. Unlike the community men in which a greater percentage of women in their network was associated with a greater proportion of intimates, no such relationship obtained for the Bowery men. Thus, for Bowery men, women do not generally serve as confidants as they commonly do in the general male population.

Other writers (e.g., Wiseman, 1979) have pointed to evidence that these men seem to "like" women and most men tend to blame themselves for earlier problems with women. As one man put it, "My wife left me because of my drinking and screwing around." It should be recalled that 57% of the men had been married previously, which, although lower than the community men (93% married), is not insubstantial and reflects a degree of affinity toward women.

Most of the men were reluctant to talk about their sexual experiences with women, and clearly many of these aging men no longer engaged in sexual relations. As Phil Parker (1970) observed,

The man on the Bowery, regardless of his status or condition, except in rare cases, has little interest in sex. There are those who do . . . but this is not the rule. Most of our men, even the younger ones, have physical and emotional problems that tend to outweigh the sex urge. (p. 13)

There are four pathways that men take to fulfill their sexual urges. The most common way is with prostitutes. However, despite the high density of men on the Bowery, prostitutes are relatively rare. This is because the prostitutes must compete with jackrollers as well as risk being victimized themselves.

Uncle Ed will occasionally go to a prostitute, although he is quite fearful of the consequences: "I get to the extent where I get horny as hell and if I've got the money I'll take a chance with a prostitute for a half-hour or so. After I'm done, I go the next day to the hospital for a check-up, just to be safe 'cause it's very easy to get yourself infected."

Ed usually goes to either Greenwich Village or some streets in Soho. There used to be a notorious pick-up spot on Delancey Street and Bowery where there was a luncheonette in which the prostitutes would proposition the male customers. That spot has disappeared but a new one has arisen nearby. Ed said it's been a while since he's gone to a prostitute. It used to cost him "ten dollars for a head job, twenty straight, fifty for the night. Now it's probably twice as much. The price is just about the same anywhere you pick up one. Pussy's still pussy, no matter what you pay for it. That's the way they figure it." Ed said that most of the men at the senior program of the Bowery Residents' Committee don't talk about sex. "Of course, if you go to bars one's gonna be braggin' to the other about the piece of ass he had last night and all that shit. But that's mostly alcohol talk."

Another way to meet women is in a bar. Because there are only two bars left on the Bowery, men generally must go uptown to find companionship. As Ed argues,

'Cause I never met a woman I drank with on the Bowery, I always drank uptown, particularly if I wanted to get doubled up with a woman. I'd go to any place that they sell booze. I could sit here for a whole week namin' different places where there's women, but on the Bowery, I can't say I've seen women too much.

A third way to find women is at Alcoholics Anonymous meetings. Ed cynically observes, "This one guy is a whore master. He's just going to AA meetings to see what cunt he can pick up. That's it, in plain English."

A final group of men seem to yearn for something more than transient sexual encounters and we found that a number of men maintained long-term liaisons with women living off the Bowery. One man had a lady friend in Connecticut whom he saw once a month, another regularly visits a woman in Brooklyn, and one street man still lives with a woman, although she doesn't let him come home when he is drinking, which he states is about three quarters of the time. A number of the men still wish for a good relationship with a woman again. Many of the men's fantasies about future escape from the Bowery involve being rescued by a woman. Although rarely do any of these older men find such a relationship, the dream is still there. As Ed wistfully puts it with respect to a woman he had been seeing at AA meetings:

I think Doris and I can develop into a long-term relationship. It's buildin' to it now. I would like that 'cause I'm so tired of being by myself and tryin' to live my life by myself, except for the AA members. I can't live in an AA meeting for twenty-four hours. And she'd be a lot of companionship, and I tend to believe that she would help me so that I'd get back on my feet and be able to leave the Bowery. Maybe we could get a nice apartment, live together, and I could live the life that I'm destined to live.

Because of the all-male environment, homosexuals are more available to these men than are women. Historically the Bowery had been a place where gays could cruise easily without fear of police harassment. However, liberalization of attitudes toward gays in recent years has made the Bowery considerably less attractive for gays who have now gravitated to other parts of the city. Among older men, there are relatively few overt homosexuals. We encountered fewer than 10 out of our sample of 281. Our findings correspond with Wiseman's earlier research that skid row men generally shun gay bars, and when some of them engaged in homosexual activities, it had the character of a money-making enterprise or of make-do sexual gratification. As one of the men in Wiseman's (1979) study put it, "Sure I've gone with some fags—when I couldn't afford women" (p. 38).

In sum, Bowery men seem to be a sociable lot—only one in six men said that they feel "ill at ease with people." However, their sociability must be tempered by their cautiousness around others in that one fourth of the men indicated that they have wanted to stay away from people. The desire for more contact was evidenced by more than half stating that they often feel lonely and by expressing a desire for more company. Loneliness was expressed as not having someone to talk to (46%) or resulting from the death or separation of someone close (48%). The profound desolation that sometimes overcomes these men was expressed movingly by Miles on his last birthday:

I recall the birthday parties that I've had. As a child I was always given a surprise birthday party. This is about the first birthday I've had in the street alone. It's very lonely out there and everyone's doin' their own thing. They have their routines so they just don't have time to sit here on the park bench with Miles and drink somethin' to celebrate his birthday.

In concluding this section we return to the debate among researchers as to whether Bowery men are sociable or not. Clearly, our investigative methods have demonstrated that these men are not complete isolates nor incapable of intimacy and complex social formations. Moreover, they are able to enlist the support of their compeers to help fulfill their daily needs. On the other hand, the skid rower has fewer social ties and fewer intimates than their aged counterparts in the general population. Hence, the contradictory statements in the literature regarding skid row sociability may have depended on the perspective of the investigator. Because the skid rower is not inept at manipulating his social world, those researchers who have studied skid row from a process or situational perspective were able to discern a panoply of interactive phenomena. On the other hand, by standards of the general population, the skid rower's social world is small and constricted. It is not difficult to see how these writers who have tried to portray the skid rower from a more normative perspective would be apt to view him as isolated and as having a detached need for others. As Wiseman (1979) has suggested, normative theories tend to view these men as pathological because they are being compared with middle-class living arrangements.

A second feature of the presumed undersocialization and disaffiliative behavior of the skid row man has been the failure to examine adequately the degree to which society has been responsible for his relative isolation. The skid rower does not bathe regularly, eat properly, dress respectable, marry, raise children, own a home, or attend school. "Skid row is the most deviant community in the United States" (Wallace, 1968, p. 144). Spradley (1970) argues, "The tramp threatens the values and security of our more respectable identities" (p. 121). Historically, when the migratory workers returned to the city they faced the full force of the attitudes of the community and were ignored as if they had never returned. The nature of his employment further isolated the skid rower as the jobs offered to him provided no advancement, no security, no social integration through work. Except for some early work by the Wobblies, the skid rower never became part of the labor movement. His only protest to exploitation has been to walk off the job. He is also isolated from political life. When the age of the political machine died and he could no longer sell his votes or get his name on a list for municipal jobs such as shoveling snow, politics no longer played a role for him. Given this history, Wallace (1965) conjectured about the skid rower, "Why should he take any interest in the community from which he is an outcast?" (p. 148).

Last, the skid rower is isolated from society's legal institutions. And until the decriminalization rulings of the 1970s, he was arrested regularly for drunkeness or vagrancy. Yet, as Spradley (1970) maintained, they were arrested more for being "offensive to the rest of society" (p. 121) than for breaking the law. Hence, the community has imposed an isolation on the skid rower that may also account for some of the earlier observations regarding his disaffiliative behavior.

## FORMAL SOCIAL SUPPORTS: AGENCIES AND OTHER INSTITUTIONS

As many traditional skid row institutions have disappeared, men have come to rely more heavily on social agencies to fulfill various needs. For example, the closing of many of the "slop joints" or "horse markets" means that the men who have meager or no incomes must depend on agency food programs. Similarly, the closing of public baths and the considerable danger that exists in using the one that remains leads many of the men to use the streets or the toilets and shower facilities of several local agencies. One notorious side street has been dubbed "shit street" because of the human excrement deposited there. During the 1970s several agencies (e.g., the Bowery Residents' Committee, Holy Name Mission, Booth House) that provide men with a lounge, socialization, food, shower facilities, and recreation opened to replace the traditional Bowery institutions that were vanishing rapidly. One elderly man summed up his reasons for going to the Bowery Residents' Committee:

Why sit in the park? The main reason I joined this group is to have a retreat. I come in to watch television, take a shower or shave, and to take a nap. Then I have my lunch and a snack, and when my friend Charlie leaves, I leave. I wait for him and we both walk out together.

The importance of formal contacts, especially agencies, in the lives of these men cannot be understated. Whereas relatively few elderly community men (17%) reported any regular formal linkages (i.e., to social workers, etc.) and formal ties accounted for only 2% of their total contacts, Bowery nonstreet men had 2.4 formal linkages and the street men 1.2 such ties; this represented between 20% and 25% of their total linkages. Moreover, 83% of the nonstreet men and 67% of the street men had a least one formal linkage. The nonstreet men had more linkages because of the inclusion of hotel staff (desk clerks, maintenance staff) in the category of formal contacts. Of their 2.4 formal ties, 1.0 were with hotel staff and 1.4 were with agency staff.

When queried regarding various hypothetical needs, 74%, 58%, 51%, 47%, and 28% of the Bowery men would use a service agency respectively for information, clothing, a place to stay, food, and medical assistance. In addition, 24% of the nonstreet men would rely on hotel staff if they were ill.

Attending these agencies is part of the socialization process of skid row—there is an internal culture with various rules, hierarchies, and behaviors that must be followed: The seating arrangements at the Seniors' Lunch Program at the BRC where the men regularly eat and congregate are illustrative of a pecking order that they impose on themselves. The cafeteria seats approximately 115 persons. Many of the men have been coming to the program for nearly a decade, sitting in the exact same seat each day. There is a small kitchen at the front of the room, a stage with tables and chairs identical to the rest at the side, and at the rear two alternate exits. The tables are arranged in the body of the room in three rows of seven rectangular tables each. Each table seats four to six for meals.

There is a number of what seems to be high status tables. A high status table is one in which the occupants are constant and invariable whatever time they arrive for the meal. These tables tend to be in the front of the room near the kitchen and the social work staff. Tables from the middle to the back of the room are of moderate status with conflicts sometimes arising over who will eat where on a particular day. The tables on the elevated stage are low status. They fill up last. There never is any friction over who sits where. The drunkest, the dirtiest, and the least psychiatrically sound tend to seat themselves in this section. A small group of lowest caste men resist seating at all, either standing or moving about until the possession of a tray of food forces them to alight on an unoccupied seat. The group of high status tables tends to have participants who are unchanged except through death, illness, or alcoholic binging that precludes attendance. The medium status tables are always in a state of flux and tension. The low status "Siberia" is tranquil and unsocial with little interaction between the men. There is never a card game or dominoes or chess going on at low status tables.

A table can be changed in status through a number of developments. An intermittent game (cards, dominoes, or chess) with a revolving cast of players can become a daily and steady game locking the table in and crystallizing its status. Less commonly, but also possible, a new man can precipitate a table set around a theme such as homosexuality or a particular ethnicity. Where the table had never been self-labeled as one for Swedes or for gay men, a charismatic Swede or gay man can attract others interested in the theme until regular seats develop and the table changes in status.

The self-imposed pecking order concerning seating arrangements is coupled with what appears to be a powerful "drive" to line up. The elderly participants seems so acclimatized to queuing up for everything that they do so at the drop of a hat. It is done reflexively and with a great internal energy whether there is anything worthwhile at the end of the line or not. Apropos, is the double meaning expressed in the title of Tom Kromer's (1935) book *Waiting for Nothing*, which encapsulates the concrete and abstract existence of many of these men's lives.

Programmatic changes that reduce the number of occasions where forming a line is necessary are resisted. If coffee, bingo cards, or numbers for lunch service are made available there is great competition and jostling for line position. This, however, is also done in a way related to status. Workers or volunteers either go to the front of the line or conspicuously wait until everyone is served, then go last. Women cut into any line at any time. The high status card playing tables actually move the card game to the location where the line is expected to form. When the payoff or the sign up sheet is produced, the game ends, and the line patiently waits for the card players to start the action. These are old men and this is not, with few exceptions, a physical thing. It is not the toughest, or the most vigorous who go first, but it's the regulars as the men themselves define them.

The lines are entities unto themselves done for the sake of lining up. If bingo cards are given out, it makes no difference whether a card is obtained early or late. Bingo will not begin until everyone gets a card. The man holding lunch ticket #5 gets an identical lunch to the man holding lunch ticket #105. Perhaps he eats ten minutes later. Most of us faced with standing 15 or 20 minutes on a line of 100 people would rather opt for staying seated, finishing the paper, and casually strolling up to get our bingo card, or our block of cheese, or our lunch ticket when the line has dwindled down to a few people. Not so with these men. They have little to entertain them, and it seems that the status implications and perhaps just the activity of queuing up is a diversion they find compelling.

Despite their extensive use of agencies, many men do not look favorably on them. Wiseman (1979) observes how these men referred to the agencies as being in the "miseries" business (p. 252). Many men believe that the agencies are mainly "looking out for themselves." They use the men to perpetuate and expand their domain, drawing government and private funds and grants and exploiting the labor of the men for food or shelter. The men know that many of these agencies must see their quota of needy persons, alcoholics, or psychotics lest they lose their funding. Phil Parker (1970), a former Bowery man, graphically depicts the circumspectuality that surrounds the skid rower's encounter with agencies:

And the worker who deals with these men must view himself as an element in this man's struggle for survival—he must see himself as clearly as possible through the eyes of the Bowery man, and he must realize that this man, no matter what category he falls into, is apt to view the worker (along with the hotel clerk, the chow server, the policeman, the man next to him in the dayroom) as first and foremost a potential enemy whom he must fend with and deceive in order to survive. (p. 10)

After living on the streets of London in the 1930s, George Orwell (1933) likewise recognized that in spite of the "abject worm-like gratitude with which they normally accept charity . . . a man receiving charity practically always hates his benefactor . . ." (p. 184).

Besides the institutions discussed above, Bowery men interact with several others as well. They regularly (at least once per month) go to food stores (85%), local restaurants (75%), clothing stores (64%), parks (76%), and drug stores (51%). Street men are less likely to use restaurants than nonstreet men (62% versus 83%), but, as one might expect, are much more apt to use parks (91% versus 70%). Obviously, for street men the park may serve as a substitute for a

room. Street men are also significantly more likely to frequent clothing stores than do the nonstreet men (71% versus 60%). This may
reflect the ability of the nonstreet men to postpone clothing purchases. Surprisingly, only a minority of the men frequent taverns at
least on a monthly basis (41% of nonstreet versus 27% street). As we
shall discuss shortly, drinking tends to be confined to rooms, street
groups, and park benches. This likely reflects the decline of taverns
as social institutions and their rapid disappearance from the Bowery.
As noted previously, only two small taverns are still open and none
serve food any longer. Even as recently as a decade ago, taverns
seemed to serve the functions that many of the newer agencies now
provide. They served light, cheap food, provided credit for reliable
men, a refuge from the weather, a place to socialize, and even a
chance to establish links with local businessmen who might become
benefactors. In 1977, Jay Sokolovsky made the following observation
in one such tavern:

It is two o'clock PM and I am sitting and drinking beers with George and Ted
who describe themselves as "Aristocratic Bums" because they keep themselves clean and seldom panhandle despite their costly drinking habits. In
walks a middle-aged man smoking a pipe who comes over to our table and
addresses George and Ted as "my wino friends." They do not seem insulted
by this but instead seem to revel in this man's attention. He is referred to
simply as Ace and is a tool and die maker who owns a shop around the block
and lives in a big house on Long Island. George introduces me to his
benefactor and to demonstrate the nature of the bond says, "Now Ace is
gonna buy us drinks" and Ace shouts to the bartender for some beers. He
remarks "these winos cost me plenty, at least eight dollars a week."

Participation in organizations/clubs is regularly engaged in by
nearly two fifths of the men; these levels are significantly lower for
street men (46% nonstreet versus 19% street). By contrast three
fourths of the elderly New York community men regularly partici-
pated in organizations or clubs. Although not generally recognized
for their religious ardor, six in ten Bowery men had gone to church
services over the past month. At times, some of these services may
have been associated with the procurement of a meal. However, by
comparison, this was still significantly less frequent than the elderly
community men, among whom eight in ten reportedly attended
religious services in the past month. Finally, the Bowery men were

seemingly a mobile group: 71% regularly used public transportation, and 82% had been in areas away from the Bowery. Street men were even more apt than nonstreet men to be in areas off the Bowery (91% versus 79%), perhaps reflecting a need to find safe parks for sleeping and good soup kitchens and to obtain temporary placements in uptown or outer borough shelters.

Popular lore views these men as runaways from the complexities of modern social life who ultimately wind up as lone, shadowy figures within the crags of skid row. As we have seen, although skid row social life is radically different from middle-class existence, it is not without its intricacies. There are missions, social agencies, flops, bread lines, taverns, and parks that form the nidus for the skid rower's social world of bottle gangs, associates, social workers, priests, loan sharks, and hotel managers. These supports may not only fill his stomach today or cheer him up tomorrow, but they also teach him how to survive the next winter or the next drunk. They teach him to be a skid row man.

# CHAPTER SEVEN

# The Physical and Mental Health
of Old Homeless Men

## PHYSICAL HEALTH

Historically, those persons with physical deformities and disabilities who have been unable to successfully compete in the work force have been found among the ranks of the homeless. The hobo argot is replete with colorful eponyms characterizing the physical deformities of these men (Anderson, 1923): "sticks" (a man who lost a leg), "peg" (a man who lost a foot), "finger" (a man who lost a finger), "blinky" (a man who lost an eye), "wingy" (a man who lost an arm), "mitts" (a man who lost a hand), "lefty" (a man who lost his left arm and leg), and "halfy" (a man who lost both legs). Anderson (1923), in his listing of reasons of why men take to the roads, described the "industrial inadequate" who were comprised of those persons with physical handicaps due to accidents, sickness, or occupational disease; alcoholics and drug addicts; and the elderly. In the first decade of the century, Alice Solenberger's (1911) study of 1000 homeless men found more than half were suffering from physical defects. Their physical state was vividly depicted by Theodore Dreiser:

Some came with thin, rounded shoulders, others with wooden legs, still others with frames so lean that clothes only flopped about them. There were great ears, swollen noses, thick lips, and, above all, red, blood-shot eyes. Not a normal, healthy face in the whole mass; not a straight figure; not a straight-forward, steady glance. (1982, *Sister Carrie*, p. 396)

More recently, Bogue (1963) identified "poor physical health" as one of four principal etiological factors explaining the existence of skid rows in the 1950s. Bogue found that four fifths of skid row men had at least one physical ailment, that they had 3.3 times the rate of illness as the general population, and that they could expect to live less than one half the number of years remaining to men of the same age in the general population. During midwinter, between one fourth and one fifth of skid row men were sick on any given day. Based on his finding that a greater percentage of teetotalers and light drinkers were suffering from chronic disease, Bogue concluded that at least for this subgroup, it was the initial breakdown of health that may have caused job loss and subsequent arrival on skid row.

For persons over age 55, Bogue found approximately one in five men suffered from arthritis or rheumatism, one in eight from heart disease, one in ten from chronic disorder of the digestive system, one in eight from impaired vision, and one in seven from asthma. Studies in the 1960s of skid row type men in other countries found high rates of gastrointestinal disease (13% to 16%) and chronic lung disease (10% to 17%) (Edwards *et al.*, 1966; Olin, 1966). By comparison, diagnosis of bronchitis and asthma are seen in 2.8% and upper gastrointestinal disease in 1.5% of ambulatory patients in the United States (Filardo, 1985). Studies in the 1970s from Sweden reported diseases of the gastrointestinal tract and nontuberculous respiratory diseases to be seven times more frequent among the homeless than in the general population (Alstrom, Lindelius, & Salum, 1975). Studies in the 1980s continue to substantiate the notion that the homeless are more physically impaired than the general population. A survey of 106 men living in New York City's public shelters revealed that 27% were suffering from a chronic medical problem that required regular physical supervision, and 24% had a physical disability that would interfere with work (N.Y.S. Office of Mental Health, 1982).

Here again, as with other factors attributed to explaining skid row, it is difficult to discern cause and effect. As Anderson observed in 1923, "Disease, physical disability, and unsanitary living conditions seem to be, as things are, the natural and inevitable consequences of the migratory risk-taking and irregular life of the homeless man" (p. 136). Phillip Brickner (1985), describing the conditions of the homeless 60 years later, comments: "Life on the streets presents stressors of a magnitude and complexity that health care professionals can seldom imagine" (p. 27). Chronic diseases require constant attention. Dietary restrictions, imposed frequently for several diseases, are nearly impossible to observe by patients who rely on soup kitchens, trash bins, and hand-outs to survive. Often lacking a watch, the homeless patient finds medication schedules difficult to follow. Once medication is obtained, storage becomes a problem—most pills must be kept dry, insulin requires refrigeration, and possibilities for sterile injection are nil. Brickner found that only half these men are able to keep clinic appointments, and 14% refused direct admission to the hospital after an ambulance had been dispatched to transport these very sick men to the hospital. Moreover, only one in four patients remained in long-term care, perhaps fearing that they would lose their room, miss their check, or be put away permanently.

With a few exceptions (Brickner, 1985; Fischer, Shapiro, Breakey, Anthony, & Kramer, 1986; Rafferty, Hinzpeter, Colwin, & Knox, 1984), the current focus on mental illness among the homeless has tended to obscure the physical health care needs of homeless persons. Even less has been written about the health of the older homeless population. Such an oversight is not trivial, since as one author (Garfield, 1982) suggested, high death rates are one of the distinguishing characteristics of the homeless population in the United States. Anthony Arce and his associates (1983) observed that like so many other needs of the homeless, general medical problems are overlooked, and this leads to further disability and more elaborate care.

Several issues arose from our review of these earlier studies: (1) Given the broader availability of health care (especially through Medicare and Medicaid) than in earlier eras, what is the current physical status of Bowery men and how does it compare with their age peers in the general population? (2) To what extent has access to medical care improved for these men? (3) Is physical illness primarily a separate entity that antedates arrival on skid row or is it a consequence of living on skid row? Given that earlier studies have generally used rudimentary statistical techniques, we will use more sophisticated analytic methods to ascertain better what factors contribute to explaining physical illness among these men.

## Skid Row Men Compared with a New York City Elderly Population

Bowery men were considerably more physically impaired than their elderly male counterparts living in the general community. On 6 of 13 health/activity scales—respiratory symptoms, ambulation, hearing disorder, hypertension, edema, somatic symptoms (which includes gastrointestinal complaints)—the Bowery men scored significantly worse than the community men (Table 5-1). On the latter three scales, the Bowery men were particularly impaired. The Bowery men also scored higher than the community men on all remaining scales. Life for a majority of the older Bowery men could be characterized as one of chronic pain, discomfort, weakness, and difficulty on exertion. For example, approximately one half of the men reported difficulties with items such as breathlessness and dizziness; one third had problems with swollen ankles, tremulousness, persistent coughing, and ambulation; one fifth had persistent fever or chills. Fully one third of men (31% nonstreet, 35% street) reported that they had been hospitalized at least once in the past year (Table 7-1). By contrast, New York City elderly men reported symptoms at rates of approximately one third to one half that of Bowery men. Roughly one in seven community men complained of dizziness, persistent coughing, or problems with ambulation; one-fifth indicated some breathlessness; fewer than one in ten reported tremulousness and 2% had persistent fever or chills. Only 12% had been hospitalized in the past year.

Except for differences on the Arthritic Scale, which included items related to pain and swelling in joints or muscles, there were no differences between street and nonstreet Bowery men on any of the physical health scales. There were no significant correlations between the men's location (i.e., street versus nonstreet) on an overall physical symptom index (derived from the summed $z$-scores of the health scales) (Appendix 1, Table 1, column 2).

Despite their relatively poor physical health, the men seemingly were not aware of their status *vis-à-vis* their age peers: 55% rated their health excellent or good for persons of their age, and only 18% rated their health as poor. These figures are roughly comparable to surveys of other populations. This was not much different from the New York City sample in which 68% reported their health as excellent or good, and 5% as poor. In Shanas and co-workers' (1968) study

Table 7-1. Comparison of Bowery and Community Men (Expressed in Percentages) on Selected Health Items

| Item | Community (N = 61) | Bowery (N = 281) |
|---|---|---|
| Chest pain in past month | 10 | 20 |
| Swollen ankles | 14 | 27* |
| Palpitations in past month | 19 | 34* |
| Trembling in past month | 9 | 37* |
| Dizziness or weakness in past month | 14 | 45* |
| Fainting or weakness in past month | 3 | 11 |
| Breathlessness in past month | 22 | 50* |
| Persistent cough | 15 | 31* |
| Fever or persistent chills | 2 | 21* |
| Nausea, vomiting | 1 | 5 |
| Persistent pain in abdomen | 5 | 7 |
| Arthritis or rheumatism | 55 | 39* |
| Difficulty ambulating | 17 | 35* |
| Seizures in past 2 years | 0 | 12* |
| History of "heart trouble" | 31 | 25 |
| History of high blood pressure | 25 | 43* |
| Memory difficulties | 24 | 43* |
| Fracture after-effects | 7 | 14 |
| Hospitalized in past year | 12 | 33* |
| Saw doctor in past year | 76 | 77 |
| Saw doctor in past month | 62 | 37* |
| Puts off seeing doctor | 28 | 44* |

*Note.* The chi-square test with Yates correction was used to compare the percentage with problems in the community and Bowery groups by testing for significance at the .05 level. Items with significant differences are indicated with asterisks.

among men aged 65 to 66, 54% rated their health "good," and 17% rated it as "poor." Street men rated their health no worse than did the nonstreet men.

## Improvements in Health Care

For the most part, nearly all the men over age 65 were able to obtain Medicare insurance. However, despite annual incomes that would make approximately one half the men eligible for Medicaid assistance (under $3900 per year), only 23% of the men had such coverage. As other studies have found (e.g., Fischer, *et al.*, 1986), coverage was especially inadequate for street people. Forty percent of the street men earned under $1000 per year, and 73% had income that made them Medicaid eligible, yet only 15% were covered.

Although most men did not have their full entitlements, 77% had been to see a doctor over the past year; 38% had gone at least twice and 23% had made ten or more visits to the doctor. The mean number of visits to the doctor was 4.3. This was roughly equivalent to the levels found in the New York City community sample, in which 76% reported having seen a doctor in the past year, and the mean number of visits was 4.7. Most visits were to family practitioners or internists, but one fourth had seen an eye or ear specialist. A relatively high percentage of men reported having received in the past 12 months a chest X ray (70%), electrocardiogram (65%), blood pressure testing (84%), eye testing (38%), and rectal exam (53%). Contrasted with 5% of the New York City community elderly men, 14% of the Bowery men felt it was inconvenient to get to a doctor's office, and, surprisingly, nearly half thought that a "doctor" would come to their home in case of an emergency, although for virtually all men this meant a city ambulance. Bowery men primarily used hospitals (73%) or neighborhood clinics (26%) for treatment. Fewer than 1 in 13 Bowery men generally seek medical care from a local doctor. This is in contrast to the community sample where three fifths saw a local doctor, one seventh used a clinic, and only one fifth used a hospital. Despite their access to care, 44% of the Bowery men tended to postpone seeking medical attention when they felt ill. This was cited by 28% of the community sample. One primary reason (23%) was because they believed doctors would not help them; 19% also cited cost as a factor. One man described the cost dilemma: "I get Medicare, the red, white, and blue card. Everytime I go to see the doctor or get medication I have to pay. I need glasses but I can't buy them right now. Glasses are very expensive and Medicare doesn't pay for them."

In contrast to medical care, there was less availability and increased resistance to psychiatric treatment. Although 23% of the sample manifested overt psychotic features or acknowledged having had a psychiatric hospitalization, only 3% reported being on a medication for "mental or emotional" problems during the previous month.

Street men reported only slightly less access to physicians than nonstreet men: 75% had seen a doctor in the past year, and 19% had ten or more visits; the mean number of visits to the doctor was 3.6. They made approximately equivalent use of local clinics and hospitals as did the nonstreet men. Perhaps not surprisingly, street men tended to be more apt to postpone seeking care than the nonstreet men (55% versus 39%). For street men, cost (24%) and feeling that they could not be helped (30%) were reasons for postponing treatment.

### Physical Illness: Antecedent or Consequence?

In trying to determine the role of physical illness in homelessness, we first examined whether there was an association between time on the Bowery and increased physical illness. The men had spent an average of nearly 17 years on the Bowery, with a range of several months to 63 years. There was a weak (nonsignificant) negative correlation between years on the Bowery and poor health, that is, men with the longest tenure on skid row had fewer physical symptoms than those with the shortest tenure.

It should be recalled that Bogue (1963) found that there was an inverse relationship between alcoholism and poor health among his broad age sample in Chicago, that is, those in poor health drank less. He concluded that there was a group of men who came to skid row because of their physical disabilities and that alcohol did not contribute to their condition. Somewhat contrary to Bogue's findings, our data indicated a weak, but significant, relationship between alcoholism and poor health (Appendix 1, Table 1, column 6). That alcohol does affect health is in keeping with the well-known physical sequelae of alcoholism. Indeed, many of the physical problems reported by these men are concomitants of alcoholism such as a history of seizure disorders (12%), tremulousness (37%), dizziness (45%), visual hallucinations (16%), and fractures in the last ten years (28%).

However, we did encounter several notable examples of men who had early histories of severe physical problems predating arrival on the Bowery or use of alcohol. The following excerpt from an interviewer's notes illustrates such a case:

John M. doesn't think that he will last much longer. He has disfiguring burns from being "blown-up" at the age of 17. He feels self-conscious about his appearance and says this has affected his life and his relationship with people. He has a long history of living on the Bowery but describes himself as a lone wolf, primarily due to his looks. He only drank infrequently. He was cooperative, and he wanted to discuss his problems. In his case the short-comings of the Bowery programs become obvious, since they focus primarily on alcoholics.

## Contributing Factors

Although earlier studies have been useful for chronicling the physical problems of the homeless population, the lack of adequate statistical analyses precluded further elaboration of the array of variables that might help explain the physical status of these men. Using the 14 variables described in the methods section that previous work had suggested were relevant to these men's physical health, we examined the zero-order correlations between these variables and physical health; we then performed a modified stepwise regression analysis with physical health as the dependent variable. Although the literature provided some guidance as to which variables might influence the health of these men, there were few data to support any particular ordering of the variables. We thus used a stepwise regression model. Correlation analysis indicated that six variables—depression, stressful life events, unfulfilled needs, being relatively younger, institutional/agency contacts, alcohol abuse—were significantly associated with more physical symptoms (see Appendix 1, Table 1, column 2). However, when the variables were entered in concert in the regression analysis five variables—depression, stressful life events, unfulfilled needs, institutional/agency contacts, and lower education—explained 39% of the variance in physical health (Table 7-2). The tetrad of poor physical health, depression, unfulfilled needs, and stressful life events often occurred concomitantly, as evidenced by their high intercorrelations, ranging between .26 and .57. Our interviewers encountered many men who were depressed, physically ill, and unable to meet their daily needs:

Mr. Charles looks about 10 years older than his 56 years. His only acquaintances seem to be the clerk and landlord of his hotel who help ensure that he has food brought to his room. He has had several serious medical problems and operations (heart attack, ulcers); he is still weak and reports dizziness and faintness. He also has prostate problems. He doesn't eat well, partly

Table 7-2. Stepwise Multiple Regression of Factors Affecting Physical Health Symptoms

|                               | $R^2$ Change | Beta In |
|-------------------------------|--------------|---------|
| Depression Scale              | .32          | .57     |
| Stressful Life Events         | .03          | .20     |
| Unfulfilled Needs             | .02          | .14     |
| Institutional/Agency Contacts | .01          | .12     |
| Education                     | .01          | −.10    |
| Total $R^2$                   | .39          |         |

because of his physical condition and partly because his income is only $128 per month. He is often, or always, depressed and lonely, and he feels life is not worth living. He said he doesn't drink much now because of his health and that there is very little that he enjoys doing.

Although certain social network dimensions such as the structural and interactional network variables did not appear to play a major role in determining physical health, a more in-depth examination of network proclivities suggests a subtle role for network supports. For example, when queried regarding a hypothetical instance of being ill and unable to get out of bed, only one in six men reported having no one to rely on. This was most noteworthy for the non-street men among whom fewer than one in ten had no one to count on. For these men, 38% could count on other hotel dwellers or outside nonkin, and another 34% depended on hotel staff. By contrast, 38% of the street men had no one to depend on in case of illness; the remainder would depend on nonkin (20%) and a combination of agencies and public hospitals (40%). Both groups of Bowery men were distinctively different from community elderly, 54% of whom would depend on relatives for assistance.

Our findings help to clarify several important issues concerning the physical health of older homeless men. With respect to the first question—how does the physical health of skid row men compare with those in the general population—we found that as in earlier studies, skid row men have significantly worse health than community men. Moreover, the principal differences occurred among those disease categories that had been identified previously as comprising "The Skid Row Syndrome," such as lung disease, hypertension, gastrointestinal disease, epilepsy, and physical trauma (Ashley *et al.*, 1976; Brickner *et al.*, 1972; Feldman, Su, Kaley, & Kissin, 1974; Scott *et al.*, 1966). Although nonstreet men currently have higher annual incomes, somewhat larger social networks, and find it easier to attend to their daily needs than do the street men (Cohen, Teresi, Holmes, & Roth, 1988), their similarities on virtually all health indices and the failure of street living to account for any variance in physical health in the regression analysis reinforce the notion of including both groups under the general rubric of "homelessness." For one thing there is flux between street and flophouses, with the median time spent at their present address of less than three years. Moreover, their similarities in socioeconomic background and education, alcohol consumption, and earlier lifestyles tend to obviate any health advantages afforded to those now living in flophouses or in local tenements.

Despite their relatively poor health, only 18% of the Bowery men perceived their health as poor, and this was comparable to percentages reported for the elderly in the general population. Interestingly, the Bowery men of today perceive themselves as considerably more healthy than did the Bowery men of 20 years ago: 20% of today's men rated their health as excellent and 18% rated it as poor, whereas in the 1960s 9% rated their health as excellent and 29% rated it as poor (Bahr & Caplow, 1973). The improvement in self-rated health over the past two decades may have reflected their enhanced access to health care. Contrary to reports pointing to inaccessibility to health care among the homeless (Filardo, 1985), our data do not generally support that notion. While it is true that 44% of the men postponed medical treatment, 28% of the elderly community sample men likewise postponed treatment. More importantly, because these men relied on hospitals and local clinics for treatment, their care was probably less consistent and perhaps qualitatively inferior to care available to middle-class patients. Nonetheless, the relatively high use of medical services by these older homeless men is in agreement with Scott and associates' (1966) earlier report of skid row men in England who were viewed as "high consumers of hospital outpatient services."

At this time, the obtaining of additional entitlements, especially Medicaid, should be a major point for intervention. Lacking Medicaid, many of these men fail to fill their prescriptions, are unable to obtain eyeglasses or hearing aids, cannot afford dental services, and are turned away from higher-quality medical services run by private clinics and voluntary hospitals. Part of the problem in obtaining Medicaid has been due to not having an address. Some street persons have used local missions as addresses, but for those who do not, the only alternative is to spend time in a public shelter. At the time of this study, clients could qualify for Medicaid benefits after spending 15 days in a shelter (Crystal, 1985). Benefits are granted for 90 days and clients can be recertified as long as they remain in the shelter system. However, most older street persons assiduously avoid shelters because of fears of muggings, abusive or insensitive staff, or concerns about being institutionalized. Certainly it is rare for them to spend 15 consecutive days in a shelter or to remain within the system for 90 days.

Our data provided some clues with respect to onset of physical disease and time on the Bowery. Given that the Bowery men's physical condition was significantly worse than their age peers in the community and that there was no significant association between length of time on the Bowery and worsening health, this would suggest that physical illness may often antedate a man's arrival on skid row. Since we found that heavy alcohol consumption began on the average nine years prior to arrival on the Bowery, it is likely that alcohol abuse may have contributed to their early physical debility, although we did encounter cases of physical disease in the absence of alcoholism.

However, there are alternate possibilities as to why there was no association between time on the Bowery and poor health. Part of the answer may be that in this sample of aging skid rowers we may be seeing the survivors. There was a significant correlation between age and *fewer* physical symptoms ($r = .18$), and age correlated highly with time on the Bowery ($r = .27$). Skid row is probably the only place in the country where reported health symptoms decrease with age. Because a certain level of health is a requisite for survival on the Bowery, sicker men may have been institutionalized or died. For instance, there was no difference on the Activity Limitation Scale between Bowery and community men. This scale assesses whether physical disabilities interfere with a person's ability to undertake social activities, do basic daily chores, and to maintain personal hygiene. Clearly, if a skid row man could not perform these activities of daily living, he could not survive very long in this setting.

Our findings also raise questions as to why there was not a greater association between alcoholism and poor health. One possible answer is that Bogue (1963) was in part correct—teetotalers and light drinkers do have a relatively high degree of physical problems. However, it cannot be discerned from our data since the now older, heavier drinkers in the sample have had time to develop levels of physical impairments equivalent to those of the light drinkers and abstainers. Alternatively, as noted above, we may be seeing the survivors. The sicker alcoholics may have died or may have been institutionalized. A third possibility is that the correlation with health was attenuated because some of the men who are currently light drinkers and teetotalers had been heavier drinkers in the past; thus, they are now suffering from the physical consequences of their imbibing.

Although it is unclear to what extent physical illness precedes arrival on skid row, it is evident that there are several factors that are associated with current health status. It was common to find men who suffered from the tetrad of poor physical health, depression, unfulfilled needs, and stressful life events. Although stressful life events have been generally shown to precede an exacerbation of physical symptoms (Rabkin & Struening, 1976), establishing causal direction for depression and needs is more difficult. Indeed, depression and inability to meet needs are often a consequence of poor health (LaRue, Dessonville, & Jarvik, 1985). Two other variables—institutional/agency contacts and poorer education—also contributed significantly to explaining physical symptomatology. Presumably, more institutional/agency contacts reflected a help-seeking response to impaired health. Since we have found no association between education and current income, its relationship to health may reflect a greater knowledge about caring for oneself or seeking help. Finally, two additional high-risk categories were identified, being relatively younger and abusing alcohol, which were significantly correlated with physical symptoms, although these did not contribute significant variance in the regression analysis.

Our findings point to several categories that are associated with higher rates of physical symptoms and thus warrant closer attention by clinicians and service providers: the depressed, those with unfulfilled needs, those undergoing more stressful life events, the poorly educated, the relatively young, and the alcohol abusers. These are not mutually exclusive categories, and several of them often are found together. The data also underscore the importance of providing additional support to skid row agencies, since men who are sick turn to agencies for assistance. By providing food, clothing, social services, toilet and shower facilities, housing, medical care, psychiatric and alcohol treatment, socialization, recreation, and outreach, the agencies provide the totality of services that can result in greater physical well-being.

In summing up this subsection, the case of Mr. James illustrates many of the issues that we have described above such as the receipt of support from fellow hotel lodgers and agencies, the use of public clinics as opposed to private doctors, and an early history of physical illness along with alcohol abuse that may have contributed to his subsequent arrival on the Bowery:

Mr. James is bald, mildly hunchbacked 77-year-old white man with thick glasses, a few missing teeth, an aluminum cane, and a constant whistling sound that emanates from his ill-fitted hearing aid.

Mr. James was born in Arkansas and spent the first 15 years of his working life as a merchant marine. He still retains much of the feistiness and rebelliousness of a seaman of the 1930s. In 1938, he was diagnosed as having tuberculosis while serving on an oil tanker in South America. Mr. James is particularly fond of castigating the medical profession, and he always points out how the ship's doctor thought he had bronchitis. He was sent home and spent the next 12 years in hospitals undergoing various treatments, including the collapsing of his left lung. With the advent of chemotherapy for tuberculosis he was eventually released from the hospital in 1950, but his residual shortness of breath left him too weak (and perhaps too old) for sea duty. The Department of Social Service sent him to a Bowery flop, and he began to drink heavily at this time. When sober, he was able to obtain various odd jobs such as distributing circulars and working in kitchens. By the 1960s he had developed severe dizziness, perhaps as a consequence of his alcohol consumption. The dizziness forced him to use a cane. He quit working and lived off his Social Security and welfare benefits. In the mid 1970s he developed cataracts in both eyes, and his hearing also began to deteriorate. Also at that time he experienced anginal pain, and in 1975 he suffered a heart attack. After the heart attack, he stopped drinking for good.

Despite his respiratory, cardiac, neurological, and sensory difficulties Mr. James manages to eke out a reasonably comfortable existence. The Bowery Residents' Committee sends him a hot lunch every weekday. He also likes to shop for food himself, which he cooks on his hotplate. To do this, he has someone from his hotel accompany him so that he doesn't fall.

This helper receives "a couple of bucks" for assisting him. He also uses runners in the hotel to pick up newspapers for him and buy him food during inclement weather. Although he has Medicare and sufficient savings that would enable him to pay for private office visits to a physician, Mr. James "prefers" to use the overcrowded public clinics at Bellevue or New York Eye and Ear. He invariably inveighs against the treatment he receives at these clinics, postpones his follow-up visits, and then reluctantly returns when he is feeling ill. This cycle regularly repeats itself. Although Mr. James has no real confidantes he is comforted by the fact that he has three "buddies" who he believes would "help him in a pinch."

## MENTAL HEALTH

Even prior to the era of deinstitutionalization, skid row men were commonly thought to have some personality defect or mental illness that could account for their condition. At times the personality theory was used to decriminalize homelessness even while it continued to "blame the victim" by attributing homelessness to a condition within the individual. For example, in 1903 the National Conference of Social Work looked back with pride at how "since 1873 [it had] committed itself to the belief that vagrancy is a curable disease" (Allen, 1903, p. 380).

Psychological and sociological studies of vagabonds in France, Italy, and Germany in the first decade of the 20th century concluded that the vagabond was primarily a "psychopathic" type (Anderson, 1923). Nels Anderson's classic work on the American hobo included "defects of personality" among the six principal causes of why men become tramps or hobos. However, Anderson cautioned that although there are large number of individuals with defects of personalities among American hobos and tramps, there are also large numbers of normal individuals: "The American tradition of pioneering, wanderlust, seasonal employment, attract into the group of wanderers and migratory workers a great many energetic and venturesome normal boys and young men" (p. 70). Anderson points out that Solenberger's (1911) examination of 1,000 homeless men found only 89 to be feeble-minded, epileptic, or insane. Sutherland and Locke's (1936) study of 20,000 men living in the public shelters of Chicago suggested that temperamental factors played an etiologic role in some of these men. For instance, some men would frequently lose jobs because they "got mad and quit" (p. 45), or breaks with family occurred because they "got mad and left home" (p. 45). On the other hand, the rates of severe psychiatric disorders were not high: 5% had psychosis, 10% were considered "pre-psychotic," 3% were "psychopathic," and 82% had no serious problems.

The post-World War II literature is much more suggestive that the skid row man is psychologically aberrant. Robert Straus (1946) viewed homelessness as an individual development problem caused by being "undersocialized," or in other words, these men are unable to adjust to "normal social ways." Donald Bogue's study of Chicago's skid row men in the 1950s concluded that there is "strong evidence that individual personality characteristics are highly correlated with the presence of the homeless men on Skid Row" (p. 390). Although only 4% of the men were rated "psychotic" and 16% were rated "neurotic," an additional 36% were classified as "aberrant." The latter was a new psychiatric category that Bogue had created to describe "odd" personality traits. Bogue further proposed that economic and related forces must interact with these personality factors to create this fate for homeless men.

In the mid 1950s psychoanalysts were also engaged in theorizing about the etiology of homelessness. Stanley Rosenman (1955), based on an analysis of one patient, concluded that these men have "negative ego images," viewing themselves as extremely unworthy, degraded, and repellant. Alcohol was described as a way to increase a man's virility. Likewise, Boris Levinson's (1958) study of 40 shelter men concluded that the "homeless man has always had personality traits differing from known normal or psychiatric groups." He maintained that living on the Bowery exacerbated but did not create these traits. Levinson described these men as having "no ego strengths," having difficulty empathizing with others, and having a fear of accepting or sharing affection.

Clearly, during the 1950s, the literature tended to attribute homelessness primarily to individual personality defects. During this era of prosperity, the underlying theme was, "How could society be held responsible for these men's states?" However, by the 1960s, the nation had discovered the "Other America," a war on poverty had begun, and there seemed to be an increased recognition of the role that societal factors play in the creation of homelessness. Typical works of the period that looked at societal and contextual relationships were Samuel Wallace's *Skid Row as a Way of Life*, Jacqueline

Wiseman's *Stations of the Lost*, and James Spradley's *You Owe Yourself a Drunk*. Below, we shall discuss their perspectives on homelessness in greater detail.

The literature of the 1970s and 1980s has been more ambiguous in the treatment of psychopathology among the homeless. Because of the deinstitutionalization movement in psychiatry there has unquestionably been an increased number of severely ill persons among the ranks of the homeless. Deinstitutionalization must be viewed as a process that involves not only discharging long-term mental patients but also shortening the stay of new cases or not admitting them at all. However, depending on the investigator's perspective or the public agency for whom he or she is working, mental illness is either viewed as one cause among several factors leading to homelessness or as the overriding causal agent. The latter perspective contends that the majority of the homeless are mentally ill and that homelessness is a result of a failure of the state's office of mental health to properly deal with the discharge and treatment of patients. An alternative perspective, usually promulgated by state agencies, is that the primary cause of homelessness is the lack of housing stock and economic factors, and that there would be fewer mentally ill homeless if these problems were addressed (Herman, 1980). As evidence, they point to the substantial lag time between the periods of rapid deinstitutionalization (1960s) and the rise in homeless mentally ill in the late 1970s and early 1980s (Fischer & Breakey, 1986; Snow et al., 1986). Even still, they maintain that the mentally ill constitute a minority of the homeless population. As we discussed previously, although some figures range as high as 80%, national surveys have placed the percentage of mentally ill among the homeless at 22% (U.S. Department of Housing & Urban Development, 1984). In New York City, the conservative estimate is that between one third and two fifths of the homeless population have been hospitalized for psychiatric illness and/or manifest overt severe psychopathology (Hopper et al., 1982).

The majority of the mentally ill homeless are under the age of 34 (Bassuk, Rubin, & Lauriat, 1984). Many are victims of the deinstitutionalization policies of the past two decades that make it more difficult to be admitted or to stay in the hospital. Despite its negative elements, long-term institutionalization had provided individuals with the security of shelter, food, medical treatment, psychiatric care, activities, and a role (albeit a stigmatized one). Now, without

the support of the hospital, individuals must have the wherewithal
to coordinate the various agencies needed for money and shelter
(welfare, SSI, SSA), food (foodstamps), medical treatment (Medicaid,
Medicare, appropriate clinics), psychiatric treatment (appropriate
outpatient clinics, obtaining medication, social rehabilitation), and
work (vocational training, psychiatric rehabilitation counseling). Because of strict guidelines regarding number and length of hospitalization, many persons are unable to qualify for professional case
managers who will help coordinate the procurement of these entitlements. The task of surviving has become especially difficult for
individuals in large urban areas such as New York City where traditional low-cost housing stock (e.g., SRO hotels, boarding houses) has
been decimated by urban renewal and gentrification. The recessions
of the 1970s and 1980s with the persistence of high unemployment
rates has made it more difficult for marginal workers, such as those
with psychiatric problems, to find employment. Therefore, primarily
as a consequence of deinstitutionalization policies, decreased housing stock, and a sagging economy, we have been seeing an increasing
number of homeless mentally ill persons.

Prior to the 1970s when psychopathology was implicated as an
etiologic factor in creating homelessness, it was often used to excuse
the social system and place the primary blame for homelessness on
the individual. Nowadays the battleground has altered: The question
becomes one of determining how many of the homeless are mentally
ill so that blame can be affixed to the appropriate point in the system.
Although today few people will blame the homeless mentally ill for
their plight, it becomes difficult to blame one aspect of the system
because each governmental sector points the finger at the other, and
they are all in part responsible for the problem.

A problem with attributing homelessness to mental illness is
that it is sometimes difficult to discern whether certain features of
the illness may in fact be derived from the stress of living on the
streets. Ernest Gruenberg (1967) has described a "social breakdown
syndrome" that occurs when individuals encounter overwhelming
stress. The syndrome, which cuts across psychiatric diagnosis, may
be characterized by aggressive behavior or apathy and withdrawal.
Thus, the features of the social breakdown syndrome can develop
autonomously or can become enmeshed in and exacerbate a previously existing condition. Ellen Baxter and Kim Hopper (1982) likewise expressed concern about the validity of diagnoses made on

individuals whose basic subsistence needs are unmet. They cautioned that "were the same individuals to receive several nights of sleep, an adequate diet, and warm social contact, some of their symptoms might subside" (p. 402).

The recent surge of interest in the homeless population has tended to focus attention on the younger segment, and particularly on the severely mentally ill such as psychotics and schizophrenics (Holden, 1986). For example, Bachrach (1984a) points to evidence that the average age of the homeless is "dropping precipitously" and attributes the rise to the postwar baby boom and development of a young chronic mentally ill population. Surveys of shelter populations by Arce and co-workers (1983) in Philadelphia and Bassuk et al. (1984) in Boston found approximately 40% suffering from psychotic illness, most being schizophrenic, and more than half being under the age of 40. Indeed, the stereotypical image of the homeless was depicted in the APA Task Force Report on the Homeless Mentally Ill (Lamb, 1984): "Ragged, ill, and hallucinating human beings, wandering through our city streets, huddled in alleyways, or sleeping over vents" (p. 2).

The emphasis on the young, schizophrenic homeless population has had two adverse effects: (1) It has drawn attention away from the plight of other subgroups of the homeless, particularly the older homeless; and, (2) it has tended to minimize the other mental health problems encountered by the homeless. Apropos, Fischer and Breakey (1986) have observed that, "The literature is pointing to the importance of defining subgroups of the homeless in terms of their psychosocial characteristics" (p. 31). Such diversity must be kept in mind by researchers, service providers, and urban planners since "it is easy to make unwarranted assumptions about the homeless mentally ill" (Bachrach, 1984c, p. 913).

One of the anomalies of recent surveys of mental illness among the homeless has been the surprisingly low level of depression and organic mental disease. Rates of affective disorder (depression and mania) ranged from 2% to 18% (Arce & Vergare, 1984; Fischer & Breakey, 1986). Similarly, rates or organic mental disease ranged from 3% to 7%, except for one study by Goldfarb (1970) done at an alcoholic treatment center where the rate of organicity was reported as 36%. This is surprisingly low given the 20% to 45% rates of alcoholism reported among shelter users in different regions of the country (Mulkern & Spence, 1984). Finally, except for the two psychoanalytic studies undertaken during the 1950s (described above), there have been no reports on the psychological defense mechanisms that homeless persons must employ to survive in such a tenuous environment.

The mentally ill homeless have been described as being "disconnected from social networks" (Bassuk *et al.*, 1984). Previous research, however, has been impressionistic or has used rudimentary measures of social interaction such as "friends," "confidants," "relatives," "marital status" (Bassuk *et al.*, 1984; Fischer, *et al.*, 1986). As we described previously, over the past decade social network analysis has been refined in its instrumentation and in the various network dimensions that can be assessed. These include structural dimensions such as size, density, and clustering along with interactional dimensions such as directionality, content of exchanges, and levels of intimacy, empathy, and friendship. Moreover, earlier research may have been vulnerable to what Bachrach (1984c) describes as asking "the right questions in culturally biased and basically inappropriate ways" (p. 913). For instance, we have found that skid row men divided their social contacts into "acquaintances," "associates," and "friends." Thus, merely inquiring about "friends" would have neglected important network ties.

Although there have been some reports regarding the physical health and socioeconomic needs of the overall homeless population, there has been no comparison of mentally ill and nonmentally ill homeless, and in turn, a comparison of both with a general community sample. Because the homeless mentally ill population consists of an overlap between two source populations, homeless individuals and the chronic mentally ill (Bachrach, 1984b), there is reason to assume that there will be diversity as well as similarity on various health and social measures; yet, we cannot predict *a priori* where they will be. Nonetheless, such data are needed to plan specific kinds of services and specific styles of service that will be useful and attractive to individuals in the various subgroups of the homeless.

Because skid row remains one of the primary areas of concentration of older homeless persons, it can serve as an excellent site to study the various aspects of mental health among aging homeless individuals. In this section we shall look at three major psychiatric symptom complexes—psychosis, organic brain disease, depression—and the relationship of these symptoms to health, socialization, and adaptation. Then we shall delineate the common psychological mechanisms and personality styles that these men employ in order to cope with their internal and external worlds.


Psychosis

For purposes of analysis we created a group which we call the Psychosis/Psychiatric Hospitalization (PPH) group. It is comprised of those individuals who scored 3 or more on the Psychotic Scale or had at least one previous psychiatric hospitalization (see Appendix 1). The Psychotic Scale included 8 items such as hallucinations, delusions, and bizarre appearance. The PPH sample consisted of 43 nonstreet men (22% of the nonstreet sample) and 21 street men (24% of the street sample). Thus there were no significant proportional differences between street and nonstreet samples. Of the overall sample, 14% (10% of street men; 16% of nonstreet men) acknowledged having prior psychiatric hospitalizations. Nine percent of the men scored 3 or more on the Psychotic Scale. Proportionately more street men manifested severe psychotic symptoms than did the nonstreet men (15% versus 7%). This finding is consistent with local service workers' observations that psychotic behavior is more common on the streets and perhaps less tolerated in the flophouses.

Bowery men had levels of psychiatric hospitalization and/or severe psychoticism that were about three fourths the level of the younger homeless samples (using the figure of 33% in younger samples). Though severe psychosis was found in only 9% of the sample, milder levels of symptoms (2 or more symptoms on the Psychotic Scale) were present in a total of 25% of the men. Hence, although psychiatric problems may not be quite as prevalent among the older men as among the younger groups, they are not insubstantial.

The mean age of the PPH men was 62 years, and they had been living on the Bowery an average of 15 years. Their income was equivalent to that of the non-PPH Bowery men. That is, most lived on income of slightly over $3900 per year, which was well below the poverty level of $5061. It is noteworthy that 16% of the PPH men (40% of the street PPH men) lived on incomes of under $1000. A description of various demographic, health, and social characteristics of the PPH Group is presented in Table 7-3.

Table 7-3. Selected Demographic, Health, and Social Variables of
64 Psychotic/Previous Psychiatric Hospitalization (PPH) Men

| | |
|---|---|
| Mean age (years) | 62 |
| Mean education (years) | 10 |
| Percent living on streets | 33 |
| Mean years on Bowery | 15 |
| Mean years in current hotel | 5.1 |
| Mean income[a] | 4.1 |
| Total network linkages | 8.2 |
| Total informal linkages | 6.0 |
| Formal linkages | 2.2 |
| Network density[b] | 42 |
| Directionality[c] | 2.1 |
| Mean exchange per linkage | 2.7 |
| Proportion of network that are sustenance linkages[d] | 0.6 |
| Proportion of network members rated as "intimates" | 0.5 |
| *Percent scoring above median of N.Y.C. elderly men:* | |
| Somatic Symptoms Scale | 90 |
| Respiratory Scale | 86 |
| Ambulation Scale | 75 |

[a]Income: 3 = $1300–2599; 4 = $2600–3899; 5 = $3900–5199.

[b]Network density: ratio of actual to potential linkage among members of the respondent's network.

[c]Directionality: direction in which aid in a dyadic relationship flows. (1 = helping; 2 = reciprocal; 3 = dependent).

[d]Sustenance linkage: linkages providing basic support items to respondent (e.g. money, food, medical aid).

As can be seen in Appendix 1, Table 1 (column 3), Table 7-4, and Table 7-5, there were no significant correlations or mean differences on various measures in physical health, demographics, alcoholism, need fulfillment, or sociability that distinguished the PPH and non-PPH men. The PPH group actually fared slightly better than the non-PPH group with its ability to meet daily needs. Perhaps their psychiatric history may have afforded them the opportunity to obtain financial and medical entitlements through interaction with institutional social workers and welfare programs. For both PPH and non-PPH groups, street men were significantly less able to fulfill their needs than the nonstreet men. Participation in psychiatric treatment was severely limited. As we had noted earlier, although 23% of the men evidenced psychosis or had previous psychiatric hospitalization, only 3% reported taking medication for "mental or emotional problems."

Table 7-4. Comparison of Mentally Ill Homeless, Nonmentally Ill Homeless, and Community Men on Selective Demographic Variables and Health Scales of the Comprehensive Assessment and Referral Evaluation

| | PPH Group[a] | Non-PPH Group[b] | Community Elderly[c] | t values PPH vs. Non-PPH[d] | t values PPH vs. Community[e] |
|---|---|---|---|---|---|
| Education[g] | 6.80 | 6.70 | 7.47 | 0.26 | 1.77 |
| Income[h] | 4.13 | 3.96 | 10.10 | 0.61 | 20.33** |
| Overall Needs | 5.06 | 5.59 | —[i] | 1.32 | — |
| Service Needs | 4.67 | 4.79 | 1.16 | 0.37 | 9.61** |
| Financial Needs | 3.45 | 3.92 | 0.82 | 1.40 | 6.86** |
| Years in SRO Hotels | 15.37 | 15.33 | —[i] | 0.02 | — |
| Years at Current Address | 5.05 | 4.05 | 17.00 | 0.99 | 8.70** |
| Somatic Symptoms | 7.53 | 6.50 | 2.56 | 1.45 | 6.05** |
| Activity Limitation | 2.78 | 3.05 | 2.62 | 0.57 | 0.23 |
| Ambulatory Difficulties | 2.87 | 2.65 | 1.75 | 0.49 | 2.00* |
| Hearing Problems | 0.97 | 0.87 | 0.34 | 0.39 | 2.39* |
| Visual Problems | 1.12 | 0.66 | 0.59 | 1.62 | 1.35 |
| Heart Disorder | 2.36 | 1.69 | 1.64 | 2.17* | 1.58 |
| Hypertension | 1.27 | 1.08 | 0.72 | 1.03 | 2.38* |
| Edema | 1.44 | 1.62 | 0.54 | 0.59 | 2.91** |
| Respiratory Disorders | 2.27 | 2.15 | 0.97 | 0.52 | 4.86** |
| Arthritis | 3.00 | 2.58 | 2.39 | 1.29 | 1.42 |
| Depression | 7.81 | 7.33 | 3.48 | 0.85 | 6.46** |
| Organic Mental Symptoms | 1.53 | 1.46 | 0.67 | 0.35 | 4.20** |
| Subjective Memory Problems | 2.80 | 2.12 | 0.85 | 2.04* | 5.10** |
| Hospitalized in past year for any condition | 0.38 | 0.31 | 0.12 | 1.03 | 2.85** |

[a]PPH Group: Scoring 3 or more on psychotic scale or previous psychiatric hospitalization. $N = 64$. Mean age = 62 years.
[b]Non-PPH Group: Scoring 2 or less on psychotic scale and no previous psychiatric hospitalization. $N = 217$. Mean age = 61 years.
[c]$N = 61$. Age = 65–69 years.
[d]$df = 279$. [e]$df = 123$.
[g]Education: 6 = 9 years; 7 = 10 years; 8 = 11 years.
[h]Income: 3 = \$1300–2599; 4 = \$2600–3899; 5 = \$3900–5199; 10 = \$10,500–15,499
[i]Item not available.
*$p < .05$ (two-tailed); **$p < .01$ (two-tailed).

159

Table 7-5. Comparison of Mentally Ill Homeless, Nonmentally Ill Homeless, and Community Men on Selective Social Network Variables

| | PPH Group[a] | Non-PPH Group[b] | Community Elderly[c] | t values PPH vs. Non-PPH[d] | t values PPH vs. Community[e] |
|---|---|---|---|---|---|
| Mean Number of Transactions | 2.66 | 2.95 | 2.98 | 1.37 | .80 |
| Multiplex | 0.80 | 0.79 | 1.00 | 0.28 | 2.73** |
| Mean Sustenance Links | 0.59 | 0.63 | 0.06 | 0.89 | 5.96** |
| Mean Frequency | 3.39 | 3.62 | 2.38 | 0.85 | 1.99 |
| Mean Directionality | 2.14 | 2.10 | 2.17 | 0.41 | 0.14 |
| Mean Very Important Links | 0.39 | 0.36 | 0.40 | 0.65 | 0.19 |
| Mean Intimates | 0.47 | 0.40 | 0.76 | 1.43 | 2.51* |
| Total Linkages | 8.19 | 8.55 | 11.08 | 0.41 | 1.61 |
| Informal Linkages | 5.98 | 6.57 | 10.83 | 0.81 | 3.30** |
| Formal Linkages | 2.19 | 1.98 | 0.25 | 0.76 | 3.22** |
| Degree | 2.07 | 2.34 | 1.68 | 0.75 | 0.60 |
| Density | 0.42 | 0.42 | 0.23 | 0.00 | 1.76 |
| Clusters | 1.47 | 1.39 | 2.75 | 0.60 | 3.74** |
| Large Clusters | 0.50 | 0.66 | 0.42 | 1.35 | 0.34 |
| Length of Linkage | 7.26 | 7.00 | 29.09 | 0.30 | 8.42** |
| Proportion of Same Sex | 0.77 | 0.77 | 0.46 | 0.00 | 4.06** |
| Proportion of Same Age | 0.71 | 0.67 | 0.63 | 0.92 | 0.87 |

[a]PPH Group: Scoring 3 or more on psychotic scale or previous psychiatric hospitalization. N = 64.
[b]Non-PPH Group: Scoring 2 or less on psychotic scale and no previous psychiatric hospitalization. N = 217.
[c]N = 12. [d]df = 279. [e]df = 74.
* p < .05 (two-tailed); **p < .01 (two-tailed).

It is also important to point out that all of the PPH group had at least one linkage (formal or informal). Only one man in the PPH group had no informal linkages, and 13 (20%) had no formal linkages (i.e., ties to hotel and agency staff). Thus, the stereotypical view of an isolated, hallucinating homeless figure was not obtained for this subgroup of the homeless population. Nonetheless, there was a small subsample of PPH men who were near isolates: 5% had one linkage, and another 8% had only two linkages. Overall, the PPH men had 8.2 linkages versus 8.6 linkages among the non-PPH men. The street men in both groups had approximately one fourth fewer contacts than did the nonstreet men.

The social networks of the PPH men provided considerable material support—three fifths of all their linkages involved sustenance aid (money, food, medical assistance)—and they saw their contacts an average of three to four times per week. Ninety-four percent of the men said they had at least one person in their network that they could count on for help, and when presented with hypothetical problems, 94%, 89%, 86%, 78% of the men would rely on others for help with obtaining information, food, illness, or cash, respectively. Also noteworthy was that more than half the PPH group expressed a desire for more contact with others.

Both PPH and non-PPH men made active use of Bowery institutions: food stores, restaurants, clothing stores, parks, agencies, and the like. However, the PPH men more often than not avoided certain "negative" institutions such as taverns and betting parlors and conversely more often belonged to local service organizations such as the Bowery Residents' Committee, AA, Holy Name Mission. Over one fourth of the PPH men's network was comprised of such formal linkages to agency, institutional or hotel staff. Indeed, there was a subgroup of relatively isolated PPH men with a moderate degree of symptoms who managed to survive because of agency support. The following excerpts from an interviewer's notes are illustrative:

Mr. Schwartz is a 57-year-old man who looks young for his chronological age. He has spent many years in psychiatric institutions. He now lives in the Pacific Hotel and is on medication. He spends a great deal of time at the Bowery Residents' Committee in the Community Support Systems Program. He is very intelligent and funny although he gets agitated very easily. His social network seems very limited. He seems to be closest with agency staff members. He didn't mention having any other close friends.

Mr. Thomas has an obvious nervous-emotional problem, he seemed very calm and mellow but in response to certain questions (memory and especially the social network section) he became very angry, at one point jumping up and saying he's going home to cut his throat. He has been hospitalized for a "nervous breakdown," as well as numerous times for physical problems. He had been badly burned about ten years ago from falling asleep with a cigarette and has third-degree burns over his lower back and buttocks. He was raised by a foster family, and they are now all dead. He depends on the Holy Name Mission, which handles his checks, finances, and other social service problems.

PPH men engaged in considerable group-oriented behavior (e.g., street groups, meal and lounge programs, hotel lobby socializing) which is common to the Bowery milieu. Such groups are major sources of material and emotional support for these men. Here again, we found a subgroup of the PPH men, despite often being overtly psychotic, who maintained the social skills and relational quality to become enmeshed in a large street based alcohol bottle gang/support group or hotel cluster. An interviewer's notes on Mr. O'Connell and Mr. Rizzuto exemplify such men:

Mr. O'Connell is 64 years old and has been living mostly on the street. He's part of a group of men that usually live on the street and sometimes in hotels. They panhandle together, feed each other, and care for each other. He spoke quietly and often mumbled. Periodically he's let out an answer that was strange and difficult to understand. There wasn't too much eye contact although there was some. He seems to be clean for a street person.

Mr. Rizzuto has been in and out of mental institutions most of his life. He actively hallucinates. For example, he says he'd be talking to somebody (somebody that he usually thinks is there at the start of the conversation), then he'll turn around and realize that he is all alone. He has a large hotel network with whom he socializes, borrows and lends money, and eats and drinks. We joked around a lot and had fun during the interview. He's never had more than a part-time job. He didn't want to come right out and say he hears voices, he got a little nervous at first when he was describing the voices. He'd say he hears them, then deny it. At times he didn't seem all that crazy to me.

Finally, the networks of the PPH men did not lack intimacy and empathy: 78% of the PPH men had at least one intimate, 86% had at least one good or best friend, and 92% had at least one person who they felt understood them and their problems. Nevertheless, there was evidence that much of the "intimacy" was superficial; nearly half the men conceded that they had no one to talk to about their problems, and two thirds said they usually kept problems to themselves.

In contrast to the minimal differences that existed between the PPH and non-PPH men there were considerable differences between the PPH group and the New York City elderly community men on various health and social measures. For example, the PPH men scored higher than the community men on all 13 physical health/ activities scales of the CARE instrument. These differences were statistically significant on six scales (Somatic Symptoms, Ambulatory Difficulties, Hearing Problems, Hypertension, Edema, Respiratory Disorders). As might be expected, the PPH men had financial and service needs that were four times those of the community men. In looking at social network measures (Table 7-5), community men had networks that were approximately one third larger; but network members were seen about one third less frequently than persons in the PPH men's networks. The PPH men had more interconnections per network member (as measured by density and degree) than the community men, reflecting the large group activities of skid row life. Community men had virtually no formal linkages, and only 1 in 20 of their linkages involved sustenance items. On the other hand, their networks contained 50% more intimate relationships. Thus, in general, the networks of the PPH men were oriented toward material support whereas those of the community men were focused on affective support.

Organic Mental Disease

Although there was a statistically significant difference between the Bowery and community men on the Organic Mental Syndrome Scale, neither group evidenced substantial organicity. The community men had a mean score of 0.7 incorrect of ten items, and the Bowery men had a mean of 1.5 incorrect items out of ten items. Since the scale approximated the Mental Status Questionnaire of Kahn and associates (1960), we could approximate levels of dementia. This test primarily assesses orientation and memory. Nine percent of the men had three or more errors, which would place them in a mild to moderate category; 5% of the men fell into a moderate to severe category of six or more errors. There were no differences between street and nonstreet men on this test (see Table 5-2). Thus, despite histories of heavy alcoholism and relatively poor health the men did not exhibit substantial organic disease. However, the more severely organic individuals would most likely have been unable to survive on the Bowery and may have been institutionalized. Perhaps this is why there was only a very weak correlation between age and dementia or between alcoholism and dementia (Appendix 1, Table 1, column 4). The following excerpt from the interviewer's notes illustrates the tenuousness of survival for an aging organicly disabled man:

Ron G. didn't know how old he was, he first said 47, then 57, then he said he was born in 1920. He had no idea of the time or date. He has been living in doorways for a long time and can't get any aid for some reason. He gets picked up and taken to detox regularly. He wasn't drunk at the time of this interview and his main concern was in getting a drink; in fact, that's all he lives for. He has no acquaintances, companions, or even drinking buddies. He doesn't want to impose himself and when he has it [alcohol], he doesn't want to share it. He said he was in "excellent" physical shape and had no problem with his memory ("he doesn't have anything to remember"), though this was not the case either for his physical or mental state. He also said he hasn't cried in the past month, but he cried several times during the interview especially when talking about his family (parents and children).

Although not evidencing substantial dementia, the men reported significantly more subjective memory problems than did the community sample, and these subjective complaints might be suggestive of more subtle underlying problems. For example, overall, 43% of the men claimed to have difficulty with their memory, and 64% said it had become more difficult to remember things. Three fifths of the men reported that they would forget where they put things, two fifths would forget what they had just read or heard, and one fifth stated that they would forget the name of close friends or relatives. Overall, one fourth of the men felt "embarrassed, bothered, or inconvenienced by memory problems."

A second small category of men with organic mental syndrome were those with mental retardation. These men have few social contacts and are able to survive on the Bowery primarily with the help of social agencies. One interviewer describes such a man:

Mr. Blass was nice, quiet, cooperative, and a little slow. His parents died when he was very young. He never met his father. He had two sisters that both died in childbirth. He has a half brother that he hasn't seen in over 15 years. He lived in orphanages and was put in institutions and a "training school." He completed one year of school. He has problems with his eyes, he hasn't been able to see too well for the past month. He's too lazy and poor to buy glasses but a social worker is now assisting him. Because he doesn't drink he has few social contacts. He's dull-witted and likes to be alone.

As can be seen from Appendix 1, Table 1, column 4, there were few significant correlations between organicity and any of the other variables. The relatively weak, but significant correlation with the structural network variables indicates that the more organic men have smaller and less interconnected networks, something that is reflected in our two case illustrations. Similarly, there was an increased level of depression with increased organicity, a finding that parallels reports in the general population (Reifler, 1986).

Depression

If, as President Reagan suggested in January, 1984, men opted to become homeless "by choice," then their level of depression certainly would suggest that they are anything but happy with their choice. Levels of depression were approximately twice that of the general New York City community elderly sample. More interesting was the level of "pervasive depression." Gurland and his associates (1983) defined "pervasive depression" as cases of a "clinical level of severity, i.e., assumed to warrant the attention of a health care professional skilled in the treatment of psychiatric disturbance" (p. 49). Gurland found that between 55% and 59% of persons with scores of 6 or more on the depression scale showed pervasive depression on clinical interviews. The depression scale consisted of 23 items such as crying, persistent sadness, and suicidal thoughts. Extrapolating from Gurland's findings we estimated that approximately one third to two fifths of our Bowery sample would be "pervasively depressed." This was based on the fact that 65% had scores of 6 or more on the depression scale. This figure is 2.5 times the level found among the New York City elderly sample.

The gravity of the depression can be appreciated by the men's responses to various questions: In the past month 41% had felt that life was not worth living, 39% were pessimistic about the future, and 38% had cried over the past month. Fully one fourth of the men reported that in the last month they had wished they were dead. Overall, two fifths of the Bowery men rated themselves "not very happy" or "not happy at all."

Most disturbing was the level of depression among the street men who manifested significantly more depression than did the nonstreet men. Seventy-eight percent scored 6 or more on the depression scale indicating that approximately two fifths of them would be considered "pervasively depressed." Nearly one third of these men had wished they were dead in the past month; 41% reported crying, and 43% were pessimistic about the future.

By contrast to the Bowery men, 11% of the overall New York City sample had felt that life was not worth living, only 3% were pessimistic about the future, 8% had wished they were dead, and 22% had cried in the past month. Only 17% had rated themselves "not very happy" or "not happy at all."

Correlation analysis yielded nine variables that were associated significantly with depression (Appendix 1, Table 1, column 5). The most potent variable was physical health, which parallels the well-established relationship found in other elderly populations (LaRue *et al.*, 1985). Having undergone stressful life events and being unable to fulfill daily needs were also highly correlated with depression. As noted previously, the tetrad of depression, poor physical health, inability to fulfill needs, and stress often occurred concomitantly as evidenced by their high intercorrelations (ranging between .26 and .57). Alcoholism was likewise associated with depression, which may reflect the chemical effects of ethanol, pre-existing depressive disorders, or the weak but significant correlations between alcoholism and other factors that predispose toward depression such as poor health, unfulfilled needs, and stress. Being older was associated with significantly lower rates of depression. This may be indicative of a resignation to their life status that many of the oldest men exhibited; they also were significantly better able to meet their daily needs. Two social network measures—the Network Structural Factor, which comprises variables pertaining to size and clustering of networks, and the Network Proclivity Scale, which assesses propensity to recruit the assistance of others—were associated with lower levels of depression. Whether having more social contacts, being in group formations, and expressing a desire to use others for support serves to prevent depression or whether depressed persons have withdrawn from their social world could not be resolved from our cross-sectional data. As noted above, depression also correlated significantly with organic mental symptoms. Last, as might be expected, those men living on the street were the most depressed. This depression was no doubt a reaction to a host of difficulties that street men encounter: more problems meeting daily needs, more stressful events, weakness in their network structure, inability to rely on others, and increased alcohol abuse. A modified stepwise regression analysis in which all 14 variables were entered in concert indicated that five of the aforementioned variables—physical health, age, network structural factor needs, organic mental symptoms, stress—contributed significantly to explaining the variance in depression. Together they accounted for 43% of the explained variance.

The profound effect that physical illness can have on the mental state of homeless men is captured in Miles's recollection of the anguish and despair that he had felt in 1972 after he had a heart attack and was out of work: "I was momentarily insane and I wanted to die. My heart was bad at that time and the doctors had me on Valium, Elavil, Seconal, plus my heart medicine." Miles slit his wrist and was discovered by a friend. He was rushed to St. Vincent's Hospital where he was treated. He vividly recalls the inspirational words of the nurse on duty: "You are a fool to cut yourself up like that. No matter how many times you may try to end your life you are not going to die unless He's ready to take you away because you were put here for a reason." Ultimately Miles began to resolve some of his hopelessness.

## Psychological Defense Mechanisms

As is found in all populations, Bowery men employ various psychological devices to ward-off the discomforts and stressors of daily life. Because discomforts and stressors are especially pronounced for Bowery men it becomes more difficult to deflect them, and consequently Bowery men are considerably more depressed than their age peers in the general population. As we noted earlier, levels of alcohol consumption were quite high, and alcohol was one of the most popular mechanisms that Bowery men use to deal with life stressors. The use of alcohol by skid row men will be described in the next chapter. Here, we will concentrate on a particularly neglected area of research: the psychological defense mechanisms used by these aging homeless men.

*Denial and Wish Fantasies.* Despite having lived on the Bowery for an average of 16 years, a substantial proportion of these aging men harbor visions of leaving the Bowery, perhaps finding some part-time work, and even reuniting with their families or establishing new liaisons. In a sense, there is a denial of their current condition (physical, mental, and socioeconomic), and they cling to the fantasy that with a little self-discipline they will be able to leave the Bowery. For instance, Ed dreams:

'Cause right now with my checks so small and living in a flophouse, I can't do much for myself. So that's why I'm hopin' that somethin' will happen in the future; I'm really prayin' to God for assistance so that Doris and I could get together. 'Cause I know she could help me and I could be a protector for her. We could help each other so that eventually I could kiss the Bowery goodbye for good.

Although six months later Ed still was in contact with Doris ("I still meet her casually off and on"), his anxiety about leaving the Bowery and its way of life unconsciously prevented Ed from forming the kind of strong bonds with this woman that would lead him off the Bowery. As he rationalized it, "We have yet to go to bed together but I'm not looking forward to that because they usually tell you in AA it's a bad policy, especially when you're coming back, to get yourself involved with the opposite sex."

Homeless men have long carried fantasies of escape. However, as Crooks told George in Steinbeck's *Of Mice and Men*:

You're nuts . . . I seen hundreds of men come by on the road an' on the ranches, with their bindles on their back an' that same damn thing in their heads. Hundreds of them. They come, an' they quit an go on; an' every damn one of 'em's got a little piece of land in his head. An' never a God damn one of 'em ever gets it. Just like heaven. Ever'body wants a little piece of lan'. I read plenty of books out here. Nobody never get to heaven, and nobody gets no land. It's just in their head. They're all the time talkin' about it, but it's jus' in their head. (p. 74)

*Rationalization or Resignation.* We have already alluded to another common defense mechanism, that of rationalization or resignation. These men have come to accept their circumstances and commonly remark how things could be worse elsewhere. Sutherland and Locke (1936) found a group of older men among their shelter population in the 1930s who developed a similar posture. The men seemed to lose any desire to leave the shelter, accepting a kind of dependent existence. For many men a position of resignation is not unrealistic, since the probability of leaving the Bowery is remote. One of our respondents, Mr. Bell, is a man who not only has learned to accept his Bowery existence but also tries to enjoy it. Our interviewer observed:

Mr. Bell is a well-dressed, well-mannered gentleman who wore a tie and suit (both fairly clean), and yellow patent leather shoes. He doesn't worry about anything anymore, leaving it all "in the hands of the Lord." He has a girlfriend in her 20s and most of his friends seem to be under 30 years old. In the '60s he spent nearly a year in the hospital with a bad heart. Symptoms of the bad heart haven't returned and he stopped drinking in the 1970s. He says he's happier now than ever, except that he misses his wife.

*Undoing or Atonement.* We have encountered a number of men who view life on the Bowery as a punishment and a vehicle to expiate the sins they have committed such as abandoning their wives and children, disappointing their parents and siblings, or not fulfilling themselves in the workplace. This defense mechanism, which psychiatrists call "undoing," is best illustrated by Bill, who we had described briefly in an earlier chapter.

Unlike many of these men, but much like the public's misconception about Bowery men in general, Bill is genuinely a loner. He is widowed and estranged from the rest of his family. He appears to have no friends other than the tablemates he regularly sits with at the seniors lunch program. He arrives alone and leaves alone in spite of the fact that a number of others in the facility live at his hotel and walk to breakfast and lunch as a group. He is, however, compassionate and helpful toward other men on the Bowery if directed by agency staff. He will visit men who are hospitalized, bringing them cigarettes or money if supplied, and is of late, a driving force on a "consumer advisory committee" at the facility he attends. Somehow, this is a business arrangement for Bill and does not seem to touch on any enduring social aspect of his life. The men he helps and the fellow committee members do not turn into casual friends, just as those at his table with which he heatedly debates religion and politics don't meet later for continuation of the debate, or for coffee, or for a movie.

The sketchy history we were able to put together of Bill's former life has been gotten with a great amount of difficulty. It is tough to glean facts from some of the others due to their constant intoxication, duplicity, or faded memory. With Bill there is the obstacle of his reserve and almost patrician air which obstructs any formal or conversational interview in that it seems like an unwanted invasion of his privacy to ask personal questions.

Bill says he's here because of a bout with alcohol following the marital breakup and the subsequent death of his wife. He will not be pinned down on the reasons for estrangement from his children and the rest of his family, but one gets a sense that embarrassment over his alcoholic episode and his ending up on the Bowery have placed a permanent barrier between him and his past.

Bill is not interested in part-time employment. There is no expressed interest in an apartment in a better neighborhood. He has no desire to travel or to live in a warmer climate. He seems to be doing penance on the Bowery. While not a drinker, he's living amongst alcoholics. He's honest and clean, but he's living amongst thieves and the unwashed. He's literate, but he's surrounded by ignorance and stupidity. Bill is not alone, however. While he's unusual in that he combines so many positive qualities, there are many drug-free bookworms mixed in with the others here. They are serving their own self imposed sentence for some crime for which they will not forgive themselves, and which they won't even discuss.

In addition to defense mechanisms another important "ego function" is that of maintaining self-esteem. At best, these men are merely ignored by the general public; they are frequently verbally or even physically abused. The inner torment that this creates makes the maintenance of self-dignity a heroic task. In *The Jungle*, Upton Sinclair (1905) described the experience of the impoverished street man:

Everywhere that he turned were prison bars and hostile eyes following him; the well-fed, sleek policemen, from whose glances he shrank, and who seemed to grip their clubs more tightly when they saw him; the saloon-keepers, who never ceased to watch him while he was in their places, who were jealous of every moment he lingered after he paid his money; the hurrying throngs upon the streets, who were deaf to his entreaties, oblivious of his very existence—and savage and contemptuous when he forced himself upon them. They had their own affairs, and there was no place for him among them. There was no place for him anywhere—every direction he turned his gaze, this fact was forced upon him. Everything was built to express it to him: the residences, with their heavy walls and bolted doors, and basement windows barred with iron; the great warehouses filled with the products of the whole world, and guarded by iron shutters and heavy gates; the banks with their unthinkable billions of wealth, all buried in safes and vaults of steel. (p. 229)

Most of the men find some way to express their self-worth. For Miles, it means not "caddying" (i.e., going to another guy's house to stay a few nights): "I have phone numbers but I stay at no one's house. I don't call anyone 'cause I feel that when a man loses his pride he lost everythin'."

Uncle Ed expresses his self-worth by helping others:

I always try to be helpful to the needy. I'm not braggin' but I'm the type that if I had one cigarette, I'd split it in half to make sure you have a smoke. My mother, God bless her soul, told me that I'd die a pauper cause I'm always givin' when I should keep for myself. I'm always tryin' to help.

However, at times these efforts to prop up their self-esteem must seem futile as these men are constantly reminded of their "worthlessness." For example, Miles sitting on his park bench must psychologically fend off verbal abuse: "People are coming by and call it bum's row and make derogatory remarks like 'Those old men should be like the old folks in Japan'. You just learn to accept the insults."

## THE SKID ROW PERSONALITY

Although antecedent personality traits may not be the key to explaining skid row behavior, living on skid row may be responsible for creating a new personality. Vexliard (1956) observes how a profound metamorphosis of personality can occur under the stress of certain kinds of life situations such as that of the hobos. Perhaps Orwell

(1933) best summarized this perspective, "I am not saying, of course, that most tramps are ideal characters; I am only saying that they are ordinary human beings, and that if they are worse than other people it is the result and not the cause of their way of life" (p. 203).

Jacqueline Wiseman (1979) in delineating some of the principal features of skid row life illustrates why researchers have often confused cause and effect. For example, skid row men usually exhibit a "today" or "now" orientation. This led some investigators (e.g., Levinson, 1958) to postulate that skid rowers inherently have poor ego strengths, and thus their "inner controls are also very poor" (p. 285). However, Wiseman contended that the skid rower's "now" orientation is based on a concern for daily survival similar to that found in other economically-deprived groups (e.g., Oscar Lewis's work on Mexicans). As George Orwell (1933) found,

You make one discovery which outweighs some of the others . . . the great redeeming feature of poverty, the fact that it annihilates the future . . . . When you have only three francs you are quite indifferent; for three francs will feed you until tomorrow, and you cannot think further than that. (p. 20)

A second aspect of the skid row man's frame of reference is his feeling of powerlessness coupled with his sense of a need for cunning to outwit a hostile and unfair world. To investigators such as Rosenman (1955) who employed a psychoanalytic approach, this hostility results from the "original, overwhelming trauma" experienced as fantasy in infancy—"of being abandoned by and isolated from good protective parental figures"—and the powerlessness stems from being "left helpless by the poisoning evil parent surrogates" (p. 448). Yet, as Wiseman (1979) and others (e.g., Parker, 1970; Spradley, 1970) have pointedly observed, the skid row man is economically and socially impotent; he is vulnerable and often exploited by merchants, employers, social workers, health care workers, and even street friends. "He suspects that his day-to-day struggle for survival will fail except for his own talents at counter exploitation" (Wiseman, 1979, p. 16).

A third aspect of their life is that of impermanence. Although there is perhaps more permanence in relationships among older than younger skid rowers, most skid row relationships are in constant flux. Men come and go, go in and out of institutions, die, are evicted from their hotels, and gain and lose money, jobs, and friends. Given this scenario, researchers looking at these men in the abstract were mistakenly apt to characterize them as "undersocialized," "disaffiliated," or "having lack of need for attachments."

Lastly, skid row men are often characterized as having "dependent" and "passive" personalities. Although they shun ordinary societal commitment and hence present a veneer of independence, many of these men accept the dependence of institutional style living, rarely break rules, doing their assigned tasks, and fit themselves into the routine of the organization. Lodge Patch (1970) noted that many of London's skid rowers seemed to have done well in the military service, often for many years. Observing this dependence, led one group of investigators to assert, "the basic problem of the homeless man is not alcohol, but a deep problem of dependency . . ." (Wiseman, 1979, p. 12). However, George Orwell (1933) reminiscing about his experience as a tramp in England remarked,

A casual ward will often admit a hundred tramps in one night, and these are handled by a staff of at most three porters . . . . Indeed, when one sees how tramps let themselves be bullied by the workhouse officials, it is obvious that they are the most docile, broken-spirited creatures imaginable. (p. 202)

He concluded, "The evil of poverty is not so much that it makes a man suffer as that it rots him physically and spiritually" (p. 204). Sutherland and Locke (1936) similarly observed a "defeatism" developing among the men living in Chicago's shelters during the Great Depression. Perhaps some of the young homeless are not as passive as Orwell's tramps or Chicago's shelter men of the 1930s. Nevertheless, over time they may eventually be transmogrified. Clearly, many of the older skid row and homeless men we encountered fit rather well into this passive/defeatist characterization.

The data presented in this chapter help resolve several important issues concerning the mental health of aging homeless persons, a group that has been generally ignored in recent years. First, we find that the tendency to focus on psychoticism among the homeless population has obscured the fact that rates of severe depression are more prevalent. Within the population under study, although the rate of psychoticism or history of mental hospitalization were relatively high (23%), the rate of significant depression was approximately 1.5 times greater. Two decades ago Bahr and Caplow (1973) observed that one of the principal distinguishing features between

Bowery and other low income men was the distinct unhappiness and lower self-esteem found among the Bowery men.

A second important finding was that contrary to reports in the literature, our data did not support the notion that the psychotic homeless differ substantially from the nonpsychotic homeless. Apart from their psychoticism and histories of psychiatric hospitalization, there were no discernible differences between the two groups on indices of physical health, socioeconomic status, or social interaction. The latter finding is particularly interesting since most studies have tended to underscore the isolation of the mentally ill homeless. However, using more sensitive and comprehensive measures of social networks than had been employed previously, we found viable support systems that were comparable to the nonmentally ill homeless. Only a small proportion of the psychotic men—about one in seven—fit the popular notion of a loner, and even these men were not complete loners.

Although there was considerable homogeneity between the two homeless groups, the mentally ill homeless men differed significantly from aging community men across all medical, socioeconomic, and social interactive scales. The homeless mentally ill were physically sicker, considerably poorer with many more unmet needs, and had smaller and less intimate social networks than did the community men. However, with respect to social interaction, contacts for the homeless men were more frequent, more materially oriented (especially toward food, money, or medical aid), and included more formal linkages than did the networks of the community men. Thus, the social networks of the homeless men were appropriate to their ecological niche.

Even some of the most severely mentally impaired men were often able to negotiate the environment. Snow and his co-workers (1986) likewise noted that "efforts of the homeless mentally ill to survive on the streets are not as chaotic and irrational as they may appear from a distance" (p. 418). Such observations also parallel reports of vagrant schizophrenics around the world who were capable of developing extraordinary survival skills despite a high level of mental disturbance (Baasher et al., 1983). For example, their report of mentally ill vagrants in Nigeria revealed that "they lack the apathy, slowness and utter disinterest seen in institutionalized patients. They were concerned about what they were going to eat, and they clutched their few belongings to carry with them" (p. 36).

Similarly, a study from Ethiopia found:

Conversation with these patients about the daily problems of survival was quite possible, but as soon as we tried to discuss their history, emotional problems or relationships they became deluded or incoherent, demonstrating a disturbance of thinking. In other words, they showed a combination of serious mental disability and quite adequate capacity for survival. (p. 36)

The data reported here are limited to one particular sector of the homeless population and therefore cannot be generalized to other homeless persons. Nonetheless, the similarities found between the mentally ill and nonmentally ill groups tend to shift the primary focus of the problems of the homeless away from the mental health arena and into a broader arena comprising physical health and socioeconomic factors: problems that exist for all homeless people, regardless of their mental status. Noteworthy is the similar conclusion that Stephen Crystal and his associates (1986) reached after a survey of a younger homeless population found in 14 New York City shelters: "the characteristics of the psychiatric group within the shelters are more like than unlike those of the non-psychiatric group. In fact, both groups have the same basic profile . . ." (p. 69).

It is not our intent to minimize the importance of psychiatric care for this population. In addition to psychotic illness, rates of depression were extraordinarily high. Moreover, only 3% of the men were receiving any psychiatric medication, and there were some homeless men who were in stages of disorganization that clearly threatened their survival. Indeed, as others have underscored, the homeless mentally ill are substantially underserved by the mental health system (Roth, Bean, & Hyde, 1986). Nevertheless, for a majority of the older mentally ill homeless it would be naive to assume that merely addressing the psychiatric problem will result in any substantial change in their overall well-being. For the most part the homeless mentally ill are suffering from the same problems of poor health, inadequate housing, and impoverishment that afflict all homeless persons.

Several analysts have warned (Estroff, 1985; Goldman & Morrisey, 1985; Hopper *et al.*, 1985; Snow *et al.*, 1986) that we must be wary of "medicalizing" the homeless problem by reducing it to a problem of psychiatric disability. Given the limited funds available for the homeless, such a view raises the specter of expending more money on mental health staff positions perhaps at the expense of commodities such as food and housing (Estroff, 1985). Furthermore, despite the considerable homogeneity between the psychiatrically disordered and nondisordered populations, the medicalizing of the homeless problem may inadvertently identify some homeless individuals as more deserving than others because those who are diseased may be perceived as not responsible for their condition, whereas the nondiseased are held more responsible for their fate (Estroff, 1985). As Leach (1979) has proposed, the mentally ill homeless must be viewed primarily as socially disadvantaged and, in addition, as having the handicap of mental illness.

The presence of high rates of depressive symptoms at levels that would warrant professional attention is especially troubling. Often these were not trivial complaints—one in four men wished they were dead, two in five felt life was not worth living, one in two reported persistent depression. Six men claimed to have attempted suicide in the previous month. These findings contravene the notions of some observers such as Bendiner (1961) who believe that the skid row man, by attaining the depths and now certain that he cannot fall farther, is "at peace" (p. 23).

Importantly, our findings suggested several potential points for intervention. Because greater network size and clustering, more institutional contacts, and ability to meet daily needs were associated with reduced levels of depression, a potential point for intervention would be the local service agencies that can provide on-site treatment for physical problems, enhance network size and interaction through lounge and socialization activities, and assist in obtaining various necessities through meal programs and social services. Within such programs, the relatively younger, more organically disabled, alcoholic homeless men especially should be targeted because of their increased susceptibility to depression. We shall return to the issue of service interventions in Chapter 10.

The post-World War II literature has often characterized homeless men as "undersocialized" (Strauss, 1946), "lacking a need for attachments" (Vexliard, 1956), having no ego strengths, having partially eroded ego defenses, and being fearful of sharing affection (Levinson, 1958). In an earlier chapter we demonstrated that these men have viable social networks that provided extensive material support and some degree of intimacy, although in comparison with a group of their age peers in the general community there was a relative isolation and a paucity of intimate contacts. In this chapter we have shown that contrary to Levinson's (1958) findings based on Rorschach Tests of 50 Bowery men, our interviews of 281 Bowery men reveal a variety of ego strengths and reasonably intact defense mechanisms. Indeed, the ability of these men to survive despite their high levels of physical impairment, poverty, public abuse, and power-lessness contrasts with the popular image of these men as helpless, inert detritus of society. Such a perspective again underscores the human qualities of these men. In referring to his first contact with poverty, George Orwell (1933) remarked, "You thought it would be quite simple; it is extraordinarily complicated" (p. 17).

# CHAPTER EIGHT

# *Problems with Alcohol*

When a man is on the street he is very nervous. His
nerves are on edge. If he don't drink he will start to.
                                                —Miles

Alcohol is essentially my friend. It is a tool to be used in
the greatest art of them all; losing certain memories,
getting rid of the excess baggage if you will. . . . But
here comes the catch: If you lose all memories you won't
have a reason to drink. . . . That is a problem isn't it?
                    —Old Bowery Man (cited in Zettler, 1975, p. 24)

## HISTORICAL CONTROVERSIES

Until recently, the general public believed that alcoholism was synonymous with skid row. This misconception did a disservice to two
populations: (1) those alcoholics in the general population who were
rarely identified as such by family and friends because they thought
alcoholics must be skid row types; (2) skid rowers who were seen as
deserving of their destitution because of their debauchery. On the
other hand, it is grossly naive to believe that alcohol has not contributed to the arrival of many of these men on skid row, their continued
existence on skid row, and their physical and mental deterioration.
To date, however, the literature has been equivocal as to what
extent alcohol explains and maintains homelessness and skid row
existence.

Nels Anderson's (1923) early work done during the height of
Prohibition noted that "drinking is responsible for keeping many

men on the road" (p. 67). Anderson further observed, "Practically all homeless men drink when liquor is available. The only sober moments for many hobos and tramps are when they are without funds" (p. 139). The study by Sutherland and Locke (1936) of Chicago's Shelter population in the 1930s suggested that alcohol was both a "cause and effect in a process of interacting factors" (p. 78). Excessive alcohol intake often resulted in marital breakup, loss of job, and eventual decline to homelessness. Correspondingly, many men, after a loss of job or marital difficulty, turned to alcohol for solace. Donald Bogue's (1963) study of Chicago's skid row in the 1950s indicated that among the heaviest drinkers (32% of his sample), four fifths of the men had started their uncontrolled drinking before their 35th birthday. Thus, based on Bogue's data, a majority of these men were already drinking heavily prior to coming to skid row. Similarly, Robert Strauss's 1946 study of 203 homeless men reported heavy use of alcohol among 80% to 85% of the men and that two thirds had begun drinking prior to becoming homeless. Strauss, however, cautioned that alcoholism was one of many contributing factors leading to homelessness and that alcohol might be a way for homeless men to adjust to the world. In other words, although heavy drinking often starts prior to entry to skid row, for many men (at least one third) heavy drinking may begin after beginning a skid row life.

While all studies have acknowledged the presence of high alcohol consumption among skid rowers and the homeless, there is considerable disagreement about the degree of consumption. Not surprisingly, a whole taxonomy and argot have developed around drinking behavior. For instance, Anderson's early study of homeless men referred to "Alkee Stiffs" and the "White Line Stiffs" as confirmed alcoholics. Next there was the "Rummy Stiff" who has impaired intellect because of habitual use of raw rum. Anderson also distinguished the "bum," who "drinks and wanders," from hobos and tramps who tended to work more frequently and drink more periodically. As noted in Chapter 2, by the 1950s investigators (Jackson & Connor, 1953) were able to identify six types of drinkers: "older alcoholics," "bums," "characters," "winos," "rubby-dubs," and "lushes." Strauss and McCarthy (1951) distinguished between the "pathological drinker," who drinks to relieve discomfort, and the "addictive drinker," who drinks persistently and who progresses toward destruction of psychological and social functioning. They maintained the pathological drinkers comprised the bulk of skid row habitués.

In addition to differentiating types of drinkers on skid row, the quantity of alcohol consumed by these men has been debated. Anderson reported that although homeless men drink, the majority are periodic drinkers who have "sober periods of a week, a month or two, or even a year" (pp. 134–135). Matthew Dumont's (1967) study of a Bowery tavern revealed that most men were plateau drinkers, that is, they established an equilibrium so that increasing amounts of alcohol would not be needed. Samuel Wallace (1965) viewed drinking as part of the way of life of skid row, but distinguished the skid row drunk from the skid row alcoholic. The drunk, who comprises the vast majority of skid rowers, regulates his drinking so that he can maintain a fairly constant level at all times, with as few dry spells as possible; he tends to drink in groups and gain approval and self-esteem from his peers. The alcoholic prefers to drink alone and achieve maximum intoxication as quickly as he can. The fact that most skid rowers share both money and drink "is perhaps the most conclusive proof that most of them are not alcoholics; alcoholics would find it exceedingly difficult to exercise the control dictated by group drinking" (Wallace, 1965, p. 187). Thus, investigators such as Wallace (1965) and Rubington (1958) believe that perhaps only 8% of the excessive drinkers on skid row are alcoholics. Although estimates as well as definitions tend to vary, in the early 1970s Howard Bahr (1973) concluded that alcoholics comprised approximately one third of the skid row population. A national survey conducted by HUD in 1984 placed the level of alcoholism among the homeless at between 27% and 63% in various regions of the country.

In general, the skid row literature of the 1960s and early 1970s tended to posit the notion that skid row drinking was a type of adaptive mechanism rather than true alcoholism. For instance, Spradley (1970) wrote:

The lifestyle of urban nomads with its drinking rituals provides men a group of friends wherever they go, men who accept them as they are. If a man stops drinking and sharing drinks, he cuts himself off from the most valuable of all resources, human companionship and acceptance. (p. 177)

For Spradley's urban nomads, bars function as churches and clubs, employment agencies and dating centers, begging places, drinking and eating places, and a place to find friendship. As one homeless man put it, "When I get into a strange new city, I head for a bar. If I want to work, I go to a bar. That's where they come to hire a man" (cited in Spradley, 1970, p. 179).

Wallace (1965) concluded that the skid row derelict requires a long socialization process to be produced. The derelict learns to

sacrifice everything to the drinking practices and needs of the group. The push of [outside] community condemnation and the pull of drinking companions, plus a habituated desire for drinking have combined to structure life around alcohol—the point at which he has now arrived. (p. 187)


## CURRENT DRINKING PATTERNS

It would seem from the literature that the pendulum has swung to the point that skid rowers and homeless men are no longer viewed as alcoholics and that their drinking serves a social and adaptive function for survival in their community. Nevertheless, our data suggest that these assumptions require some modification, especially among older skid row men. First, alcohol use was widespread and consumption was substantial. Fewer than 2% of the men claimed that they never drank alcohol and 80% reported that they still drink. By their own estimates (which are certainly conservative), 21%, 22%, and 20% of the men reported that they are moderate, heavy, or spree drinkers, respectively; 49% of the men drink daily, and another 33% drink several times per week. Drinking among the street men was exceptionally high, 90% of the men were either moderate, heavy, or spree drinkers; 37% classified themselves as "heavy" consumers. We found that 58% of the street men drank daily, and 36% drank several times a week.

Men who drank only wine comprised 16% of our sample, while 25% drank only beer, 19% drank only hard liquor, and 41% drank a combination of alcoholic beverages (usually wine and something else) or as several men put it, "whatever is available." The popular brands of wine on the Bowery are Thunderbird ("T-Bird"), Wild Irish Rose, and Night Train. A good part of the popularity of these brands lies in their price: $1.30 or $1.35 for a pint. The taste or drunk that you get purportedly varies between brands. Miles critiques the wine:

I like the light wine, Thunderbird. It makes me drunker than vodka. I don't like the dark wines, Wild Irish Rose and Night Train, though they are stronger. They had this wine called Mad Dog 20/20. Oh my goodness, it was horrible. I think they took it off the market.

The kind of "drunk" one gets—whether it is a "good" or "bad" one—is important. As Ed explains:

A "good drunk" is when the alcohol wipes out all of my problems. A "bad drunk" is when you would wake up on a park bench all cut-up or all beat-up, jack-rolled, with no room and no money in your pocket and you have to start all over again. "Hitting the skids" is when someone is almost helpless. Their ass is rubbin' up against the ground. They have no home and no means of support, and usually they're dirty, and they're out on the streets. You've hit rock bottom. You can't go down no farther.

When bars and liquor stores are closed—in the early mornings or late at night—the men use bootleggers. Two notorious boot-leggers are "Moms" and "Pops": Ed and Miles, respectively, recall visits to Moms and Pops:

I just went to Momma Green, the bootlegger. She's uptown off Sixth Avenue. It's an apartment buildin' but you go up one flight and knock on the door. She looks through a peephole and you just tell her what the hell you want.

I buy my bottle at the bootlegger, the Spanish guy, "Pops" who is a couple blocks off the Bowery. He has a little grocery store. He sells cigarettes, soda, and wine. He charges $1.50 for a bottle. Most places charge less.

Though drinking is part of the social matrix and folklore of the Bowery, more than half the men (51%) reported drinking mostly alone. The remainder drank in groups (38%) or bars (33%). (There was some overlap of responses.) The percent drinking alone was considerably greater than the one third reported by Bahr and Cap-low (1973), but this may reflect the somewhat older age of our sample. It was our observation that many of the men tended to move toward solitary drinking behavior as they aged. Also, with only two taverns remaining on the Bowery (one of which is notoriously dan-gerous), bar drinking has been curtailed.

Typical of the men who drink alone is Mr. Watts, who like many of the solo drinkers tends to be quite despondent. The following is an excerpt from the interviewer's notes:

Tim Watts is a very depressed, isolated, self-educated older man who is going through a drinking bout. It seems like he has been drinking intensely for the past several months. With the exception of two associates down the hall he keeps to himself and hides in his room. He does most of his drinking by himself in his room. All connections with his family have been destroyed. His marriage broke up because his wife had an affair. Most of his family is dead, and his living daughter is not in touch with him. The lack of connection with the daughter is a cause of grief for him.

As the following narrative reveals, some of the oldest men depend on runners, buddies, and hotel staff to sustain their drinking behavior:

Sid is old, has bad feet, and can't get around. He is taken care of by people in the hotel, especially the manager who keeps his money and buys him his food (not much) and drink (one bottle of wine per day). He has a good memory and a good sense of humor; he's a lovable old guy and that's the reason he gets "special" treatment in the hotel. He never leaves the hotel because he is afraid and he really has no desire to go out.

Other men may drink alone or with one good associate or friend. Uncle Ed often drank with Jeff. Ed feels close to Jeff because he believes that they are "birds of a feather." He's also a periodic drinker: "With a snap of the finger he can go off and get drunk." Two weeks before Thanksgiving they both took off on "a bender." They had been sitting in Spring Street Park and Ed offered to get him a cup of coffee. Jeff said no. Ed asked, "What do you want?" "A bottle." So Ed gave him some money and they drank a fifth of T-Bird together.

We have described previously how a number of the men drink in regular groups, which often provide members with money, food, and emotional support in addition to alcohol. Some men, however, belong to true "bottle gangs," which are transient entities formed for the sole purpose of procuring and consuming a bottle or two of alcohol. This interviewer's notes on Mr. O'Reilly, a street man, exemplify the elderly "bottle gang" participant:

Mr. O'Reilly is an alcoholic. He was separated from his wife 20 years ago and has lived here ever since. He hasn't seen his family since he left his wife. His only income is odd jobs, and when he's drinking he can't work, so he often ends up not having money and unable to afford a room. About half of the time he winds up on the street, staying in various parks in the area. He looks to be in fairly good physical condition considering his drinking problem. He has a few long-term acquaintances and very few other relationships. He says that he always drinks with other people, but usually different ones, and he doesn't know their names.

The men generally had been abusing alcohol for long periods of time. The moderate, heavy, or spree drinkers reported having begun such patterns on the average of 25 years ago. Noteworthy was that one fifth of these drinkers had begun such patterns relatively late in life (i.e., past age 50). Primary reasons for beginning later in life included "living alone," "nothing else to do," "gave-up, depression, frustration," or "I don't know." As contrasted with the Bowery group as a whole, few street men began drinking patterns after age 50 (about 1 in 10). As with the group as a whole, the street men's current drinking patterns began about 25 years ago.

A number of the late onset drinkers attributed their alcoholism to the isolation following the death of a wife. The following narrative is illustrative:

Mr. Kirsch lost his wife four years ago. Ever since then he's been drinking almost all the time. He always thinks about her. He sees her face and thinks of things that she used to say. He was in tears when he talked about his wife. Any friends and family that he had don't talk to him because of his drinking; therefore, last Easter he took a pledge not to drink for 90 days. If he can stop drinking his family will have him back or at least provide some support, but if he calls now and he sounds as though he's been drinking they hang up on him. His mother, who was 15 when he was born is his closest contact. They still talk to each other weekly. He has emphysema and arthritis. He has cramps in his legs, and last week he was given a cane to use by a doctor. He was in tears when we talked about his wife.

Despite the current levels of heavy consumption, levels were even greater when they were younger: Nearly three fourths of the men rated themselves as heavy, moderate, or spree drinkers in the past; fully one third of the men had considered themselves "heavy" drinkers in the past. Reasons for having diminished consumption over the years in order of frequency were: poor health, loss of interest, or inability to afford the habit.

Alcohol has played a powerful role in these men's lives. Nearly one fifth of the men listed alcohol specifically as a primary or secondary reason for coming to the Bowery, although it also contributed indirectly through impoverishment (the major reason most men came) and family problems. These men had been drinking moderately or heavily on the average of nine years prior to coming to the Bowery. This is consistent with the early studies of Robert Strauss (1946) who found that two thirds of homeless men had begun their heavy drinking prior to arrival on skid row.

For many men, drinking began early and created a lifetime of instability. For example, Uncle Ed first began drinking as a teenager when he ran away from home and ended up in Newark. There, he started hanging around with the "bottle boys." As he put it, "What started me drinkin'? Just kind of hangin' around with the guys. What the hell, they're drinkin'. I'll drink too. That's all. No real reason. Just to be one of the boys."

Several of the men who started early in life echoed Ed's sentiments. Alcohol was a way to belong, of becoming part of the group:

I started drinkin' at 15 but it wasn't nothin' serious 'cause I was goin' to school at that time and I drank only on Saturday. I never really knew why I drank. I used to like it at first when I was a kid. I started as a lark. I still don't know why I drink now. I don't like it. I really don't.

A number of the early onset drinkers began imbibing heavily because drinking was a common pastime among their fellow-workers. Ed, while working as a dishwasher in Boston, used to go out drinking with his co-workers on the weekend. Also, beer was usually passed around when the men were working the night shift. Miles also began drinking heavily after losing his steady job and had to accept seasonal jobs working in the kitchens of the Catskill hotels. Most of the kitchen men drank heavily. Miles viewed alcohol as medicinal: "You know I need it. It calms my nerves." Other men claimed to have begun their heavy consumption after their marriage broke up or after a family death or tragedy:

Mr. Rodriquez lost his entire family, uncles, aunts, parents, grandparents, and so forth in a flood in Texas in 1957. He then started falling apart, and in 1961 he said he became a full fledged alcoholic. He drank extremely heavily for four years during which time he said he was hospitalized from "300 to 400" times (unbelievable?!) for alcoholism. He was finally put in intensive care a couple of times and from that scare or shock, quit drinking and thereafter started smoking a lot of pot. He smoked up most of his earnings and has recently quit that.

As these interviewers observed, the price that alcohol has exacted on their families and in missed employment opportunities is legion:

Mr. Davis blames his situation on the booze. He sees patterns in what he does and really wants to get it together before it's too late. He has a summer job in the mountains and wishes not to return to the Bowery. Most of his life he worked as a tractor-trailer driver. He sees rigs drive by, looks at the driver and says to himself "Now why aren't I still doing that." Then he says, "I think the quart of booze per day took its toll."

Mr. George was forced to leave home after separating from his wife. He attributes most of his problems to alcohol abuse. He seems fairly isolated living on the Bowery and often spoke about his wife and relatives who live in Mount Vernon, N.Y. He is unhappy about the infrequent contact he has with them.

As noted previously, many of the men had symptoms associated with alcohol abuse: 12% had seizure disorders, 37% were tremulous, 45% had dizziness, 16% had visual hallucinations, and 28% had incurred fractures in the past ten years. We developed a scale comprised of 3 items: age of onset of heavy drinking (before age 35), quantity, and frequency of alcohol consumption. The alcohol scale was found to have a weak but significant relationship with poor physical health, failure to fulfill material needs, increased social interaction, depression, and an inverse relationship to age (see Appendix 1, Table 1, column 6). In other words, within our sample, those who drank the most tended to be younger, in poorer physical health, more depressed, and less capable of meeting their daily needs. Because of the prevalence of group drinking patterns, their level of social interaction tended to be higher than that of light drinkers. Perhaps this increased social interaction serves a protective function by concomitantly providing a modicum of assistance with food, medical aid, and money along with the exchange of alcohol. This may in part account for the relatively weak correlations of the other variables such as physical health and depression with alcohol. A more powerful contributory explanation is the fact that depression and poor health are widespread on the Bowery, regardless of current alcohol consumption. Although the statistical association between current alcohol consumption and poor physical health was weak, we encountered numerous instances of individuals who were physically wracked by the consequences of alcoholism. Such a man is George, who attends the senior program at the Bowery Residents' Committee.

George is the personification of what most people think of as a "Bowery Bum." Burly, sloppy, and florid, we see him daily at the BRC and have never seen him sober; George has maintained a pathetic alcoholic equilibrium for years. In those few instances when we can talk to him, he describes a hostile, self-destructive, and seemingly rock-bottom existence.

George claims to have been a solid 100 pounds heavier than his current soft 250. He talks of years in prison due to a volatile temper, poor timing, and poorer luck. He has a fearsome countenance, perpetually covered in scrapes, scars, and bruises. Many of these abrasions and contusions are self-inflicted from the simple act of toppling over backwards or sideways, late in the day, blasted out of his mind. Only early in the morning, after his "eye opener" but before heavy drinking sets in, can any sense be made of what George has to say.

He lives the ultimate alcoholic nightmare: too drunk to defend himself, too addicted to hostility to stop requesting beatings from policemen, hospital workers, and fellow Bowery dwellers. George's bigotry (he's white) is probably the primary reason he gets a solid thrashing a week. We have seen him repeatedly challenge black men by slobbering racial epithets at them. They invariably pelt him with food, humble him with umbrellas, and frequently he arrives at the BRC early in the morning with scars and open wounds providing evidence of more serious beatings. He is apt to call the social workers attempting to help men regardless of race "nigger lovers." We've seen him scream "kike" and "Jew bastard" at men; yet on the next day, when slightly more sober, he'll admit that he too is Jewish.

As drunk, abusive, and crazy as George gets he never misses a meal, is never hospitalized, is never arrested. The equilibrium of his existence is the truly remarkable thing about him and about those men who are like him on the Bowery. He says he has cancer. He obviously has brutal circulatory problems which any elderly middle-class man would call "a serious heart condition" to which he would be forced to adapt. His color changes are quite dramatic: flushed, cyanotic, pale, livid. He goes through all, sometimes daily. He can hardly get through the soup kitchen line, but he does. At times he seems as if he can't get it up for one more argument, he can't take one more beating. But he does. He must mellow or he must die. But he does neither.

George is 68 years old. He claims to have lived essentially this way for the last 20 years. Panhandling, cashing in bottles, sleeping in gutters, doorways, and parks, going from pint to pint, he never has enough money for a room or for a quart bottle. And yet something about his constitution, some quirk of fate, of ill luck, keeps him suspended—half dead, half drunk, half asleep, half homicidal, half suicidal, forever. He can't have a pound of liver left. He can't have been missed by all those cars in the street. He can't have escaped that one fatal blow from an enraged black man or Jew (or social worker). He has, however, and after years of observing him there seems to be no change, no drift in his condition. On his best days, early in the morning he can be found in the park, a pair of nonprescription magnifying glasses on his nose scoping out the racing form. On his worst days, he's face down in the gutter, his beefy hand still clutching a tiny empty vodka bottle. He neither gets better nor worse, the ultimate alcoholic in Dante's Inferno.

## TRYING TO STOP

Virtually all the men whom we encountered said that they were going to stop drinking shortly or claimed that they had recently stopped. Nearly every agency on the Bowery offers some sort of alcohol counseling program or an AA program. There are also several detoxification units as well. Numerous AA groups could be found in the area, but many Bowery men reviled AA with comments such as "Ya know what AA stands for? American Assholes." Despite this, probably every skid row drinker has attended at least one AA meeting, and one fourth of the men reported having attended at least one meeting in the past month (this percentage was identical for street and nonstreet men).

Uncle Ed is a strong proponent of AA and several of his closest friends are AA members. Ed's first experience with AA was 25 years ago when he was imprisoned at the Riker's Detention Center for "breaking and entering." Ed had been drunk and had broken into a store. Or at least that's what they told him: "I don't remember doing it, I had a blackout." While Ed was in prison he met Jack, an outside speaker from AA. He said to Ed, "Maybe I can help you when you get out of here. Do you have a sponsor?" Jack explained that, "A sponsor is a 'winner' in AA. You confide in him more than anybody else. He'll take you under his wing." Several months later, as Ed was leaving the jail, he was told someone was waiting for him. "Well lo and behold it was Jack. He took me under his wing and that's how I got started with AA."

Uncle Ed has three sponsors now. One of the things that helps him through difficult periods is "twelve-stepping" and calling up his sponsors for support. "Twelve-steppin' means that you take a person on the side and tell him what he's doin' wrong, or if he's headed for a drunk, talkin' about it. Thus, if he has problems, you twelve-step him and try to help him find an answer to his problems." Ed says that's why he has three sponsors. By having just one sponsor, he won't have all of the answers. So Ed might call a sponsor if he has a problem: "'Oh, man, I'm havin' a problem,' I'd say. 'What is it, man? Where are you?' 'I'm at the BRC.' 'Can you come up to the house?' I'd say, 'Yeah.' 'Come on up. And don't forget, you pass four bars on the way up here. Don't stop in any fuckin' one of them. If you've got to piss, piss between two cars.'" When he arrives at a sponsor's house, there will usually be a pot of coffee waiting for him. Then Ed will sit down and tell him his problems. In this way he'll be twelve-stepping Ed by trying to help him get answers to his problems.

Telephone therapy is also very important to Ed:

Whenever I need help or I feel depressed, or when I'm ready to say 'the hell with it,' I throw a quarter in the telephone and call up some AA member and talk it out. Chances are, after I've talked it out, the party I've talked to will tell me, "How's your problem now?" More than one time, I really forgot I had a problem. In other words, I'm givin' him my problem and he carries it after that because he had more strength than I did.

Miles, on the other hand, is cynical about AA like many Bowery men. He was in an AA group at a local hospital in 1971, and he recalls how the two principal speakers had boasted that they had been sober for many years. A few nights later, Miles passed a bar with a friend and cried, "Look, there's the same two bums who spoke about how they haven't been drinkin' for umpteen years and they're in there throwin' shots up their face like there's no tomorrow." Since then, Miles considers AA "a bunch of crock. I don't believe in it 'cause they lied. To me it's a pack of lies."

Virtually all the moderate and heavy drinkers have had to be detoxified (withdrawn) from alcohol at some point in their lives. Many of the men have been detoxified dozens of times. As men consume regular quantities of alcohol, their body builds a tolerance to a particular quantity of alcohol. They then must consume more alcohol to get the desired high. Eventually they may run out of money to pay for the increased quantities of alcohol, and become physically deteriorated, or they simply see that they have had enough. At this point, they may begin to experience withdrawal symptoms such as tremulousness, nausea, vomiting. More serious and sometimes life-threatening symptoms include seizures, hallucinations, blood electrolyte abnormalities, and delirium tremens (DTs). Until about a decade ago, the men often had to go to hospitals to detoxify. More recently, a number of small clinic units ("Sobering-up Stations") have opened up as an alternative to the expensive and sometimes impersonal care of large city hospitals.

Uncle Ed animatedly recounts his positive experience with one sobering-up unit that he used a few years ago. As he was coming out of a subway station near the Bowery, Ed encountered an old acquaintance. Ed had been spending the nights on the subways at that time. "You look in bad shape Ed," the acquaintance said. Ed replied, "I am. I need detox, but I don't know where the hell to go." So he took Ed across the street to the Lafayette Street Detoxification Unit. Inside, Ed was given a cup of coffee, and about ten minutes later another worker brought him some lunch. As he recalls, "I was so sick, I couldn't eat." Shortly, a nurse appeared. She assessed Ed's condition, and took him inside to be showered, deloused, and put to bed. "I slept the rest of the day." On the third day his withdrawal tremors and dry heaves had stopped. During this time he was told that he had experienced three grand mal seizures, although Ed could recollect nothing except some snippets of conversations or being turned in bed. He now felt well enough to "consume a good meal," and he was able to get to the bathroom and to the area where they serve food, watch television, and play cards. After he finished his first meal, he felt considerably better: "I knew I was over the brink then; I knew I was going to get back to reality." He stayed another five days, the last of which was the day before his check arrived. One of the social workers told him, "Ed, we've contacted the manager of your old hotel; he says that you can have your room back." To Ed, the staff at Lafayette Detox are just "beautiful people."

The most difficult challenge for these men is to fend-off the craving for alcohol. Not only is there a psychological craving, but the role of alcohol in the everyday interactions of many of these men makes it nearly impossible to abstain. For many of them, as this interviewer observed, ceasing to drink may mean ceasing to have friends:

Mr. Johnson is a quiet man who's been living on the street for 7 years, and on the Bowery for about 28 years. I found him in the park on Mulberry and Prince streets. He ended up on the street because he was drinking so much that he couldn't go anywhere else. One of the things that keeps him drinking now is his friends. He'll stop for a few days, but when he gets lonely and wants to be with his friends, they make him drink. Since he's bored and needs people, he drinks.

Some men, like Uncle Ed, have been able to substitute AA friends for drinking friends. Nonetheless, the frustrations of daily life often build to the point that he succumbs:

It started when I had the problem with the food stamps. I got depressed. It lasted for me close to a month and a half. I was really goin' through a tedious time. I just felt like sayin' "The hell with everythin', I'm better off being drunk." I even talked to Doris [his girlfriend] one time and I told her, "As far as I'm concerned I'm just as well being drunk as the way I am." She said, "No don't take that attitude Ed. What good will it do ya being drunk. For one thing you'll say the hell with food stamps. Then you'll say the hell with your check and the next thing you know you'll be without a room. You'll be on the streets and that'll be no good for you."

A few days later Ed seemed to be caving in:

"Say Joe, I had a hell of a day. I feel like I need a drink. Can you lend me a couple of dollars." Joe responded, "Well Uncle Ed, you're good for it. I'll lend ya two dollars that's all I can afford." Ed recalled that he believed "that without a doubt I was headed down. So he went over to Oscar's, the liquor store, to buy himself a bottle. In the back of his mind he was saying, "Ah the hell with every fuckin' thing."

On the way to the liquor store Ed met his friend Kenny. They decided to split a bottle. While they were sitting on a bench drinking, Kenny turned to Ed, "It just takes one bottle and we could become 'stary' shit. I don't want no more after this, I don't need it." So they both called it quits after that. Ed proudly recalls how there have been several times when he has been still sufficiently sober to say, "What the fuck am I doin'?" And then he usually calls it quits. "You might laugh," he says, "More than one time I remember seein' myself take two pints up to the room, drink about half of a pint, and there'd still be a pint and a half left the next mornin'. I couldn't even look at the shit."

For Ed, the unceasing battle to remain sober torments his life:

You go through a lot of hell and devastation of tryin' to sober up and get back on your feet. You had promised yourself a thousand things. Then you let yourself get down and say "the hell with it"—the AA meetings and the teachings of AA members who've had more sobriety than you. You go off on the first drink and you're back on that damn merry-go-round.

# CHAPTER NINE

# What Makes a Skid Row Man?

There must be something wrong . . . or I wouldn't be on
the Bowery.                                        —Uncle Ed

This chapter serves as a review and synthesis of the various elements that go into the making of a skid row man. In earlier chapters
we have treated these threads separately but now it is time to weave
them together.

## POVERTY

Poverty or being marginally poor was the hallmark of most of these
men's early lives. Their parents were poor or near-poor, and most of
the men received relatively inadequate schooling. They entered the
work force as either unskilled or semiskilled laborers. Because of
their inadequate skills, many assumed jobs in cyclical and seasonal
industries such as construction, the merchant marines, farm work,
hotel work, and day labor of various sorts. On these jobs or in the
military, the men often had their first exposure to heavy drinking
and, in between jobs, those who were not married sought the inexpensive housing and services of skid row. Consequently, many became exposed to skid row quite early in life, even though they might
have been repulsed by their initial visits and may not have stayed
permanently at that time. The reader should recall the biographies of
Miles and Ed, who are illustrative of men from marginally poor
families, who had few skills, and who came to use alcohol primarily
through their early work (and unemployment) experiences.

Poverty also played an important role in forming the skid row man once he had arrived on the Bowery. Two thirds of the men claimed that they had come to the Bowery for economic reasons— for its cheap housing, food, second-hand shops, missions, social agencies, day labor centers, and truck pick-ups. As we shall argue shortly, these institutions of poverty force new life patterns on these men. For example, a sense of powerlessness and dependency arises in the face of breadlines, exploitation by hotel managers, muggings, or a lost or stolen welfare check. Recall how Miles walked "thirty miles a day" merely to keep clean and to obtain food. Moreover, living amidst a community of the poor places strains on one's physical health—increased vulnerability to tuberculosis, a likelihood of infestation, personal injuries due to assaults, poor nutrition, decreased access to high-quality immediate health care—that further serve to weaken body and spirit. As we have suggested, the overwhelming stressors of street and flophouse life can create a "social breakdown syndrome" which is characterized by either withdrawal or aggressivity. It is difficult to determine how much these concomitants of poverty become enmeshed in the psychiatric syndromes found among the homeless.

Impoverishment creates a new kind of social world for these men. Often they must form temporary groups to obtain alcohol or food. Borrowing money from a fellow skid rower creates a powerful obligation to repay in the near future—a failure to repay can result in a cut-off of sources of survival or provoke physical assault. Some men become dependent on hotel managers and other exploiters who lend them money at 40% to 100% interest rates.

Finally, poverty truly transforms the individual's physiognamy. If a man happens to arrive on skid row with relatively decent clothing and jewelry, he learns quickly that he is at risk for assault in such garments.The dirt and filth of skid row clings to clothes like a magnet. Hence, even clothes serve to create the Bowery man:

For the first time I noticed, too, how the attitude of women varies with a man's clothes. When a badly dressed man passes them they shudder away from him with a quick frank movement of disgust, as though he were a dead cat. Clothes are powerful things. Dressed in a tramp's clothes it is very difficult, at any rate for the first day, not to feel that you are genuinely degraded. You might feel the same shame, irrational but very real, your first night in prison. (Orwell, 1933, p. 129)

## ALCOHOL

Alcohol also plays a key role in the formation of the Bowery man. We found that moderate and heavy alcohol consumption preceded by nearly a decade a man's permanent arrival on the Bowery. Here, it is possible to see how several factors can potentiate each other. Marginal poverty and periodic unemployment creates personal and family stressors which in turn produce increased exposure and desire for alcohol; increased alcohol consumption makes it more difficult to hold a job, as well as further exacerbating family strain. Upton Sinclair (1905) graphically describes this battle:

One day, however, he took the plunge, and drank up all that he had in his pockets, and went home half "piped," as the men phrase it. He was happier than he had been in a year; and yet, because he knew that the happiness would not last, he was savage, too—with those who would wreck it, and with the world, and with his life; and then again, beneath this, he was sick with the shame of himself. Afterward, when he saw the despair of his family, and reckoned up the money he had spent, the tears came into his eyes, and he began the long battle with the specter. (p. 139)

Nearly one in five men listed alcohol as their primary or secondary reason for coming to the Bowery, although alcohol was implicit in other reasons such as economics, family problems, or feeling comfortable on the Bowery.

Once on the Bowery, or shortly thereafter, the long years of alcohol consumption begin to take their toll. Roughly two in five men report tremulousness or dizziness, one in eight have seizure disorders, one in six have had visual hallucinations, and one in seven were suffering from the aftereffects of a fracture. The physical effects of alcoholism in combination with the squalid environment and close quarters in the flops make these men especially susceptible to various contagion. Consequently, a startling one third of the men were hospitalized at least once in the past year.

Alcohol, like the need for money, generates certain social patterns that facilitate its procurement. Bottle gangs form; some are transient whereas others remain together for long periods. Some men, like Roland, become "runners" and earn money or part of the bottle as their tip. Some men build up close friendships with one or two men with whom they regularly share a bottle. The reader should recall Ed's friend Jeff, whom he describes as being a "bird of the same feather" and with whom he often will share a bottle. The reader might also remember that Miles is part of a group of four men with whom he regularly sleeps and shares food and a bottle.

Alcohol is a commonality that binds skid row men together. It provides men with friends wherever they go. Those men who stop drinking cut themselves off from human companionship and acceptance. And although the prominent role of the tavern in Bowery life has diminished, men entering many cities will head to a bar because it still serves as a place to pick up information, find jobs, make friends, and to eat and drink.

Several authors (Dumont, 1967; Rubington, 1958; Wallace, 1965) have argued that most skid row men are able to regulate their drinking to maintain a constant level with as few dry spells as possible, and further, that they tend to drink with others to gain approval and self-esteem from their peers. These men are thought to contrast with "alcoholics" who prefer to drink alone and achieve maximum intoxication as quickly as they can. Our findings suggest that this picture may be misleading. First, more than two out of five men rated themselves as heavy or spree drinkers. Second, the extensive physical consequences of alcohol consumption found among these men indicate that their level of consumption is not benign.

## IDIOSYNCRATIC FACTORS

A third variable that contributes to the formation of the Bowery man is an idiosyncratic factor. In other words, some additional social, psychological, or physical variable in the person's biography further tipped the scale toward skid row life. For example, a physical impairment occurring in a middle-aged man who had engaged primarily in manual labor can be the final blow that pushes a man from marginal poverty into abject poverty and ultimately skid row. The reader should recall how Miles lost his kitchen job after his heart attack, or how Mr. James became unfit for sea duty after a long bout with tuberculosis.

For other men it may be long-standing psychiatric problems that kept them chronically unemployed and periodically undomiciled. Eventually they arrive at the Men's Shelter or sleep on nearby streets in order to be near the various service agencies and food programs in the skid row area. Several writers (Mayhew, 1851;

Sutherland & Locke, 1936) have postulated that some of these men were extremely temperamental and that this characterological trait made it difficult for them to accept supervision at work or live peacefully with a spouse. Recall how Roland's angst around machinery caused him to flee from any foul-ups. Two decades ago, he took flight from his sister's house after he thought he had damaged her lawn mower and hasn't spoken to her since.

Stressful family events also seemed to have played a role in many of the men's life histories: Deaths of spouse or parents, chaotic marriages, divorces, and separations were commonly reported. Skid row has always been a zone of refuge for those who for a variety of reasons flee from or cannot survive in other parts of the city.

The key point is that all three factors implicated in the pathway to the Bowery—poverty, alcohol, idiosyncracy—frequently occurred together, feeding on each other, and engendering a cycle of despair, deterioration, and descent to skid row. Leach and Wing (1980) arrived at a similar conclusion after studying homeless men in Great Britain: "If neither disability nor social disadvantage is sufficient to cause destitution, the combination is often deadly" (p. 154).

## THE BOWERY MILIEU

Whereas these factors contribute to bringing a man to the Bowery, the final ingredient in the production of the Bowery man is the Bowery itself. As we have already alluded, the Bowery milieu—its social agencies, missions, shelters, second-hand stores, food programs, slop joints, loan sharks, and social formations (e.g., bottle gangs, flophouse interaction, group activities)—compels the newcomer to conform to the structure in order to survive. These structures act to restructure the man's character. While these men often claim to be free and independent, in reality they become increasingly dependent. They begin to adjust to institutionalized settings, rarely break rules, do their assigned tasks, and fit themselves into the routine of the organization. The old timers have developed a compulsion to line-up for activities; and as we previously noted, programmatic changes that reduce the occasions where forming a line is required are usually resisted. Similarly, along with dependency is a sense of powerlessness. These men develop feelings of impotency in the face of dominance and exploitation by social service workers, merchants, employers, hotel managers, and other Bowery men. Many are enmeshed in monthly cycles in which they must turn over part of their checks to loan-sharks; other men feel helpless in the face of frequent muggings; often the mentally and physically weak kowtow to the bullies of the flops and streets. Added to this is a feeling of impermanence, as people come and go out of flophouses, shelters, and hospitals; as men gain and lose money, job, or friends; and as men go off on a binge and then return. This external flux along with the internal demands of one's body creates a "now" orientation. With little money in their pockets, many men are intensely occupied with problems of daily survival, such as getting to the next food line, finding a shower, taking care of an oozing leg ulcer, finding shelter, obtaining a bottle. We are reminded of Orwell's (1933) observation that poverty "annihilates the future" (p. 20).

In addition to the Bowery's effect on personality structure is its effect on personal relationships. Whereas in middle-class elderly populations social ties revolve around emotional bonds, advice giving, informational exchanges, common social activities, and occasionally small material transactions (e.g., lending a few dollars, helping with repairs, etc.), in the skid row culture there is a dramatic shift toward material support (e.g., money, food, medical aid) as a prominent feature of most relationships. Reciprocity becomes crucial, and with such a material focus, failure to reciprocate the aid in the future will assuredly result in termination of the relationship. Although the popular stereotype depicts these men as shunning the material world, ironically, it is material things that dominate these men's lives.

Men also find themselves constantly in groups, whether it's to procure a bottle, to eat their lunch, or sit in the lobby of a hotel. Although some men avoid group ties, five of six men are actively engaged in at least one group comprised of three or more men, and nearly half were engaged in a large grouping comprised of five or more men. This contrasts with community elderly who are commonly engaged in small groups but who are about one third less likely than the Bowery men to be a member of a large group formation. Hence, the Bowery man's more material-oriented, large-group dominated social world contrasts with his age peers in the general population whose social world is more emotionally oriented and comprised of multiple small groups.

Finally, the Bowery itself is a stigmatized section of the city. Although men may regularly leave the Bowery for sojourns into other quarters in order to go to a hospital clinic or a welfare office, their visits are brief. Their personal appearance, their lifestyles, and their time away from mainstream society make them feel unwelcome and uncomfortable away from skid row. As one skid row man told Jacqueline Wiseman (1979):

You see, you don't feel welcome in any other part of town. Landladies don't like to rent you a room because sometimes a guy looks pretty rough. And if he has no luggage—that's all, brother. In those neighborhoods you can't go for a walk without attracting a lot of attention. You are a man without a family, a fifth wheel, suspicious. On top of that, there's no one to be with, nobody you know lives there. Everyone is married, so they don't have no time for a lot of talking. If you're not working they wonder why not. If they find out you drink, they ask you to leave. Why bother in the first place? (p. 23)

Thus, despite the men's assertions that they would like to leave the Bowery, the transformations in personality and social interaction that have been wrought by their life on skid row make escape unlikely. We found several men who were given the opportunity to leave but recoiled. It was not easy to accept the fact that they were shackled to the Bowery; often a rationalization for their immobility had to be devised. For example, Miles balked at such an opportunity to leave skid row. He had received a message that his grandmother had died, and she had bequeathed her Alabama home to him. By the time he arrived to claim the home a cousin was living in the house with her children:

She started cryin' the blues. "Oh you come to take the house and where am I to go?" I said, "Honey, take the house 'cause I'm goin' back to New York and don't want to be bothered with it. I can go back to the city and do the same thing I was doin' before."

However, about a year later Miles went down to Alabama again:

Next time I went down there she wasn't there; someone else had the house. I don't know what happened to it. Anyway, I'm not worried about this house. It would have been a long hassle 'cause I had lost my grandmother's Social Security number that I need in order to claim the house.

# CHAPTER TEN

# Strategies for Intervention

## SHORT-TERM APPROACHES

The aim of this chapter will be to look at some of the more immediate causes of difficulty for these men and to suggest strategies for alleviating them. Our empirical analyses identified ten variables that put individuals more at risk for poor physical or mental health or for having trouble meeting their needs (see Table 10-1). These data provide empirical support for many of the interventions that have been advocated in the past but which have sometimes been dismissed because of lack of "hard data." For two variables—age and education—there is obviously no way to alter these characteristics. Service workers, however, should be made aware that the "younger old men" and, in the case of physical health, the poorly educated, are more at risk for developing problems. Age, which was a fairly potent variable, creates a paradoxical problem in which more intensive efforts must be concentrated on not the very old but rather on the younger elders. Frequently, these men were still drinking heavily, and they are at an age when their bodies can less easily endure the ravages of alcohol, homelessness, poor nutrition, and the like. As we suggested above, the oldest men on the Bowery are survivors—mentally and physically—and they have accommodated relatively well to their environment.

There were eight variables that placed men at risk but were potentially alterable, at least to some extent. The potent tetrad of poor physical health, unfulfilled needs, stressful life events, and depression should be a prime focus for intervention. First, there are particular subgroups—men living on the street, alcohol abusers, and

## Table 10-1. Potential Intervention Points[a]

| At-risk category | At-risk but potentially alterable | Outcome variable |
|---|---|---|
| Age | Depression<br>Physical Health<br>Stressful Life Events<br>Alcohol Abuse<br>Living on Street (weak)<br>Institutional/Agency Contacts (weak) | Need Fulfillment |
| Age<br>Education (weak) | Depression<br>Stressful Life Events<br>Need Fulfillment<br>Institutional/Agency Contacts (weak)<br>Alcohol Abuse (weak) | Physical Health |
| Age | Physical Health<br>Need Fulfillment<br>Stressful Life Events<br>Network Structure<br>Living on Street<br>Alcohol Abuse<br>Proclivity to Use Others (weak)<br>Organic Mental Symptoms | Depression |

[a]Based on significant variables in correlation and regression analyses. (Variables significant at the .05 level are listed as "weak.")

the "young old"—who are more vulnerable to this tetrad (see Appendix 1, Table 1). If any further justification is needed for providing housing to the homeless, our data cogently support the notion that such housing could reduce the physical and mental disturbances found among the undomiciled men. We found that even the marginal housing provided by Bowery flops and tenements gave the men sufficient stability to help reduce life stressors, diminish alcohol consumption, and increase informal and formal social networks. Of course, it is possible that inability to fulfill needs, stressful events, and depression are causes of rather than consequences of living on the street; however, the fact that virtually all street men spend some time in flops, the similarities in biographies between street and nonstreet men, and the lack of any significant differences between the two groups with respect to levels of psychosis tend to refute this argument. Indeed, there are some men for whom this alternative hypothesis clearly does obtain (to some extent for all street men these factors at times contribute to keeping them on the streets), but in general we do not believe it is the overriding causal factor. Hence, housing for the homeless can be justified not only on moral and humanitarian grounds but on economic grounds as well: The cost of health care and social services incurred because of the physical, psychiatric, and social morbidity associated with street living could be reduced by providing men with adequate, permanent shelter.

Given the high rates of physical and psychiatric illness, emphasis should be placed on making high-quality medical and psychiatric care available to these men. Currently, many men delay treatment and then use the crowded clinics of large public and voluntary hospitals. Many of these facilities are blatantly hostile toward skid rowers, and the men often fail to return for follow-up visits or to comply with instructions. Institutional/agency contacts and need fulfillment can be enhanced by strengthening and broadening the services provided by existing skid row agencies and creating new ones where gaps in services exist. This becomes especially important as traditional skid row institutions (e.g., slop joints, used clothing stores, bathhouses) disappear. Agencies must be available not only to fill the gap, but to make services available in a way that will not "crowd-out" seniors because of fear of younger men or bureaucratic impediments.

Several variables that we examined were only weakly or not significantly related to any of the three outcome variables, but nonetheless, these must be viewed as objects for intervention. Our Alcohol Scale was such a variable; however, our case histories as well as the physical symptoms that we uncovered clearly implicated alcohol as a major component in these men's physical and mental decline. We suggested above that the Alcohol Scale, which is based on age of onset of heavy drinking and current quantity and frequency of consumption, may not be a very meaningful index for a population in which most men drink heavily for substantial periods of their lives. In other words, although they may not be drinking heavily now (either temporarily or even permanently), the effects of long years of abuse have already left behind physical and psychological scars.

Based on the levels of alcohol consumption that we identified, alcohol treatment programs should be included as part of any service program for older skid row men. Nevertheless, our findings suggest that service programs might begin to divide their alcohol treatment into two subgroups: those men who are still-active moderate, heavy, or spree drinkers and those men who were formerly in those categories but who have now quit or dramatically curtailed their drinking due to health, economic, or psychological factors. This second group suffers from the physical and emotional consequences of alcoholism but does not require the same kind of counseling and treatment interventions as the active drinkers. In dealing with active drinkers, the primary goal before any significant physical, psychiatric, or social interventions can be made must be to curtail (usually eliminate) the alcohol ingestion.

Second, our data indicate that street men were heavier drinkers than nonstreet men. Although the street men are more difficult to engage, they may be a more important group to target with respect to alcohol treatment. Of course, given the role that alcohol plays in the social interaction of street men in particular, this can become a frustrating exercise. Only in combination with a more global intervention to get these men off the street and into suitable housing can the problem of alcoholism be addressed realistically.

Being in the Psychosis/Psychiatric Hospitalization (PPH) Group had no significant associations with the three outcome variables. In part this may have reflected the construction of the variable, which required either a history of psychiatric hospitalization or actively severe psychotic symptoms for inclusion. Consequently, some persons were included who were not severely psychotic at the time of the study. Also, a relatively small percentage of persons were excluded from the interview because they were too flagrantly psychotic or disorganized to answer the questions. Nonetheless, our data suggest that this group is no more at risk than the rest of the older Bowery men. In other words, all the men have substantial health and psychosocial problems; the PPH Group has approximately the same level of problems. Being on the Bowery versus other urban areas may afford some advantage to the men in the PPH Group since there is a higher density of service agencies in the area. Consequently, at least some of their basic needs can be addressed, there may be opportunities to receive treatment, and the nonsheltered men can sometimes be placed into residential programs whose qualities are a cut above the flops and public shelters. One major problem will be to overcome the men's resistance to psychiatric treatment. Even in programs where psychiatric services are available, workers have had considerable difficulty engaging these men in treatment. Despite the widespread prevalence of severe mental illness, this resistance accounted for part of the reason why only 3% of the men were receiving psychiatric medication.

There are several variables that warrant further discussion because of their failure to figure in any of the causal models. The social network variable—Interactional Factors—was not associated directly or indirectly with any of the three outcome variables. The Interactional Factor was especially surprising since it is comprised of network dimensions related to both material and emotional support (see Appendix 2). Apparently despite the substantial material exchanges that go on between men as well as the modest level of intimacy that was present, these factors were not sufficiently powerful to affect significantly either physical health, emotional well-being, or their ability to fulfill needs. Perhaps these exchanges were neither quantitatively adequate nor sufficiently reliable to influence the outcome variables. Even the Network Structural Factor, which was related to depression, may have been an effect rather than a cause of depression. That is, the smaller nonclustered networks that were associated with depression may have been the result of depressive withdrawal rather than an antecedent of future depression. Thus, the more regularly reliable sources such as agencies, stores, clinics, and the like (i.e., "Institutional Agency" Contacts) proved to be considerably more important in that they were significantly associated with two of three outcome variables.

As an outgrowth of the research findings presented here, our project administrator, Eric Roth, began to envision an expansion of the senior lunch program at the Bowery Residents' Committee as a vehicle for reaching more homeless and flophouse men. At that time (1984), Eric was serving as coordinator of the lunch program which served approximately one hundred meals per day. Impetus for the expanded program was further provided by reports that seniors were not uncommonly "crowded out" of existing service and shelter programs because of insensitive shelter staff or fear of muggings and/or being institutionalized. Moreover, as we noted earlier, it is rare to find a senior center which serves the homeless. A report by the Aging Health Policy Center (1985) could identify no program that specifically targeted the elderly homeless mentally ill. The 1984 Coalition for the Homeless/Gray Panthers report recommended that "existing drop-in centers be strengthened . . . and that additional drop-in centers of this type be supported in Manhattan, where they are already effectively reaching the homeless elderly" (p. 21).

Therefore, a new program was conceived, Project Rescue, which was to build on current contact with seniors through an existing nutrition program and expand to cover a full range of the needs of homeless seniors. The overall aim of Project Rescue was the following:

1. To operate a Respite Center for Bowery seniors as a place where they can find refuge, acceptance, social interaction, and welcome.
2. To meet the nutritional needs of Bowery seniors by providing balanced meals.
3. To improve the health of Bowery seniors by linking them with professional health care.
4. To provide psychiatric and alcohol counseling services to the Bowery seniors.
5. To assure shelter and housing for Bowery seniors by providing advocacy, referral and placement services to those who are homeless or in danger of becoming homeless.
6. To help stabilize the finances of Bowery seniors by assisting in securing and maintaining government benefits for which they qualify.
7. To avoid isolation and abandonment of Bowery seniors through outreach to people on the streets and the homebound.
8. To provide opportunities for work and vocational rehabilitation.
9. To serve as a training, educational, and resource center for other agencies servicing homeless persons.

To meet these objectives, the following services were developed:

*Respite.* A specific area at the BRC on Chrystie Street, one block from the Bowery, had been previously set aside for the use of the seniors. It is open 9 AM to 5 PM (2 PM Saturdays), six days per week. It includes a large cafeteria and activities area as well as a smaller area for TV viewing and peace and quiet. There are shower facilities for men. Seniors are free to come and go as they please during the day. The area is reserved for their use. This became the base of operations for Project Rescue.

*Nutrition.* With the support of the New York City Department for the Aging and donated foodstuffs, the BRC provides breakfast, lunch, and a snack for 115 seniors six days a week, Monday through Saturday. The meals are nutritionally balanced and hot.

*Physical Health.* The BRC has a medical clinic on site operated in conjunction with the Robert Wood Johnson Healthcare for the Homeless Project. A four-member health team is available three mornings a week. The seniors, however, do not take advantage of this service without encouragement and follow-up, and Project Rescue provides this. Individual work with seniors helps them overcome their fears of receiving medical attention and helps them follow medical instructions with regard to medication and follow-up visits. Without this type of assistance, seniors remain isolated from health services.

*Psychiatric and Alcohol Services.* The BRC has a part-time psychiatrist available for seniors. Here again, the mentally ill elderly need encouragement and support before seeing the psychiatrist. There is also a Community Support System program linked to the BRC that can assist the mentally ill seniors with case management issues such as obtaining entitlements, specialized housing, long-term psychiatric care, and the like.

The BRC has a very large alcohol rehabilitation program with many counselors, group meetings, and an AA program. Seniors are encouraged to participate in these programs.

*Housing.* Project Rescue staff assist homeless seniors and seniors facing eviction in securing or maintaining shelter and housing. The BRC works with Mobilization for Youth Legal Services so seniors have access to the legal help they need. Project Domicile, an effort of the Partnership for the Homeless with which the BRC works, makes available city-owned apartments to the homeless. Project staff work with seniors to avoid the loss of present housing and to find alternative housing. Efforts are underway to secure several apartments that can temporarily house homeless seniors so that they can attain medical, psychiatric, and social stability and while also finding suitable permanent housing.

*Finances and Vocational Assistance.* Most Bowery seniors are eligible for government benefits on which to live. However, not all receive the benefits to which they are entitled, and others are cut off due to unwarranted bureaucratic actions. Project Rescue staff assist seniors to obtain and retain government entitlements by helping them in the paperwork and advocacy generally needed in the application and appeals processes. Counselors assist those able-bodied individuals for jobs or vocational training. Various prevocational activities, such as volunteer work, are available at the BRC.

*Training/Resource Center.* The workers from Project Rescue make available to other agencies their expertise in dealing with homeless seniors. They provide training programs and lectures, are available for telephone consultation, and accept referrals from other agencies.

Utilizing a schema of services developed by Baxter and Hopper (1984) we can summarize in six broad categories (listed in Table 10-2) the types of services provided by Project Rescue.

Although Project Rescue is still in its infancy, the implementation and early history of the program deserve some elaboration because the project has potential for replication in other settings. (Indeed, a recent report by Joseph Doolin [1986] indicated that a service program for homeless elders in Boston had been similarly built around a senior lunch program.) Project Rescue began operation in early 1985. Initial project activities were of two types: (1) putting the programmatic elements of the project in place; and (2) expanding previous services and introducing special project services.

Project phase-in began with the appointment of the Project Rescue Director (Eric Roth), who had been the Director of Senior Nutrition Program. The director then set about the tasks of continued fund raising, development of the staffing pattern and job descriptions, staff recruitment and hiring, and development of a data collection and record keeping system for the project. At the same time current nutrition services were expanded from one to three meals and from five to six days a week.

The next position filled was that of full-time caseworker which effectuated a major advance in project implementation. The Respite Center was established, thus providing for the seniors a warm, safe space. In addition to being at the Center, seniors could obtain showers and receive a change of clothing. At the same time the first specialized project services were offered: entitlement counseling, general social service referrals, and escort.

During the second half of the year, three part-time outreach workers were recruited, and additional senior volunteers were recruited from among the project's participants. Initial project activities were expanded, and new activities were added to the project, particularly outreach to seniors in the streets and to homebound seniors. Outreach workers worked together with senior volunteers to find elderly in the Bowery area who could benefit from Project Rescue. Referral work became more specialized by focusing on the

## Table 10-2. Types of Services Provided by Project Rescue to Clients

1. *Concrete*
   Showering
   Delousing
   Transportation to home
   Money (when welfare check is late)
   Loans (when food stamps are late)
   Money (daily allowance until client
     is put on welfare)
   Grooming articles
   Clothing (e.g., thermal underwear,
     shoes, coat, sweater, socks)
   Blankets
   Plastic bags

   Food
   Meals
   Cigarettes
   Items for housing (clock, radio,
     hotplate)
   Carfare
   Magazines, newspapers
   Miscellaneous: provision of mailing
     address; photocopying of legal
     papers; Christmas gifts or birthday
     parties.

2. *Clinical*
   Engagement and trust-building
     (talking with clients, etc.)
   Crisis intervention
   Supportive interpretation of
     delusions
   Social-medical counseling (before
     operation, after radiation
     treatment, etc.)
   Psychological counseling
   Family counseling
   Orientation to alcoholism programs

   Counseling after victimization
     (mugging, etc.)
   Contacting "network" members
     (sister, cousin, former room-
     mate, friend, etc.)
   Job counseling
   Counseling on finding housing
   Physician's services
   Dental services
   Psychiatric services

3. *Case Management*
   Making appointments
   Helping client keep appointments
   Escorting to new program
   Escorting to appointments
   Discussion, liaison with other
     community support system
     program workers
   Negotiating with hotel manager
     about handling of funds
   Persuading private shelter to keep
     client until public assistance
     check arrives

   Negotiating with superintendent
     (e.g., to fix broken locks, replace
     broken windows, fumigate)
   Representing client in welfare
     hearing
   Arranging transfer of client to
     hospital closer to his home
   Getting attention for client in
     emergency room
   Advocating for client with doctor
   Persuading shelter to shower and
     delouse client

4. *Socialization*
   Opening savings account for client
   Showing client how to do banking
   Teaching management and
     budgeting of funds
   Supervising funds
   Taking client to thrift shops
   Helping client move into room
   Supervising maintenance of client's
     room
   Counseling client about living
     conditions

   Explaining importance of
     showering and/or delousing
   Helping client keep calendar (time
     orientation)
   Preparing client for interview (job,
     housing intake, etc.)
   Preparing client for court case
   Social outings

*(continued)*

Table 10-2. (Continued)

5. *Housing*

| | |
|---|---|
| Providing room | Discussing housing possibilities |
| Looking for alternative housing | (adult home, SRO, etc.) |
| (before eviction, hotel closing, | Explaining rent, dispossession |
| etc.) | notice, etc. |
| Explaining tenants' rights | |

6. *Public Assistance/Economic Assistance*

| | |
|---|---|
| Filling out forms | Helping client prepare for fair |
| Writing letters of referral, | hearing |
| introduction | Accompanying client to welfare |
| Re-opening closed cases | office and advocating for client |
| Tracking down lost checks | Interpreting regulations |
| Advising about lost checks | |

health and housing needs of the seniors. Respite Center activities were expanded to include art therapy and recreational activities. The first trips out of the area were on the Day Line cruise around New York and to baseball games and the zoo. A clothing room was formally opened to meet the seniors' growing need for clothes.

Two events exemplify the type of work that Project Rescue is doing and underscore the needs and exigencies faced by the seniors. First, five of the men served by the project reside in the Pioneer Hotel. During a "remodeling," the hotel suffered a partial collapse. The owners seemed to desire a closing of the hotel in preparation for its demolition, an illegal activity which is fueled by gentrification. Project staff worked with these men to provide emergency housing, counseling, and advocacy in this crisis. The men were able to join with other advocacy groups, and, with legal help, the hotel owners were forced to make repairs and reopen. While this was a Project Rescue success, it underlined the scarcity of housing resources, since long-term housing alternatives for these men were impossible to locate.

Second, one of the project's senior volunteers brought to the attention of an outreach worker the situation of "Benny," a 64-year-old man living in the White House Hotel. Benny looked sick and was having difficulty walking, so he could not come out of his room. The senior volunteer signed him up for a homebound meal and agreed to bring a worker over to meet Benny. After several visits the worker convinced Benny to come to Project Rescue to see a doctor. A medical exam discovered bronchitis. Medication was obtained and the volunteer and worker made sure Benny took it regularly. After several months Benny was back on his feet and started to come regularly to the Respite Center on his own.

A number of noteworthy events also occurred in that first year. The opening of the project was reported on in various newspapers. A special grant was received from Chemical Bank to pay for weekend trips and recreation. A grant of $6,000 was received from the state Supplemental Nutrition Assistance Program to bolster the food program. More recently, the program has received additional funding from the National Institute of Mental Health.

First year results reflect accomplishments based on the project's partial implementation in the first six months and full implementation in the second six months. Currently, the project director, a supervising case worker, and three outreach workers are joined by a dozen regular senior volunteers and a volunteer-donations coordinator to staff the project. Each day 175 seniors are involved in project activities. Table 10-3 presents an accounting of the project's work with the seniors.

The results of the first year include some that were anticipated and some that were not. The meals program expanded, the Respite Center opened, and new activities were implemented. Referring to the project's purposes described in the original proposal, we find the areas of greatest effort focused on outreach, health, and finances. The most problematic area was housing.

Table 10-3. Project Rescue: First Year Client Contacts

| | | |
|---|---|---|
| Breakfasts served | 8,011 | |
| "4 PM Snacks" | 4,508 | |
| Showers | 537 | individuals |
| Outreach contacts | 119 | " |
| Health referrals | 36 | " |
| Social service referrals | 14 | " |
| Escort services | | |
|   Health | 6 | " |
|   Entitlements | 2 | " |
|   Housing | 5 | " |
| Entitlements advocacy | 27 | " |
| Housing and shelter | 14 | " |
| Clothing | 89 | " |
| Counseling and psychiatric assessments | 37 | " |
| Miscellaneous | 51 | " |

Outreach contacted 119 individuals, a number greater than had been anticipated, but which accentuates the need among the seniors. This had a significant impact on the homebound meals program. During our outreach forays we repeatedly discovered elderly persons who were unable to leave their rooms, who would eat only if they could coax someone "for a charge" to bring them back some food. Project Rescue provided the data to spur the City to expand the homebound meal program from 5 in 1983–1984 to 43 in 1986. This is the type of multiplier that Project Rescue is expected to generate.

Health referrals and escort were provided in 36 instances, a substantial number, but these also require greater attention. Clients remain resistant to health and nutritional counseling, and a significant number of sick clients refuse medical help. Continued and consistent work with them is needed to elicit their trust.

Work in the area of finances revolved around government entitlement advocacy. Twenty-seven individuals were assisted, some to apply for benefits and others to retain them. This activity was uniquely tied to efforts to obtain or retain housing, since without government entitlements these seniors have no way to pay rent.

Housing remained the most problematic service area precisely because finding alternatives remains so difficult amid the City's housing crisis. While the program continued to work with Project Domicile of the Partnership for the Homeless, efforts were begun to look for ways to sponsor alternative housing. Potential funding has been identified for a residential project, and work on locating a site continues.

In its first pilot year Project Rescue has infused a new energy and direction into the Senior Services program. A complex hierarchy of services to the homeless and homebound elderly is now offered. A senior is brought into the Center with the promise of food or clothing. The senior is then encouraged to shower and to apply for entitled benefits. A visit to the doctor and follow-up visits, if necessary, are arranged. The staff then works to improve his housing situation. The approach is to offer the basic services first, and then to encourage clients to work with staff toward higher level services.

With the aid of governmental and philanthropic grants, Project Rescue is now moving toward a second level of service. Plans for the second level include the establishment of several group apartments that will be used as transitional residences to stabilize the seniors medically or psychiatrically and to prepare them for placement in permanent housing. The notion is to tap into the growing diversity of model housing programs being established for the homeless.

A second feature of the expanded program will be to reach out to elderly women. Homeless women are an especially high-risk group according to several reports that indicated higher rates of psychiatric illness than among men (Aging Health Policy Center, 1985; Bassuk, Rubin, & Lauriat, 1984). At present, only four or five women regularly use Project Rescue services. This largely reflects the all-male Bowery environment. However, there are many homeless women living in the streets and neighborhoods contiguous to the Bowery (Barrow & Lovell, 1987). A third new element to the program will be a mobile van that will enable the staff to move more easily outside the perimeter of the Bowery to bring food, clothing, or medical aid to homeless individuals, as well as to bring homeless persons to the center for service. With the use of the van, Project Rescue will be able to seek out homeless seniors in the area of Manhattan below 42nd Street.

In developing programs such as Project Rescue for elderly homeless persons we have found the hierarchical schema presented below to be conceptually useful. Several programs in this country and in the United Kingdom have adapted such an approach (Fischer & Breakey, 1986; Goleman, Nov. 4, 1986; Goleman, Nov. 11, 1986; Leach, 1979). The first service provided by the program is *contact*. The program should aim to attract as many persons as possible. Informality and permissiveness are essential. There should be a "no questions asked," accepting environment. Hours should be flexible and restrictions on drinking should be minimum (e.g., no overt drinking on premises, no verbally or physically abusive behavior). Too much red tape will result in the exclusion of men who might otherwise use the program. Project Rescue used the meal and respite components as the initial hook. One imaginative tack used to attract men was to distribute handbills to older men on the streets with a coupon that read, "This entitles you to one free meal at the Bowery Residents' Committee." Of course, they were entitled to free meals anyway, but the coupon was the "carrot" that drew some of the more resistant men into the program.

The second level of service should be to provide the homeless person with *basic life necessities* such as shelter, food, clothing, and toileting. Many men do not express a desire for help and avoid contact with the program staff. Such attempts by staff to engage the persons should be made on a regular basis. Considerable patience is required, and the pace of the relationship should not be forced. As John Leach (1979) observes, "Changes in [the men's] attitudes are unlikely to occur quickly" (p. 100). Project Reachout, a Manhattan based program regularly visits 479 street people each month. After many visits, about 25% of the street clients finally accept an invitation to come to the project office where they receive anything from a cup of coffee to a room, financial aid, or psychiatric care (Goleman, 1986a).

The final level of service is to provide the homeless person with *specialist help* such as medical and psychiatric treatment, vocational counseling, social work assistance, or alcohol or drug treatment. Such services usually begin once the person becomes engaged within the program and can be expected to attend on a regular basis since these services often necessitate continuing treatment and follow-up. Daniel Goleman (November 11, 1986), a writer for the New York Times, chronicled the laborious task of moving a homeless man living amidst a pile of garbage from his initial encounters with an outreach program through his eventual engagement and subsequent placement in a community residence—a multi-agency, multi-disciplinary effort that took nearly 12 months. Despite such bureaucratic delays, well-run programs can make a very significant impact on the quality of life of the homeless. A recent evaluation (Barrow, Hellman, Plapinger, Lovell and Struening, 1986) in New York City of several community support programs for the mentally ill homeless showed that once persons were incorporated into the programs a majority eventually entered long-term housing. The earlier the time of intervention since becoming homeless, the greater the probability of becoming domiciled. Moreover, it was found that people who received entitlements, and thus gained a stable form of income were the most likely to be housed.

What about self-help? With back-up support can older Bowery men help themselves? As we have already described, a great deal of material support and advice-giving already goes on among these men. Is it possible, however, to stimulate the social networks to expand to provide additional services? In another study we attempted to address this issue for persons living in an SRO hotel in Midtown Manhattan. For 15 months an experimental service program using two social workers operated within the hotel. The social workers attempted to treat all problems brought to them by tenants through a network intervention rather than through direct service. In other words, if someone came requesting assistance in going to a clinic, the social worker would review the person's social network and assist that person in obtaining help from someone in the network. If no one was available in that person's network, informal helpers in the hotel would be identified who could help with the problem.

The results of this intervention were mixed. On the negative side only about one sixth of the 519 presenting problems could be successfully addressed through such an intervention. On the positive side, one third of the 156 persons who approached the social workers had at least one successful network intervention. Interventions for problems that involved interaction more common to the folkways of the SRO hotels had better outcomes, such as information exchange, food exchange, or small-money lending (Cohen & Adler, 1986).

The difficulties that we encountered in the SRO project are probably transferable to skid row populations. First, many of the problems presented to the project staff came after the individual had already exhausted his or her social network. Hence, a network approach to the problem was not always well accepted. Second, many problems were perceived as emergencies and were therefore less amenable to a slower network intervention approach. A third problem entailed a "perceived isolation" on the part of the client. Although most persons had fairly extensive informal support systems, they were seemingly unaware of the supportive nature of their social ties. As one staff member observed, "It all added up for the worker to be, in a sense, searching for something others couldn't perceive." A fourth problem involved "trust." Many clients were reticent about discussing their personal networks in detail with project staff. In some instances they remained guarded because they believed the workers were connected with governmental programs. Conversely, a final problem was that some needs (e.g., money) were thought to be only appropriate to discuss with a social worker or professional and that they were too private to be handled by the client's friends or associates.

This earlier study suggests that although network interventions could at times be successful, it is certainly not for every problem or everybody. Problems that are regularly handled by the social networks and those that can be handled in a more casual fashion have a much better chance for success.

A somewhat related approach has been to work with some of the natural helpers in the neighborhood. For instance, Matthew Dumont (1967) provided informal supervision to a Bowery bartender who served as "psychologist" to many of the men. He also gave the bartender some vitamins to hand out to his customers. Similar interventions have been carried out in SRO hotels with the maids, desk clerks, and management who provide lodgers with material and emotional support (Cohen & Sokolovsky, 1979).

Some of the men have proposed their own solutions to the problem of homelessness. For example, Miles posited this remedy:

What if we could get together and write to the Mayor's office when they have the next auction. We would buy a deteriorated house from the city and renovate it. They have to get us off the street. All these broken down buildings could be renovated 'cause I know a person that's a carpenter; we could get a carpenter, electrician, and a plumber that's what we need. If a man can drive a nail he's a carpenter. He can drive a nail from this beam to that beam, then he knows how to fix up a wall. When it comes to furnishing you can go to the Salvation Army and get a whole living room section of furniture for forty dollars. I would spend my money that way instead of runnin' around tryin' to survive. I'd much rather have the responsibility of a home than to have to sleep on a park bench 'cause it's cold. A lot of those fellas out there in the park have been in Viet Nam. I don't pry in their personal life, they volunteer to tell me things. They are very unhappy and angry. All they were given was a parade out there a couple of years ago. On the Lower East Side they have squatters. Those people put up tents. They eat and sleep there, and that's their home. Mayor Koch believes you lock these people up.

Perhaps there are a few older homeless men who could realize Miles's dream. Maybe there are more among the younger homeless men. But, as we suggested in the previous chapter, for the older men (and increasingly for the younger men) the years on skid row create a sense of dependency, helplessness, powerlessness, and despair. One should recall Orwell's observation that the evil of poverty is not that it makes a man suffer but that "it rots him physically and spiritually."

Self-help approaches may hold some promise for alleviating a limited number of problems faced by these men. However, it is imperative to eschew pronouncements that tout the use of indigenous support systems as a panacea for service delivery problems. As the Task Force on Community Support Systems (1978) warned, we must guard against using natural supports to "justify public policies which could withhold from various communities and individuals the resources they need to obtain professional and formal institutionalized services" (p. 144).

Can the homeless organize themselves to demand services? During the early part of the century the Wobblies and the International Brotherhood Welfare Association made serious attempts to organize the nation's hobos, tramps, and day laborers. The Wobblies boasted a membership of 100,000 men during their heyday. Reminiscent of these earlier movements has been the rise of the Union of the Homeless (Hope & Young, 1986). Founded in 1985 in Philadelphia, the union, which requires unemployed workers to pay dues of one dollar a month and those with a job to pay five dollars, attracted 4500 members within a few months. The founder and first president of the union is Chris Sprowal, a middle-class professional who was himself on the streets during the recession of the early 1980s. Sprowal's dream is to create "a broad movement that would include all kinds of groups working to change the priorities of this crazy government." He adds, "We can't say we're successful 'till all Americans realize that food and shelter are entitlements. If they don't realize this, these problems will simply grow while we continue looking at symptoms and dabbing away at them with Band Aids" (cited in Hope & Young, 1986, p. 247).

The Union of the Homeless has taken an aggressive position and has staged sit-ins at the Transportation Authority to ask for reduced fares for the homeless and poor, organized a sit-in at Temple University to demand that it convert a vacant armory it owned into a shelter for the homeless, and pressured the University of Pennsylvania to provide free health care to 50 union members. The union has begun establishing chapters in other cities. Chris Sprowal's well-received visits to several shelters in New York City indicate that homeless persons are searching for ways to overcome their powerlessness and diminished self-esteem.

Advocates for the homeless have a guarded optimism about the potential for success of the new union movement. It should be recalled that even at its acme the Wobblies did not reach many hoboes (Wallace, 1965, p. 80), and Samuel Wallace has maintained that historically the homeless man is "almost by definition unorga-nizable" (p. 82). Despite the historical failures to successfully orga-nize the homeless, the new union movement at least offers the possibilities of empowerment.

## LONG-TERM APPROACHES

As "benchworkers" on the Bowery it is easier for us to pinpoint the more immediate problems for these men than to suggest global solutions. Many of the immediate solutions, however, tend to be palliative and fail to address more fundamental forces. In looking at the broader sociohistorical forces that shape these men, complexities abound with respect to etiology and solution. Nonetheless, in any study of homelessness it is critical to address at least briefly these systemic forces. As we described in Chapter 3, governments have historically attempted to shift the blame for homelessness from society onto the individual. Indeed, we are currently seeing such a swing in public discourse from talking about the problem of "home-lessness" to talking about the problem of "the homeless." In this subtle shift we can see that the latter term implies that the problem is an individual's whereas the former suggests a more global focus (Hopper, 1987). Our aim, therefore, will be to present in schematic form some of the more egregious causal factors that have emerged from our research and to propose some general steps toward solving these problems.

### Poverty

Once every few years a man dies in a Bowery flop with thousands of dollars in the bank. The newspapers get hold of it and as one hotel manager put it, "Right away, everyone thinks these guys got mil-lions." The manager adds,

Recently a reporter came down to write a story about the Bowery. In the article I guarantee it, all the clichés—defrocked priest, kicked-out lawyer, guys with millions. It never changes, they'll come down here and ask all the questions they want, but it'll have all the clichés. No matter how much you tell 'em they are still gonna write it that way.

Poverty is far and away the major cause of a man's descent to skid row and, in part, his inability to leave it. The size and composition of the homeless have changed dramatically over recorded history—it has included actors, priests, scholars, families as well as the more traditional categories of unemployed men, the aged, and the mentally and physically impaired. And even these "traditional" categories have appeared only with the full development of capitalism. The aged and handicapped were afforded protection in peasant and feudal societies, and an "able-bodied unemployed" was an oxymoron in these early societies. Our data, as well as numerous investigations over the past 50 years, have repeatedly found that homeless men are spawned from poor and marginally poor families. As is well established by now, children of poverty do not easily escape. In adulthood, the men enter unskilled and semi-skilled jobs. The burdens of family, borderline poverty, periodic unemployment, and the use of alcohol created a highly unstable life pattern for these men. The break-up of a marriage, the loss of a job, or a physical injury were common precipitating events that preceded arrival to skid row.

We have described the effects of living in the squalor of skid row. The effects on the body and soul further serve to entrench these men there. Possibilities for employment become even more limited in our society as these men become physically frailer and older. Most of these men are considered "old" by 50. Their lives mirror those of persons in third world countries who prematurely age as they are caught in the inescapable cycle of poverty.

Unless serious attempts are made to relieve poverty and to aid those who are no longer competitive in the workplace, the principal ingredient for generating homelessness will remain operative. During President Johnson's "War on Poverty" the number of Americans below the poverty line dropped from 36 million to 24 million, or from 19% to 12.5% of the population. Contrary to President Reagan's quip that "poverty won the war" in the 1960s, the evidence indicates that a substantial impact had been made to seriously alter those factors that contribute to the poverty cycle (Takaki, 1986). Between 1969 and 1980, however, the number of poor people rose from 24 million to 29 million; an increase of 5 million over 11 years. The number of Americans below the poverty line remained at 12.9% in 1980. However, during the period 1980 to 1983, (corresponding to the beginning of the Reagan presidency), the number of poor Americans increased by 6 million in three years and the poverty rate soared to

15% (Takaki, 1986). During this period, one American fell below the poverty line every 12 seconds (Perales, 1983). Furthermore, a startling one in four children in this country now lives below the poverty line (U.S. Bureau of the Census, 1984), and the percentage of broken or female-headed households rose more than 100% between 1970 and 1983, further destabilizing these youngster's existence.

Economic safety nets and entitlements necessary to provide some security and stability for these individuals have diminished over the last decade. For example, in 1983, the average monthly welfare payment for a family of three was only $312.84 compared with $581 a month earned from a minimum wage job (Perales, 1983). It should be noted that both these amounts were below the official poverty level for that family which was $7,693. The ability to secure such entitlements has also been under assault. For example, the Reagan Administration has waged a battle to make it more difficult for persons to obtain Social Security disability. This has been a devastating blow to the mentally and physically impaired, and the aged, all of whom are especially over-represented on skid row. Finally, the availability of low-cost housing and federal funds for building such housing has been cut drastically during the Reagan years.

Beatrice Webb once pointed out that preventing poverty was immeasurably more humane, more practical, and more economic than trying to relieve it (cited in Leach & Wing, 1980). Perhaps the saddest commentary on our times is that until recently a concatenation of factors and events preceded a person's descent into homelessness, today children are born into it (see Chavkin *et al.*, 1987).

## Alcohol

We have emphasized the role that alcohol has played in destabilizing these men's lives prior to coming to the Bowery and the subsequent effects on physical and mental health after their arrival. This is not to deny that alcohol is a common bonding agent and thus indirectly serves to promote material and emotional support between the men. Nevertheless, its deleterious effects, particularly those contributing to a man's arrival on skid row, must be addressed. Serious efforts must be made to curtail the level of alcohol consumption in this country. Cross-national studies have demonstrated that rates of alcoholism in a country correlate with the production of alcohol. Consequently, alcoholism is very high in France and rates have risen dramatically in the United States as production has increased. Research on alcohol beverage advertising indicates that exposure to such advertising is second to peer pressure as a correlate of teenage alcohol consumption, especially beer and wine (Secretary of Health and Human Services, 1987). Similarly, it is thought that favorable portrayals of alcohol consumption in the entertainment media can induce increased consumption of alcohol. Moreover, there is evidence that measures to increase the price of alcohol such as through taxation, can reduce consumption. The effect of educational programs on alcohol consumption is inconclusive, although several reports from college campuses are encouraging (Secretary of Health and Human Services, 1987).

We are not so naive to believe that reducing alcohol consumption alone will have a dramatic impact on reducing homelessness. However, just as alcoholism interweaves and potentiates the other causal factors, curtailing alcoholism in combination with efforts to reduce poverty and family instability can indeed produce change.

## Support Services

A final broad goal must be to expand support services to vulnerable persons in our society. This means that family counseling as well as economic support must be readily available for families in crisis. It means that deinstitutionalized patients must not be left to flounder while attempting to negotiate the welfare system, the psychiatric service system, or the job and housing market. Job counseling, vocational training, and employment opportunities must be expanded for the physically and psychiatrically impaired, the middle aged, and the "young old." Perhaps government incentives could be given to companies to hire such individuals. Last, safe, clean inexpensive housing must be given highest priority. Any visitor to New York City is immediately struck by the irony of homeless persons sleeping under the lee of one of the scores of luxury high-rises that have mushroomed in the past few years. Nearly all these high-rises have been subsidized by the public through special tax incentives. On the other hand, as the Senate was poised to approve its first major housing bill in seven years, President Reagan threatened to veto it because it was a "budget buster" (Rasky, 1987).

Unless an intensive effort is made to address the three elements outlined in this chapter it is likely that today's young homeless will come to resemble the older men that we have studied. In fact, for many it may be too late to rectify the situation. Their background of poverty and lack of work skills, their heavy use of alcohol and drugs, their psychiatric disabilities, their nascent physical infirmities, their adaptation to the social world of the street, flops, and shelters, and the ineluctable effect of these elements on the individual's psychological make-up are the same ingredients that acted to produce the older homeless men. There are more men like Uncle Ed, Miles, and Roland incubating in our shelters and on our streets. The longer these young men stay homeless, the less likely will they be capable of readapting to mainstream life. Yet shelters are already gearing up to house men to the year 2000 (Stern, 1984; Torres, 1986). Like his older counterparts, the young man will continue to harbor fantasies of escape but in reality he has received a lifetime sentence: "all outdoors, all life, was to him one colossal prison. . . . He had lost in the fierce battle of greed, and so was deemed to be exterminated; and all society was busied to see that he did not escape the sentence" (Sinclair, 1905, p. 229).

# Postscript

Approximately 18 months after study had been completed, we attempted to determine the fate of three men whose lives are depicted in Chapter 1. When last seen, it seemed that each was poised at a key juncture in his life. The physical limitations of old age were colluding with the multiple miseries of homelessness and poverty to set the stage for calamitous events.

It took almost five hours to track down Uncle Ed. Despite the strong efforts of a new social worker at the BRC to involve Ed in part-time work at the center and to helping him handle his meager monthly income, over the past six months Ed had slowly begun to drink again. Consequently he became increasingly indebted to his hotel manager and a friend, Jack, at the BRC. After repeated arguments with his friend over the unpaid loans, Ed decided to "escape" to the "Holy Mountains" for the specified 3 weeks where he hoped to save some of his monthly check and thus regain his dignity and repay his friend.

Uncle Ed, almost immediately on his return to the Bowery went looking for Jack with $50 to pay off much of his debt. However, as he asked around the street for Jack, he was repeatedly told that this man had spread word around that Ed was a welcher and could not be trusted by anyone. Leaving the message with everyone that Jack could get repaid by coming to his hotel, Ed waited in vain for a few days before he started spending this pot of money. Depressed by the situation, Ed began the third "small drunk" of the year. Like the others this one lasted two to three days and ended with him locking himself in his cubicle and, for several days, consuming nothing but water and cigarettes. This was at the end of July, and now in the last week of August he felt that perhaps his luck had changed at least a little. He had found a new senior center near Chinatown where they served good 25-cent lunches, and better yet, Ed started receiving some food stamps again. Although, the stamps amounted to only $10 a month, for Ed this was a great triumph "over the system."

Like Ed, the Super-Runner had not been seen at the BRC for many months. Although Roland had not gone back full-time to living in the streets over the past year, he had begun to renew his seemingly endless cycle of running away from life. Having become a daily fixture as a worker at the BRC, Roland all of a sudden began to find strange reasons why he could no longer work there. Chief among these was that Charlie, a retarded man who also helped out at the BRC, never bathed and was too smelly to be around. The staff were not eager to lose Roland and made a serious attempt to keep Charlie as clean as possible. Despite these efforts, one day almost a year ago Roland simply declared that he had had enough and walked out. To date, he has not returned.

Yet, much of his daily cycle remains the same. He still lives in the same flop, spends much of his time walking on the city streets and works in at least one mission. The problem with his leg that caused him to crawl for sanctuary to this same mission had healed amazingly well almost immediately after Roland stopped sleeping on the streets. One cannot help speculating about whether the pain in his limb was a psychological means of enforcing a change in his life which he could not confront directly.

Of the three men, Miles's past year and a half had started off the least promising. The rumored reopening of the Brooklyn restaurant he had worked at many years ago turned out to be just a bad joke. His dreams of once again being a fry cook vanished as fast as the availability of affordable housing in Manhattan. With little prospect of employment or a tolerable roof over his head, Miles renewed his cycle of moving around the city's parks and periodically sojourning to the "Holy Mountains." Returning to Manhattan in early March, he spent his days in parks and slept in Grand Central Station. One night he spent his last money getting quite drunk at the bar in the station and began to tell the bartender about how he was going to cut his throat. The bartender called a group called the "Night Riders" who tend to the homeless mentally ill. They came and asked Miles if he would like to stay for a while in a small shelter set up in Bellevue Hospital. A very despondent Miles was taken to the shelter, and in a few days he was talked out of his suicidal state by a social worker. Miraculously, she was able to locate a tiny but available city-owned apartment in the Bronx which rented at just $107.75.

Miles borrowed the first month's rent from friends and is now living in this apartment. Several days a week are spent making some extra money by collecting and selling aluminum cans. Although, he still lives in one of the poorest, most crime-ridden parts of New York, he turned 65 with a roof over his head, something neither he nor we thought would happen.

# Scales Used in Analyses

## PHYSICAL HEALTH

The measure of physical health symptoms is the sum of a respondent's z-scores on 11 health scales derived from the CARE. These scales are Somatic Symptoms, Heart Disorder, Edema, Sleep Disorder, Arthritis, Stroke, Respiratory Problems, Hypertension, Cancer, Hearing Problems, and Visual Disorders.

## NEED FULFILLMENT

A 40-item scale ($\alpha = .70$) based on Lawton's (1970) taxonomy of needs list. The scale comprises six major areas: physical health needs, mental health needs, physical self-maintenance, instrumental self-maintenance (e.g., finance, transportation), effectance (recognition, creativity), and social needs. Higher scores indicate that fewer needs are being met. Items were based on self-report rather than external objective criteria. The scale focuses primarily on material tasks and correlates highly with Gurland and associates' Activities of Daily Living Scale ($r = .62$). Illustrative of the items that were used are "Goes without bath because of lack of help," "Essential shopping not done," and "Cannot do leisure activity because of mobility problem."

## ALCOHOLISM

A 3-item scale based on level of drinking, frequency of intake, and age person began drinking at moderate, heavy, or spree levels.

## PSYCHOSIS/PREVIOUS HOSPITALIZATION (PPH)

This variable is scored positive if the respondent had a previous psychiatric hospitalization or scored 3 or more on an 8-item scale of psychotic symptoms ($\alpha = .63$). The scale consists of items such as current levels of auditory and visual hallucinations, current delusions, derealization, and presentation of bizarre appearance.

## DEPRESSION

A 23-item scale ($\alpha = .78$) that consists of items such as persistent sadness, crying, suicidal thoughts, pessimism, decreased energy, and anhedonia.

## ORGANIC MENTAL SYMPTOMS

A 10-item scale ($\alpha = .47$) that resembles the Mental Status Questionnaire (Kahn, Goldfarb, Pollack & Peck, 1960). The items test for orientation, memory, and ability to do simple calculations.

## STRESS

A 10-item scale based on categories derived from Dohrenwend and associates' (1977) life events list. Typical items are "deterioration in the neighborhood," "family illness," "mugging in past year," "personal injury due to crime," and "financial problems." Items that were redundant with social variables were removed.

## STRUCTURAL NETWORK

Comprised of five structural network variables—size (informal), size (formal), number of clusters, number of large clusters, degree (average number of linkages per network member)—which was created by factor analysis.

## INTERACTIONAL NETWORK

Comprised of nine interactional network variables: mean transactions (numplex), sustenance aid, number of multicontent linkages (informal), number of multicontent linkages (formal), importance, intimacy, under-standing, availability for help, length of linkage. This scale was created by factor analysis.

## INSTITUTIONAL CONTACTS

A 13-item variable based on at least monthly contact with various Bowery institutions such as social agencies and commercial establishments.

## NETWORK PROCLIVITY

An 8-item variable based on whether respondent would attempt to utilize his social contacts when confronted with eight hypothetical problems.

## DEMOGRAPHIC VARIABLES

1. Age
2. Race—white versus nonwhite
3. Location—street versus nonstreet
4. Education

## Table 1. Zero Order Correlations of Selected Variables

| | NF | PH | PPH | OMS | D | AL | S | SN | IN | IC | NP | A | E | R | LS |
|---|---|---|---|---|---|---|---|---|---|---|---|---|---|---|---|
| Need Fulfillment | — | .34 | -.07 | -.01 | .35 | .18 | .26 | -.05 | .09 | -.11 | -.03 | -.17 | .01 | .01 | .14 |
| Physical Health | .34 | — | .10 | .09 | .57 | .11 | .35 | -.05 | .01 | .12 | -.03 | -.18 | .10 | .02 | .04 |
| Psychosis/Previous Psychiatric Hospitalization (PPH) | -.07 | .10 | — | .02 | .05 | -.03 | .01 | -.02 | .01 | .02 | .09 | .03 | .02 | -.02 | .03 |
| Organic Mental Symptoms | -.01 | .09 | .02 | — | .25 | -.01 | -.03 | -.13 | -.08 | -.10 | -.02 | .03 | -.09 | .01 | .02 |
| Depression | .35 | .57 | .05 | .25 | — | .17 | .31 | -.19 | .00 | .01 | -.11 | -.28 | .00 | -.08 | .18 |
| Alcoholism | .18 | .11 | -.03 | -.01 | .17 | — | .13 | -.02 | .13 | -.11 | -.09 | -.16 | .01 | .01 | .33 |
| Stress | .26 | .35 | .01 | -.03 | .31 | .13 | — | -.07 | .03 | .06 | -.16 | -.05 | .04 | .01 | .19 |
| Structural Network | -.05 | -.05 | -.02 | -.13 | -.19 | -.02 | -.07 | — | -.02 | .14 | .32 | .03 | .08 | -.07 | -.25 |
| Interactional Network | .09 | .01 | .01 | -.08 | .00 | .13 | .03 | -.02 | — | .08 | -.03 | -.04 | -.01 | .17 | .20 |
| Institutional Contacts | -.11 | .12 | .02 | -.10 | .01 | -.11 | .06 | .14 | .08 | — | .09 | -.08 | .03 | .06 | -.15 |
| Network Proclivity | -.03 | -.03 | .09 | -.02 | -.11 | -.09 | -.16 | .32 | -.03 | .09 | — | .19 | .06 | -.05 | -.36 |
| Age | -.17 | -.18 | .03 | .03 | -.28 | -.16 | -.05 | .03 | -.04 | -.08 | .19 | — | -.11 | -.13 | -.27 |
| Education | .01 | .10 | .02 | -.09 | .00 | .01 | .04 | .08 | -.01 | .03 | .06 | -.11 | — | -.18 | .07 |
| Race (Black) | .01 | .02 | -.02 | .01 | -.08 | .01 | .01 | -.07 | .17 | .06 | -.05 | -.13 | -.18 | — | .20 |
| Living on Street | .14 | .04 | .03 | .02 | .18 | .33 | .19 | -.25 | .20 | -.15 | -.36 | -.27 | .07 | .20 | — |

*Note.* Values in italics are statistically significant at the following levels: $r = .11$ ($p < .05$); $r = .15$ ($p < .01$), two-tailed. NF = Need Fulfillment; PH = Physical Health; PPH = Psychosis/Previous Psychiatric Hospitalization; OMS = Organic Mental Symptoms; D = Depression; AL = Alcoholism; S = Stress; SN = Structural Network; IN = Interactional Network; IC = Institutional Contacts; NP = Network Proclivity; A = Age; E = Education; R = Race (Black); LS = Living on Street.

Table 2. Mean Values and Standard Deviations of Scales Used in Analyses

|  | Mean values | Standard deviation |
|---|---|---|
| Physical health (summed z-scores) | 0.00 | 5.07 |
| Need Fulfillment (summed z-scores) | 0.00 | 2.17 |
| Alcoholism (max. = 5) | 2.56 | 1.87 |
| Proportion with psychotic/previous psychiatric hospitalization | 0.23 | 0.42 |
| Depression Scale (max. = 23) | 7.44 | 3.93 |
| Organic Mental Symptoms (max. = 10) | 1.48 | 1.39 |
| Stress Scale (max. = 10) | 3.78 | 1.47 |
| Structural Network (summed z-scores) | −0.01 | 3.86 |
| Interactional Network (summed z-scores) | −0.02 | 5.01 |
| Institutional/Agency contacts (max. = 13) | 7.42 | 2.48 |
| Network proclivity (max. = 8) | 6.59 | 1.60 |
| Age | 61.51 | 6.24 |
| Education[a] | 6.72 | 2.69 |
| Proportion white | 0.69 | 0.46 |
| Living situation[b] | 1.69 | 0.46 |

[a]Education. 6 = 9 years; 7 = 10 years.

[b]Living situation: 1 = street; 2 = nonstreet.

# Social Network Dimensions

Numerous criteria have been employed to examine the multifaceted aspects of social networks (Barnes, 1954; Boissevain, 1974; Mitchell, 1969). For use here we have identified three dimensions comprised of 19 variables. The three dimensions encompass various material and emotional aspects of exchange (Interactional), morphological features of the network (Structural), and characteristics of the network members *vis-à-vis* the respondent (Member Attribute).

| Dimensions | Variables | Description |
|---|---|---|
| A.  Interactional | | |
| | 1. Numplex | Mean number of transactions (e.g., food exchange, advice-giving, etc.) per linkage in respondent's network. |
| | 2. Sustenance | Mean proportion linkages providing basic support items to respondent (e.g., money, food, medical aid). |
| | 3. Very Important | Mean proportion of linkages rated "very important" or "most important." |
| | 4. Frequency | Mean frequency of contact per linkage; this was scored on a continuous scale (7.0 = daily contact; 1.0 = weekly contact; 0.25 = monthly contact). |

| Dimensions | Variables | Description |
|---|---|---|
| | 5. Directionality | Direction in which aid in a dyadic relationship flows; mean directionality was calculated for the hotel, nonkin, and kin sectors of the respondent's network. Overall directional flow for each relationship was scored: 1 = helping; 2 = reciprocal; 3 = dependent. |
| | 6a. Multiplex-informal | Proportion of linkages that have more than one type of transaction with respondent (informal = hotel nonkin, outside kin) |
| | 6b. Multiplex-formal | Proportion of linkages that have more than one type of transaction with respondent (formal = hotel staff, agency/institutional staff). |
| | 7. Length of Linkage | Mean number of years persons have known the respondent |
| | 8. Intimacy | Mean proportion of linkages rated as an intimate |
| | 9. Understanding | Mean proportion of linkages rated as understanding respondent's problems |
| | 10. Availability for Help | Mean proportion of linkages rated as being counted on for help. |
| B. Structural | | |
| | 1a. Size-informal | Total number of linkages in respondent's network (informal = hotel nonkin, outside kin). |
| | 1b. Size-formal | Total number of linkages in respondent's network (formal = hotel staff, agency/institutional staff). |
| | 2. Density | Ratio of actual to potential linkages, excluding linkages with respondent. |
| | 3. Degree | The average number of linkages each person has with others in the respondent's network, excluding linkages with respondent. |

| Dimensions | Variables | Description |
|---|---|---|
| | 4. Number of Clusters | Number of subunits of network with 100% linkage density |
| | 5. Large Clusters | Number of clusters with five or more members |
| C. Member Attribute | 1. Gender Homogeneity | Percentage of network members of the same sex as the respondent |
| | 2. Age Homogeneity | Percentage of network members aged 50 years or older |

# References

Aging Health Policy Center (1985). *The homeless mentally ill elderly* (Working Paper). San Francisco: University of California.

Allen, W. H. (1903). *The vagrant: Social parasite or social product?* Proceedings of the National Conference of Social Work.

Allsop, K. (1972). *Hard travellin'.* Middlesex: Penguin.

Alstrom, C. H., Lindelius, R., & Salum, I. (1975). Mortality among homeless men. *British Journal of Addiction, 70,* 245–252.

Anderson, N. (1923). *The hobo.* Chicago: University of Chicago Press.

Arce, A. A., Tadlock, M., Vergare, M. J., & Shapiro, S. H. (1983). A psychiatric profile of street people admitted to an emergency shelter. *Hospital and Community Psychiatry, 34,* 812–816.

Arce, A. A., & Vergare, M. J. (1984). Identifying and characterizing the mentally ill among the homeless. In H. R. Lamb (Ed.), *The homeless mentally ill* (pp. 75–89). Washington, DC: American Psychiatric Association Press.

Ashley, M. J., Olin, J.S., le Riche, W. H., Kornaczewski, A., Schmidt, W., & Rankin, J. G. (1976). Skid row alcoholism: A distinct sociomedical entity. *Archives of Internal Medicine, 136,* 272–278.

Baasher, T., Elhakim, A. S. E. D., El Fawal, K., Gise, R., Harding, T. W., & Wankiiri, V. B. (1983). On vagrancy and psychosis. *Community Mental Health Journal, 19,* 27–41.

Bachrach, L. L. (1978). A conceptual approach to deinstitutionalization. *Hospital and Community Psychiatry, 29,* 573–577.

Bachrach, L. L. (1984a). Interpreting research on the homeless mentally ill: Some caveats. *Hospital and Community Psychiatry, 35,* 914–917.

Bachrach, L. L. (1984b). Research on services for the homeless mentally ill. *Hospital and Community Psychiatry, 35,* 910–913.

Bachrach, L. L. (1984c). The homeless mentally ill and mental health services: An analytic review of the literature. In H. R. Lamb (Ed.), *The homeless mentally ill* (pp. 11–53). Washington, DC: American Psychiatric Association Press.

Bahr, H. M. (1967). The gradual disappearance of skid row. *Social Problems, 15,* 41–45.

Bahr, H. (1973). *Skid row: An introduction to disaffiliation.* New York: Oxford University Press.

Bahr, H. M., & Caplow, T. (1973). *Old men drunk and sober.* New York: New York University Press.

Barnes, J. A. (1954). Class and committees in Norwegian island parish. *Human Relations, 7*, 39–58.

Barrow, S., Hellman, F., Plapinger, J., Lovell, A. M., & Struening, E. L. (1986). Residence outcomes, preliminary findings from an evaluation of programs for the mentally ill homeless, 1986. Executive summary. New York: New York State Psychiatric Institute.

Barrow, S. M., & Lovell, A. M. (1987). Homelessness and the limited options of older women. *Association for Anthropology and Gerontology Newsletter, 8*(4), 3–6.

Bassuk, E. L. (1984). The homelessness problem. *Scientific American, 251*,1, 40–45.

Bassuk, E. L., & Gerson, S. (1978). Deinstitutionalization and mental health services. *Scientific American, 238* (2), 46–53.

Bassuk, E. L., Rubin, L., & Lauriat, A. (1984). Is homelessness a mental health problem? *American Journal of Psychiatry, 141*, 1546–1550.

Baxter, E., & Hopper, K. (1982). The new mendicancy: Homeless in New York City. *American Journal of Orthopsychiatry, 52*, 393–407.

Bendiner, E. (1961). *The bowery man.* New York: Thomas Nelson.

Bhaskar, R. (1978). *A realist theory of science.* Atlantic Highlands, NJ: Humanities.

Bhaskar, R. (1979). *The possibility of naturalism.* Atlantic Highlands, NJ: Humanities.

Blumberg, L. M., Shipley, T. E., & Moor, J. O. (1971). The skid row man and the skid row status community. *Quarterly Journal of Studies on Alcohol, 32*, 909–941.

Blumberg, L., Shipley, T. E., & Shandler, I. W. (1973). *Skid row and its alternatives.* Philadelphia: Temple University Press.

Bogue, D. J. (1963). *Skid row in American cities.* Chicago: University of Chicago Press.

Boissevain, J. (1974). *Friends of friends.* New York: St. Martin's.

Breakey, W. R., & Fischer, P. J. (1987, May). *Alcoholism in homeless people.* Paper presented at the 140th Annual Meeting of the American Psychiatric Association, Chicago.

Brickner, P. W. (1985). Health issues in the care of the homeless. In P. W. Brickner, L. K. Scharer, B. Conanan, A. Elvy, & M. Savarese (Eds.), *Health care of homeless people* (pp. 3–18). New York: Springer.

Brickner, P. W., Greenbaum, D., Kaufman, A., O'Donnell, F., O'Brian, J. T., Scalice, R., Scardizzo, J., & Sullivan, T. (1972). A clinic for male derelicts. *Annals of Internal Medicine, 77*, 565–569.

Chavkin, W., Kristal, A., Seaborn, C., & Guigli, P. E. (1987). The reproductive experience of women living in hotels for the homeless in New York City. *New York State Journal of Medicine, 88*, 10–13.

Coalition for the Homeless (1984). *Crowded out: Homelessness and the elderly poor in New York City.* New York: Author.

Cohen, C. I. (1984). Schizophrenia and work. *Hospital and Community Psychiatry, 35*, 1040–1042.

Cohen, C. I., & Adler, A. (1986). Assessing the role of social network interventions with an inner-city population. *American Journal of Orthopsychiatry, 56*, 278–288.

Cohen, C. I., & Briggs, F. (1975). A storefront clinic on the Bowery. *Journal of Studies on Alcohol, 37*, 1336–1340.

Cohen, C. I., & Sokolovsky, J. (1979). Clinical uses of network analysis for psychiatric and aged populations. *Community Mental Health Journal, 15*, 203–213.

Cohen, C. I., & Sokolovsky, J. (1981). A reassessment of the sociability of long-term skid row residents: A social network approach. *Social Networks, 3*, 93–105.

Cohen, C. I., & Sokolovsky, J. (1983). Toward a concept of homelessness among aged men. *Journal of Gerontology, 38*, 81–89.

Cohen, C. I., Teresi, J., Holmes, D., & Roth, E. (1988). Survival strategies of older homeless men. *Gerontologist, 28*, 58–65.

Cohen, N. L., Putnam, J. F., & Sullivan, A. M. (1984). The mentally ill homeless: Isolation and adaptation. *Hospital and Community Psychiatry, 35,* 922–924.

Crystal, S. (1985). Health care and the homeless: Access to benefits. In P. W. Brickner, L. K. Scharer, B. Conanan, A. Elvy, & M. Savarese (Eds.), *Health care of homeless people* (pp. 279–287). New York: Springer.

Crystal, S., Ladner, S., & Towber, R. (1986). Multiple impairment in the mentally ill homeless. *International Journal of Mental Health, 14,* 61–73.

Dohrenwend, B. S., Krasnott, L., Askenasy, A. R., & Dohrenwend, B. P. (1978). Exemplification of a method for scaling life events: The PERI life events scale. *Journal of Health and Social Behavior, 19,* 205–229.

Doolin, J. (1986). Planning for the special needs of the homeless elderly. *The Gerontologist, 26,* 229–231.

Drake, M., O'Brien, M., & Biebuyck, T. (1981). *Single and homeless.* London: Her Majesty's Stationery Office.

Dreiser, T. (1982). *Sister Carrie.* New York: Bantam.

Dumont, M. P. (1967). Tavern culture, the sustenance of homeless men. *American Journal of Orthopsychiatry, 37,* 938–945.

Dunham, H. (1953). *Homeless men and their habitats: A research planning report.* Detroit: Wayne State University Press.

Edwards, G., Williamson, V., Hawker, A., & Hensman, C. (1966). London's skid row. *Lancet, 1,* 249–252.

Erickson, J., & Wilhelm, C. (1986). Introduction. In J. Erickson & C. Wilhelm (Eds.), *Housing the homeless* (pp. xix–xxxvii). New Brunswick: Center for Urban Policy Research, Rutgers University.

Estroff, S. E. (1985). Medicalizing the margins: On being disgraced, disordered, and deserving. *Psychosocial Rehabilitation Journal, 8,* 34–38.

Feldman, J., Su, W. H., Kaley, M., & Kissin, B. (1974). Skid row and inner-city alcoholics: A comparison of drinking patterns and medical problems. *Quarterly Journal of Studies on Alcohol, 35,* 565–576.

Feyerabend, P. K. (1975). *Against method.* London: Verso.

Filardo, T. (1985). Chronic disease management in the homeless. In P. W. Brickner, L. K. Scharer, B. Conanan, A. Elvy, & M. Savarese (Eds.), *Health care of homeless people* (pp. 19–31). New York: Springer.

Fischer, P. J., & Breakey, W. R. (1986). Homelessness and mental health: An overview. *International Journal of Mental Health, 14,* 6–41.

Fischer, P. J., Breakey, W. R., Shapiro, S., & Kramer, M. (1986). Baltimore mission users: Social networks, morbidity, and employment. *Psychosocial Rehabilitation Journal, 9,4,* 51–63.

Fischer, P. J., Shapiro, S., Breakey, W. R., Anthony, J. C., & Kramer, M. (1986). Mental health and social characteristics of the homeless: A survey of mission users. *American Journal of Public Health, 76,* 519–524.

Foucault, M. (1965). *Madness and civilization.* New York: Random House.

Foulks, E. (1975, December). Revitalization and social change: Contributions from psychiatric epidemiology. Paper presented at the 74th annual meeting of the American Anthropology Association, San Francisco.

Garfield, E. (1982). On beggars, bagladies, and bums. *Current Contents, 6,* 5–15.

Gillin, J. L. (1929). Vagrancy and begging. *American Journal of Sociology, 35,* 424–432.

Gilmore, H. W. (1940). *The beggar.* Chapel Hill: University of North Carolina Press.

Goldfarb, C. (1970). Patients nobody wants: Skid row alcoholics. *Disease of the Nervous System, 31,* 274–281.

Goldman, H. H., & Morrisey, J. P. (1985). The alchemy of mental health policy:

Homelessness and the fourth cycle of reform. *American Journal of Public Health, 75,* 727–731.

Goleman, D. (1986, November 4). To expert eyes, city streets are open mental wards. *The New York Times,* p. C-1.

Goleman, D. (1986, November 11). For mentally ill on the streets, a new approach shines. *The New York Times,* p. C-1.

Gruenberg, E. M. (1967). The social breakdown syndrome: Some origins. *American Journal of Psychiatry, 123,* 1481–1489.

Gurland, B. J., Copeland, J., Kuriansky, J. B., Kelleher, M., Sharpe, L., & Dean, L. L. (1983). *The mind and mood of aging.* New York: Haworth.

Gurland, B. J., Kuriansky, J. B., Sharpe, L., Simon, R., Stiller, P., & Birkett, P. (1977). The Comprehensive Assessment and Referral Evaluation (CARE): Rationale, development, and reliability. *International Journal of Aging and Human Development, 8,* 9–42.

Hartman, C. (1983). Introduction: A radical perspective on housing reform. In C. Hartman (Ed.), *America's housing crisis: What is to be done?* (pp. 1–28). Boston: Routledge & Kegan Paul.

Heckler, M. (1984, May). Statement in "Shelter" (television broadcast), KCTS-Seattle.

Herman, R. (1980, December 30). New York City resists state on shelters for homeless in residential areas. *The New York Times,* B-7.

Holden, C. (1986). Homelessness: Experts differ on root causes. *Science, 232,* 569–570.

Hope, M., & Young, J. (1986). *The faces of the homeless.* Lexington, MA: Lexington Books.

Hopper, K. (1987, June). *Overview on the homeless.* Paper presented at the Conference on Health Care for Homeless People, New York.

Hopper, K., Baxter, E., Cox, S., & Klein, L. (1982). *One year later: The homeless poor in New York City, 1982.* New York: Community Service Society.

Hopper, K., & Hamburg, J. (1984). *The making of America's homeless: From skid row to new poor.* New York: Community Service Society.

Hopper, K., Susser, E., & Conover, S. (1985). Economics of makeshift: deindustrialization and homelessness in New York City. *Urban Anthropology, 14,* 183–236.

Human Resource Administration. (1987, October). *Comprehensive homeless assistance plan.* Washington, DC: Author.

Jackson, J. D., & Connor, R. (1953). The skid row alcoholic. *Quarterly Journal of Studies on Alcohol, 14,* 468–486.

Kahn, R. L., Goldfarb, A. I., Pollack, M., & Peck, A. (1960). Brief objective measures for the determination of mental status in the aged. *American Journal of Psychiatry, 117,* 326–328.

Kasinitz, P. (1986). Gentrification and homelessness. The single room occupant and the inner-city revival. In J. Erickson & C. Wilhelm (Eds.), *Housing the homeless* (pp. 241–252). New Brunswick: Center for Urban Policy Research, Rutgers University.

Kennedy, W. (1984). *Ironweed.* New York: Penguin.

Kromer, T. (1935). *Waiting for nothing.* New York: Knopf.

Kuhn, T. S. (1970). *The structure of scientific revolutions* (2nd ed.). Chicago: University of Chicago Press.

Lamb, H. R. (Ed.). (1984). *The homeless mentally ill.* Washington, DC: American Psychiatric Association Press.

LaRue, A., Dessonville, C., & Jarvik, L. F. (1985). Aging and mental disorders. In J. E. Birren & K. W. Schare (Eds.), *Handbook of the psychology of aging* (2nd ed.) (pp. 664–702). New York: Van Nostrand Reinhold.

Lawton, M. P. (1970). Assessment, integration, and environments for older people. *The Gerontologist, 10*, 38–46.

Leach, J. (1979). Providing for the destitute. In J. K. Wing & R. Olsen (Eds.), *Community Care for the Mentally Disabled* (pp. 90–105). Oxford: Oxford University Press.

Leach, J., & Wing, J. (1980). *Helping destitute men.* London: Tavistock.

Levinson, B. M. (1958). Some aspects of the personality of the native-born white homeless man as revealed by the Rorschach. *Psychiatric Quarterly Supplement, 32*, 278–286.

Levinson, B. M. (1966). Subcultural studies of homeless men. Transactions. *New York Academy of Science, 29*, 165–182.

Levinson, D. (1974a). The etiology of skid rows in the United States. *International Journal of Social Psychiatry, 20*, 25–33.

Levinson, D. (1974b). Skid row in transition. *Urban Anthropology, 3*, 79–93.

Lipton, F. R., & Sabatini, A. (1984). Constructing support systems for homeless chronic patients. In H. R. Lamb (Ed.), *The homeless mentally ill* (pp. 153–172). Washington, DC: American Psychiatric Association Press.

Lodge Patch, I. C. (1970). Homeless men: A London survey. *Proceedings of the Royal Society of Medicine, 63*, 436–441.

London, J. (1905). *War of the classes.* New York: Regent.

London, J. (1970). *On the road: The tramp diary and other hobo writings.* Logan: Utah State University Press.

Love, E. G. (1956). *Subways are for sleeping.* New York: Signet.

Lovell, A. M. (1984). *Marginality without isolation: Social networks and the new homeless.* Presented at the 83rd annual meeting of the American Anthropology Association, Denver, Colorado.

Mayhew, H. (1851). *London labor and the London poor: A cyclopedia of the condition and earnings of those who will work, those that cannot work, and those that will not work.* New York: Harper Brothers.

Merton, R. K. (1949). *Social theory and social structure.* Glencoe: Free Press.

Meyerson, D. J., & Mayer, J. (1966). Origins, treatment, and destiny of skid row alcoholic men. *New England Journal of Medicine, 275*, 419–425.

Mitchell, J. (1969). *Social networks in urban situations.* Manchester, UK: University of Manchester Press.

Morgan, M. (1951). *Skid row: An informal portrait of Seattle.* New York: Viking.

Mulkern, V., & Spence, R. (1984). *Alcohol abuse/alcoholism among homeless persons: A review of the literature. Final report.* Washington, D.C., Superintendent of Documents, U.S. Government Printing Office.

Murray, H. (1986). Time in the streets. In J. R. Erickson & C. Wilhelm (Eds.), *Housing the homeless* (pp. 53–69). New Brunswick: Center for Urban Policy Research, Rutgers University.

New York City Human Resources Administration (1983). *Project future: Focusing, understanding, targeting, and utilizing resources for homeless mentally ill, older persons, youth and employables.* New York: Author.

New York State Office of Mental Health (1982). *Who are the homeless?* New York: Author.

Olin, J. S. (1966). "Skid row" syndrome: A medical profile of the chronic drunkenness offender. *Canadian Medical Association Journal, 95*, 205–214.

Orwell, G. (1933). *Down and out in Paris and London.* San Diego: Harcourt Brace Jovanovich.

Parker, P. (1970). A view from the Bowery. Unpublished manuscript.

Pepper, B., Kirshner, M. C., & Ryglewicz, H. (1981). The young adult chronic patient: Overview of a population. *Hospital and Community Psychiatry, 32*, 463–469.

Perales, C. A. (October 26, 1983). *Myths about poverty* (p. A27). New York Times.

Peterson, W. J., & Maxwell, M. A. (1958). The skid row "wino." *Social Problems, 5,* 308–316.

Pittman, D. J., & Gordon, T. W. (1958). *Revolving door: A study of the chronic police case inebriate.* Glencoe: Free Press.

Popper, K. R. (1963). *Conjectures and refutations.* London: Routledge & Kegan Paul.

Rabkin, J. G., & Struening, E. (1976). Life events, stress, and illness. *Science, 194,* 1013–1020.

Rafferty, M., Hinzpeter, D. A., Colwin, L., & Knox, M. (1984). *The shelter worker's handbook: A guide to identifying and meeting the health needs of homeless people.* New York: Coalition for the Homeless.

Rasky, S. F. (1987). Senate nears vote on housing bill; Reagan vows veto. New York Times, November 16, A1.

Reifler, B. V. (1986). Mixed cognitive–affective disturbances in the elderly: A new classification. *Journal of Clinical Psychiatry, 47,* 354–356.

Ribton-Turner, C. J. (1887). *A history of vagrants and vagrancy and beggars and begging.* London: Chapman & Hall.

Rooney, J. (1961). Group processes among skid row winos: A reevaluation of the undersocialization hypothesis. *Quarterly Journal of Studies on Alcohol, 22,* 444–460.

Rooney, J. (1976). Friendship and disaffiliation among the skid row population. *Journal of Gerontology, 31,* 82–88.

Roscoe, J. T. (1969). *Fundamental research statistics.* New York: Holt, Rinehart, & Winston.

Rosen, G. (1968). *Madness in society.* New York: Harper & Row.

Rosenman, S. (1955). The skid row alcoholic and the negative ego image. *Quarterly Journal of Studies on Alcohol, 16,* 447–473.

Roth, D., Bean, G. J., & Hyde, P. S. (1986). Homelessness and mental health policy developing an appropriate role for the 1980s. *Community Mental Health Journal, 22,* 203–214.

Rubington, E. (1958). The chronic drunkeness offender. *The Annals of the American Academy of Policial and Social Science, 315,* 65–72.

Rubington, E. (1968). The bottle gang. *Quarterly Journal of Studies on Alcohol, 29,* 943–955.

Rubington, E. (1971). The changing skid row scene. *Quarterly Journal of Studies on Alcohol, 32,* 123–135.

Schneider, J. C. (1986). Skid row as an urban neighborhood, 1880–1960. In J. Erickson & C. Wilhelm (Eds.), *Housing the homeless* (pp. 167–189). New Brunswick: Center for Urban Policy Research, Rutgers University.

Scott, R., Gaskell, P. G., & Morrell, D. C. (1966). Patients who reside in common lodging-houses. *British Medical Journal, 2,* 1561–1564.

Secretary of Health and Human Services (1987). *Alcohol and health.* Washington, DC: U.S. Department of Health and Human Services.

Sexton, P. C. (1986). The life of the homeless. In J. Erickson & C. Wilhelm (Eds.), *Housing the homeless* (pp. 73–81). New Brunswick: Center for Urban Policy Research, Rutgers University.

Shanas, E., Townsend, P., Wedderbum, D., Friis, H., Milhoj, P., & Stehouwer, P. (Eds.). (1968). *Old people in three industrial societies.* London: Routledge & Kegan Paul.

Sinclair, U. (1905). *The jungle.* New York: New American Library.

Snow, D. A., Baker, S. G., Anderson, L., & Martin, M. (1986). The myth of pervasive mental illness among the homeless. *Social Problems, 33,* 407–423.

Sokolovsky, J. (1986). Network methodologies in the study of aging. In C. Fry & J. Keith (eds.), *New Methods for Old Age Research* (pp. 231–261). South Hadley, Mass: Bergin and Garvey.

Sokolovsky, J., & Cohen, C. I. (1981). Toward a resolution of methodological dilemmas in network mapping. *Schizophrenia Bulletin, 7*, 109–116.

Solenberger, A. W. (1911). *One thousand homeless men: A study of original records.* New York: Charities Publication Committee.

Spradley, J. P. (1970). *You owe yourself a drunk: An ethnography of urban nomads.* Boston: Little, Brown.

Spradley, J. P. (1972). Adaptive strategies of urban nomads: The ethnoscience of tramp culture. In T. Weaver & D. White (Eds.), *The anthropology of urban environments* (Monograph 11; pp. 21–38). Boulder, Colorado: Society for Applied Anthropology.

Steinbeck, J. (1938). *Of mice and men.* New York: Viking Press.

Stern, M. J. (1984). The emergence of the homeless as a public problem. *Social Service Review, 58*, 291–301.

Stone, M. (1983). Housing and the economic crisis: An analysis and emergency program. In C. Hartman (Ed.), *America's housing crisis: What is to be done?* (pp. 99–150). Boston: Routledge & Kegan Paul.

Strauss, R. (1946). Alcohol and the homeless man. *Quarterly Journal of Studies on Alcohol, 7*, 360–404.

Strauss, R., & McCarthy, R. G. (1951). Nonaddictive pathological drinking patterns of homeless men. *American Journal of Orthopsychiatry, 37*, 938–945.

Sutherland, E. H., & Locke, H. J. (1936). *Twenty thousand homeless men.* Philadelphia: Lippincott.

Takaki, R. (March 3, 1986). *Letters to the Editor.* New York Times.

Task Force on Community Support Systems (1978). In President's Commission on Mental Health, *Report to the President from the President's Commission on Mental Health* (Vol. 2). Washington, DC: U.S. Government Printing Office.

Torres, J. (1986, November). The health of the homeless: Strategies for empowerment. Presentation at the New York Marxist School.

U.S. Bureau of Census (1982). *Statistical abstract of the United States.* Washington, DC: U.S. Government Printing Office.

U.S. Bureau of Census (1984). *Statistical Abstract of the United States.* Washington, DC: U.S. Government Printing Office.

U.S. Department of Housing and Urban Development (1984). *A report to the Secretary on the homeless and emergency shelters.* Washington, DC: U.S. Government Printing Office.

Vera Institute of Justice (1981). First time user's of women's shelter services: A preliminary analysis. New York: Author.

Vexliard, A. (1956). The hobo: Myths and realities. *Diogenes, 16*, 59–67.

Wallace, S. (1965). *Skid row as a way of life.* Totawa, NJ: Bedminister.

Wallace, S. E. (1968). The road to skid row. *Social Problems, 16*, 92–105.

Whiting, W. A. (1915). *What the City of New York provides for the homeless.* New York: Department of Public Charities.

Wiseman, J. P. (1979). *Stations of the lost.* Chicago: University of Chicago Press.

Wray, L. B. (1984). On skid row: Just who are the "Bowery boys" of the 1980's? *University of Maryland Chronicle, 18*(3), 3–6.

Zettler, M. D. (1975). *The bowery.* New York: Drake.

# Index